More Than Marriage

More Than Marriage

FORMING FAMILIES AFTER
MARRIAGE EQUALITY

John G. Culhane

UNIVERSITY OF CALIFORNIA PRESS

University of California Press
Oakland, California

© 2023 by John G. Culhane

Cataloging-in-Publication Data is on file at the Library of Congress.

ISBN 978-0-520-39165-9 (cloth : alk. paper)
ISBN 978-0-520-39166-6 (pbk. : alk. paper)
ISBN 978-0-520-39167-3 (ebook)

Manufactured in the United States of America

32   31   30   29   28   27   26   25   24   23
10   9   8   7   6   5   4   3   2   1

This book is dedicated to my family, in the broadest sense of that word.

Contents

Tables

Preface

This book is a tribute to the many people who gave generously of their time in sharing with me (and now with you) eloquent testimonials to their roles in creating and *living in* the various legal relationships that I discuss throughout this volume: domestic partnerships, civil unions, domestic beneficiary agreements, and, of course, marriages. The countless fruitful hours I spent talking with them via phone, Skype, or Zoom or through long email chains not only were necessary for illustrating the arguments I wanted to make on the law's need for growth and flexibility but also ended up honing and improving those arguments. I can't imagine the book without their stories. Remember their names: Tom Brougham and Barry Warren; John Kennedy; Tom Gibson (pseud.); Leah Whitesel and Justin Gates; Alex Rifman and Jennifer Tweeton; Emil Roe and Margaret Koe (pseuds.); Lisa Goodman; Sheila Blackburn; Colorado State Senator Pat Steadman; Patricia Yarrow and Liz Gettings; Marilyn McCord; May and April Doe (pseuds.); Anne Quinn and Terry McKeon; and John Hunter and Hal Kooden.

Like the marriage equality movement that spawned these legal alternatives, this book's gestation has been a long and, at times, difficult process. I greet its completion with a mixture of joy and—let's face it!—relief. And like the hard-fought path to the Supreme Court's ultimate recognition of the rights of gay and lesbian couples to marry, the proposals I put forth here will require sedulous effort and deep dedication to a fuller, fairer legal recognition of all adults in committed relationships. But obstacles will not daunt those determined to carry this fight forward and to continue to protect marriage equality from a Supreme Court that now seems bent on rolling back decades of increasing recognition of fundamental rights and liberties. (That's another whole book.)

In addition to the everyday heroes whose stories form its spine, so many others have helped to push this book across the finish line that I'm sure I'll omit some of them from the acknowledgments to follow. For that, I apologize in advance. But let's give it a try.

First, thanks to my editor nonpareil, Maura Roessner. She's believed in this book from the first time she read it and has been my sounding board, coach, and confidant. Her suggestions and contributions, along with her patience and good humor, have been wise and comforting. The anonymous reviewers she selected, whom I wish I could thank personally, spurred me to think more deeply about the tough issues I raised and led to important changes. And Maura's assistants, Madison Wetzell and Sam Warren, were quickly responsive to my questions and very helpful. Juliana Froggatt is a careful and thorough copy editor, whose attention to every detail of the writing process has significantly improved this book.

Thanks too to Jessica Feinberg and Jean Eggen, who read and commented extensively on earlier drafts. Nancy Polikoff provided indispensable information on and context for the early days of domestic partnerships. My colleague and friend Alicia Kelly convinced me of the importance of including a more comprehensive treatment of cohabitation. I also benefited enormously from workshopping portions of this book at various events over the past several years. In particular, my presentation at the Nonmarriage Roundtable at Arizona State University in 2019 elicited helpful comments and suggestions from many of the panelists, especially Kaipo Matsumura, Naomi Cahn, Albertina Antognini, June Carbone, and Barbara Atwood. I have gained invaluable insights from discussing earlier work leading to this book at the Midyear Meetings of both the Family and Juvenile Law Section and the Sexual Orientation and Gender Identity Issues Section of the Association of American Law Schools, during a presentation to faculty and students at the University of Akron School of Law, and in two presentations to my own faculty at the Delaware Law School. Thanks also to Dahlia Lithwick, who somehow found the time to read and comment favorably on the book. I am also grateful for my role as an official observer for the Uniform Law Commission's work that led to the adoption of the Uniform Cohabitants' Economic Remedies Act (although I am disappointed that the drafters did not include a registration option in their final draft).

I also thank my long-suffering family, friends, and random passersby who have had to listen to me talk about this book for the past several years. In particular, thanks to Paulette Greenwell; Iris, Douglas, and Lisa Culhane; Alexa and Courtnee Girasole-Culhane; and—especially—my husband, David Girasole.

Introduction

The nature of marriage is that, through its enduring
bond, two persons together can find other freedoms,
such as expression, intimacy, and spirituality. This is true
for all persons, whatever their sexual orientation. There
is dignity in the bond between two men or two women
who seek to marry and in their autonomy to make such
profound choices.

Supreme Court Justice Anthony M. Kennedy

There are almost as many kinds of relationships as there are
people in combination. . . . The marriage issue . . . seems to
be a way of denying recognition to [most] relations.

Michael Warner

What do adults in committed relationships need from government?

This vital question has been submerged for far too long by the focus on
marriage as the ideal—no, the *only*—form of adult relationship that
deserves recognition. That's not a healthy or realistic view, but there's been
little appetite at either the state or (especially) the federal level for sober
consideration of how people in all sorts of interdependent relationships
might be legally supported.

A moment's reflection reveals some of the problems with elevating
marriage to its unique and unchallenged status. First, marriage is too
bossy. It comes with a strong set of default rules. Although couples can

1

modify the terms of marriage through prenuptial agreements, these are rarely executed and are often seen as antithetical to the promise and premise of marriage by the couples choosing to wed. By and large, then, married couples don't actively select (and are often not even aware of) all of the terms and conditions of their union. Second, continuing with marriage as the unique status is willfully blind to the many millions of adults who are *in fact* in committed relationships other than marriage but nonetheless need and deserve support. Third, marriage is just the wrong status for many couples.

This book provides a foundation for creative thinking about how we might build something new and more capacious—perhaps even sprawling. The inspiration for this model is an institution called *the designated beneficiary agreement.* This legal creature is currently in effect only in Colorado, but it deserves to be expanded and exported to every state. Its unwieldy name notwithstanding, some version of this status stands to do immeasurable good for many—perhaps millions of—people. As we'll see, a retooled designated beneficiary agreement law provides people with the greatest flexibility to organize their relationships and, if it is properly designed, to gain state support for them.[1]

This reckoning with the deficiencies of marriage is long overdue and has been obscured for at least the past thirty years by the laser focus on a different but related legal disability: the exclusion of gay and lesbian couples from the institution of marriage. That spotlight diverted focus from the wider issues with the marriage-only concentration. Yet the step-by-step path to marriage equality led to an unintentional but providential spin-off. It has inspired the creation of several compromise legal statuses designed to provide same-sex couples with some of the rights and benefits of marriage. The debates that led to those statuses, as well as their content, have allowed for a clearer focus on how the law might better help all committed adults—not just gay and lesbian couples.

We begin at the end of the momentous battle for marriage equality.

On June 26, 2015, many Americans—gay and straight alike—celebrated victory in the decades-long struggle for marriage equality. On that day, the United States Supreme Court issued its seminal decision in *Obergefell v. Hodges.*[2] By a slim 5–4 vote, the justices held that same-sex couples have a constitutional right to cement their love and commitment through marriage. The decision is rightly seen as one of the great triumphs in the perpetual movement toward ever greater civil rights, because marriage was the one place where members of the LGBTQ community were denied an important government benefit—and a coveted status—by virtue of their willingness to be open about their lives and their love.

As many predicted when *Obergefell* was decided, the conversation has now shifted to what might be considered questions collateral to marriage. Some of these should be easily answered. Married gay and lesbian couples must be entitled to the same government benefits as straight couples, for instance—even though the Texas Supreme Court has held otherwise.[3] Other questions are more challenging, such as whether business owners can claim religious or "expressive" exemptions to their obligation to serve gay and lesbian people—often in connection with the very wedding ceremonies that cement the status that these couples are finally entitled to enjoy.[4]

Despite these post-*Obergefell* skirmishes, most observers seem to take marriage equality itself as settled and not likely to be upended—even with a more conservative SCOTUS in place.[5] There's an understandable inclination to move on, and, for the most part, that's happened. Victory has been achieved.

Yet the marriage equality movement is in an important sense incomplete. While successful on its own terms, it mostly avoided raising broader questions. Gay and lesbian couples were placed on equal footing with other marriage-eligible folks, but *Obergefell*—and the movement that led to it—ended up reinforcing the divide that separates married couples from everyone else. As Professor Melissa Murray has said, the *Obergefell* decision promoted "marriage—and only marriage—as the normative ideal for intimate life."[6] This insight concisely states one of the persistent criticisms of marriage equality: by emphasizing the rights of gay and lesbian couples to be granted the perquisites of marriage on the same basis as their straight counterparts, the marriage equality movement implicitly reinforced the strong legal fence that separates married couples from others in committed relationships.

The movement also mostly sidestepped questions about what marriage *is*. What does it mean, and how should it be supported in the twenty-first century? And what other types of adult relationships—intimate and otherwise—should the law recognize?

These questions are more vital than ever today. Misty-eyed paeans to marriage can't disguise the fact that an ever-increasing number of people are choosing not to wed. A watershed moment was reached in 2013, when, for the first time, the number of unmarried adults exceeded the number of married adults in the United States.[7] Of perhaps greater significance is the uneven distribution of marriage within society. While marriage rates were once relatively even across socioeconomic classes, over the past forty years or so those with higher levels of education and greater wealth have married at significantly higher rates than the less well educated and the poor.[8] There is also now a sharp distinction between marriage rates between races—Black men and women are far less likely to marry than white men and women, for instance.[9] Laws and policies that ignore such large and diverse parts of the population need serious rethinking.

A useful way to begin thinking about the place of marriage and the limitations of focusing too narrowly on that singular status is to consider *United States v. Windsor*, decided just two years before *Obergefell*.[10] The litigation involved a challenge to the Defense of Marriage Act (DOMA), a federal law that applied to same-sex couples who were legally married in their home state.[11] Through DOMA, their rights faded at the state border, because the act fenced them out of the many, many *federal* goodies that are showered on their different-sex counterparts. These include income tax benefits, preferential immigration status, and certain social security benefits, as well as a host of other advantages that come to a spouse under a variety of social programs. In *Windsor*, the Supreme Court declared DOMA unconstitutional and held that the federal government had to recognize marriages that were legal at the state level.[12]

The case was powerful precisely because of the side-by-side contrast between the plaintiff, Edie Windsor, and other surviving spouses. When her wife, Thea Spyer, died, in 2009, Windsor didn't qualify for an exemption from the federal estate tax, even though she would have had she been married to a man. The story was made more compelling by the sheer length of the two women's relationship. Although they had been legally married for only six years, they had been together for almost four decades.[13] For all that, Windsor and Spyer were legal strangers under federal law—and Windsor was slapped with an estate tax bill of $363,000.

So the fact that the two women were married under state law didn't do them much good—especially financially, and especially after Spyer's death. During oral argument on the case, the late justice Ruth Bader Ginsburg memorably referred to the women's union as a "skim milk" (federal-benefit-free!) marriage.[14] The comparison was devastating. How could Congress get away with creating such rank inequality? A purer denial of basic justice would be harder to imagine, so striking down DOMA was an easy call. Windsor got her tax exemption, and all gay and lesbian married couples were able to share in the victory—their marriages were now just as good as everyone else's.

But are everyone else's marriages *too good*? Perhaps Justice Ginsburg's metaphor was more apt than she realized. If straight marriages are "whole milk," as she implied, then they contain an unhealthy amount of fat. Maybe the solution should be skim-milk marriages for all.

What ingredients would such fat-free marriages contain? We can start thinking about that question by acknowledging that marriage contains too many benefits (fat), some of which aren't closely related to why the state supports the institution. During the litigation over whether same-sex couples should be allowed to marry, the Government Accountability Office estimated that marital status was a factor in determining rights, benefits, and obligations in some 1,138(!) statutory provisions.[15] The best known and most significant among these are federal income tax and estate tax rules that treat married and unmarried couples differently, eligibility for Social Security survivor and retirement benefits, and the allowance in immigration law for US citizens to sponsor their spouses into the country as permanent residents.[16] Marriage is also the trigger for many benefits at the state level, including inheritance rights, economic protection at divorce, the right to sue for wrongful death under tort law, and the right to hold property in a privileged legal form.[17] And it's not just the government that privileges marriage either—as anyone who receives spousal health or life insurance benefits from a private employer will attest.

But while these benefits are showered, indiscriminately, on those who are married, others have no access to them at all—no matter the depth or length of their commitment to another person. The marriage laws are problematic, then, and neither *Windsor* nor *Obergefell* addressed this divide. The decisions added gay and lesbian couples to the privileged side of the ledger but left untouched the disparity the law has erected between the married and the unmarried. Because the inclusion of these newly eligible pairs into the marriage club was in one sense radical, it was easy to miss that the movement was, in another sense, quite conservative. The velvet rope was unclasped for gay and lesbian couples but not for others. While the voices of the more creative opponents of this formal equality were hard to hear over the celebrations, the seeds of a more expansive view of relationship recognition and state support had already been planted. We'll take a close look at some of these efforts over the course of this book.

None of this should detract from recognizing the extraordinary, and swift, accomplishment of marriage equality. In the earliest cases challenging the exclusion of gay and lesbian couples from marriage, courts were uncomprehending and unsympathetic. But as the LGBTQ community became more visible over the past thirty years, so too did its members' relationships. Courts and then lawmakers began to take notice.[18] *Windsor* isn't the only case where a profile of the law's effect on actual people insinuated itself into a judicial opinion. The Massachusetts Supreme Court foregrounded its pathbreaking 2003 marriage equality decision, *Goodridge v. Department of Public Health*, by telling the stories of the fourteen couples seeking marriage licenses—a committed, responsible, and in some cases child-rearing group of unfairly treated citizens.[19] Justice Anthony Kennedy's majority decision in *Obergefell* followed a similar path, revealing heartbreaking details about James Obergefell's marriage in Maryland to a dying man and the state of Ohio's subsequent refusal to acknowledge that union by placing his name on his deceased partner's death certificate. Also featured was a lesbian couple who had not been able to jointly adopt two seriously ill babies, so that each child had only one legal parent.[20]

This book follows this narrative approach, presenting profiles of people in adult relationships that the law does not consistently recognize or support. For instance, the lifelong bond between two elderly sisters from Philadelphia underscores the dichotomy between Edie Windsor and Thea Spyer and other adults in committed relationships. These siblings, who appear in chapter 4, have lived together all their lives. They are emotionally and financially interdependent, no less than were Windsor and Spyer. But since they are sisters, they of course remain ineligible for marriage—

meaning that the survivor will not enjoy the estate tax exemption that Windsor ultimately received. Is that fair? Why or why not? And is the estate tax exemption fair in the first place? More broadly, how should the law support couples in relationships of different kinds?

Although the marriage equality movement achieved victory without answering these questions, it did not quite manage to avoid raising them—in two different but related ways. First, in tackling the issue of whether government had a valid reason for excluding same-sex couples from marriage, courts and legislatures were occasionally drawn into a broader discussion of what marriage means—what is it for, and why does the state support it? I address these crucial questions and make suggests for reforming the institution. Second, the growing realization among gay and lesbian couples that they were being treated unfairly in their relationships led them to advocate for "consolation prizes": other legal statuses that conferred benefits on them (and sometimes on other unmarried couples) short of marriage. These statuses began to appear in the 1980s and now flourish in cities, counties, and states. They carry several names and varying legal incidents, with attendant uncertainty and confusion. But they have the potential to serve as auguries of a more comprehensive alternative to marriage—one for which I enthusiastically make the case in this book.

In searching for real, defensible reasons for barring same-sex couples from marriage, defenders of traditional marriage could not avoid delving into existential issues about marriage itself. For instance, Supreme Court Justice Samuel Alito, in dissenting from the ruling in *Obergefell*, identified two competing views of marriage. The traditional view (which, he argued, states had a right to maintain) is that marriage is to encourage procreation in a stable setting—and since only different-sex couples can procreate without assistance, states can limit marriage rights to those couples. He went on to express a concern that once the marriage-procreation link was sundered, over time the institution might be "seriously undermine[d]."[21]

The other side of the debate, for Alito, was the modern view that marriage is mostly about "promot[ing] the well-being of those who choose to marry." This, he acknowledged, results in good things for society too: by providing "emotional fulfillment and the promise of support in times of need . . . marriage indirectly benefits society because persons who live in stable, fulfilling, and supportive relationships make better citizens." That's why "states encourage and formalize marriage, confer special benefits on married persons, and also impose some special obligations."[22] Alito concluded that the contest over the meaning of marriage had not been resolved and was best left to the political process.

The triumph of the marriage equality movement signified at least that marriage no longer meant *only* what traditionalists maintained was its one, true purpose—whether that was a version of Alito's natural law view, that the institution exists only to bring men and women together in recognition of their "biological complementarity,"[23] or, more dismally, the view of people like the conservative political commentator Maggie Gallagher, for whom it is a way of keeping men from leaving the children they'd otherwise be tempted to run from.[24]

Even on its own terms, Justice Alito's perception misses a few things— like the tenuous connection in the twenty-first century between procreation and marriage, or the government's interest in supporting *adoptive* families too—but it is a useful starting point for a discussion about what marriage does and should signify. Marriage equality didn't end that debate; it just represented the legal triumph of the more modern view. It also failed to address the more practical question of how far the state should go in privileging marriage above other forms of relationships— intimate and otherwise—and whether the benefits attached to it are central to its purpose.

Beyond forcing at least a limited debate on the meaning of marriage, the struggle for gay and lesbian equality did something else that could stand to remake life in the twenty-first century. Although the issue was mostly avoided by marriage equality advocates, the movement triggered the creation of several new legal statuses—sometimes indirectly and sometimes quite directly. The earliest of these was the *domestic partnership*. This status resists concise description, because it is actually a polymorph of sometimes distantly related things, conferred by different authorities. There are local domestic partnerships, offered by some cities and towns; statewide domestic partnerships; domestic partnership benefits provided by employers to employees as part of their compensation packages; and even de facto domestic partnerships created by courts to protect people whose reasonable expectations of support are defeated when their cohabitating partners skip out. And they're just as diverse in the benefits and rights they establish. Among these are health benefits, rights to hospital visitation, the ability to be named as a beneficiary of various pension plans—and many more, depending on where the partnership is formed and who's doing the conferring. Finally, domestic partnerships vary in the classes of couples eligible for them, as we'll see.

Chapter 1 profiles Tom Brougham and Barry Warren, the pioneering couple who invented the term *domestic partnership* and have been joined in that status since it became legal—way back in the 1980s. Their struggle and the explosion of domestic partnerships for which they lit the fuse have important implications for the future of nonmarital relationships.

A much tidier legal status arrived in 2000: the *civil union*. Perhaps the best known of the marriage alternatives and a direct outgrowth of the marriage equality movement, the civil union was specifically designed to be marriage in all but name. (That didn't work. The only thing equivalent to marriage is . . . marriage.) This clever compromise was created in Vermont as a way to give gay and lesbian couples legal rights without the charged label *marriage*.[25] My now husband, David, and I were among the early adopters. I tell our story in chapter 2.

Civil unions soon evolved in an unexpected way, when Illinois and Hawaii (later joined by Colorado) allowed *different-sex* couples to enter into them too.[26] This later variation turned out to have deep significance for some revolutionary couples who were willing to throw marriage aside for something they saw as having greater transformational potential. As it turns out, though, the civil union, which generally provides all of the state-based rights and obligations of marriage but is not recognized by federal law, is unlikely to be exactly the right vehicle for a movement investing in flexible legal alternatives to marriage. We'll explore why that is.

Other legal statuses have also emerged. Though not all of these were direct outgrowths of the struggle for gay and lesbian marriage, each was a response to the law's failure to see the lived reality of gay and lesbian couples and, increasingly, their children. Among these are "reciprocal beneficiaries" and something called the "designated beneficiary agreement."[27] Unfortunately, very few people have even heard of them. That's not surprising, since each is currently recognized in one state only: Hawaii has had its reciprocal beneficiary law in place for more than twenty years, while Colorado has offered designated beneficiary status since 2009. The latter status—itself inspired, in part, by Hawaii's law—has greater potential, as we'll see. It sets up a sort of do-it-yourself group of options for each couple, allowing the beneficiaries to pick and choose the rights and obligations they'd like to confer on each other.

Chapter 3 focuses on a few people for whom the designated beneficiary status was the best option—including Colorado State Senator Pat Steadman, who both drafted the law and became one of its earliest adopters, and Marilyn McCord, an intrepid senior citizen who found that marriage wasn't quite the right fit for her and her not exactly husband.

In other words, there's a market for other forms of relationships beyond marriage. But the marriage equality movement performed the neat trick of seeding the ground for these laws while mostly ignoring them.[28] So although American society is in fact in the midst of another, wider discussion about how to create legal structures that support all families, it's been conducted in a whisper. And conversations conducted at a low volume are easily drowned out.

The movement toward giving people options other than marriage has lost momentum, and some of these statuses are in danger of disappearing in the wake of full marriage equality. Some of the civil union laws have been repealed. Domestic partnership laws and company-conferred private equivalents are just as inconsistent in their persistence as they are diverse in structure. And the designated beneficiary agreement law—the greatest legal advance for partners since marriage itself—sits in splendid isolation, hemmed in by Colorado's majestic Rockies. These developments are not surprising. Since the statuses were often created to give some rights to couples who were not permitted to marry, there has been little appetite to extend them—or, in some cases, even to retain them.

Yet there's still time to build on the successes and to learn from the failures of these newbie statuses. Perhaps ironically, their viability has mostly been tied to whether they were also made available to *different-sex* couples. Those that were have mostly survived, while the laws created solely to accommodate same-sex couples have been blinking out, like dying stars. For instance, every state except New Jersey that granted civil union status to same-sex couples only has by now done away with that option, while the three states that extended the right to different-sex couples have kept it. Some of these still-extant laws address a wider range of issues than the same-sex-only laws. There they sit, waiting for analysis, improvement, and expansion.

Working through the stories of real couples, this book is one effort to bring attention to issues that marriage equality pried open to inspection without systematically examining. The chapters that follow move more or less chronologically through the various legal statuses that have surfaced in a sort of informal competition with marriage. The profiles of pioneers of domestic partnerships, civil unions, and then designated beneficiary agreements put into relief the promise and limitations of these ways of legal coexistence.

All of these problem-solving options have lasting value as part of the broader debate about how best to protect and empower people in their most important relationships. But because they were pieced together to solve specific problems, they fall short of realizing their own revolutionary potential. I attempt a synthesis of these statuses, putting together a sort of "greatest hits" package of their features while adding a few bonus tracks to the album.

Toward this end, in chapter 4 I introduce a final three couples as a way of pulling marriage apart into its myriad legal and social pieces to reveal how "busy" the institution is—and how it needs to be taken down a peg or two. At its vital core, marriage protects the expectations and commitments of couples—and signals that commitment to the broader society. Other features and benefits are mostly unfair, unprincipled accretions that need to be examined from the broader perspectives of equity and limited resources.

We'll go into greater detail about the two elderly sisters who have spent their lives together and are as emotionally and financially tied to each other as any married couple—indeed, likely closer than most. A gay man and a lesbian who decided to raise their biological children together have a story to tell about the difficulty of making existing legal options work for them. And we'll look in on one last gay couple, whose long wait for legal marriage led them to thoughtfully examine the institution as outsiders looking in. Their perceptive, deeply contextual view contains important truths about what marriage has meant, how it's changing, and how it might be reformed.

Once emptied of its bilge water, marriage can then be fruitfully compared to its new legal competitors and to relationships that exist without

any consistent protection. Even if marriage is destined to continue to signal the strongest adult commitment that the law recognizes, many other
forms of human connection need—*deserve*—protection too. Chapter 5
makes the case for a more systematic and fair approach to informal cohabitation and then lays out one vision for a new legal status. The proposal
borrows liberally from the several legal creatures that populate the first
three chapters, but creates something new and more flexible. It's an
improvement on the ingenious designated beneficiary status currently
recognized only in Colorado. Think of it as a kind of turbocharged designated beneficiary law.

The modular, adaptable approach I advocate stands to do a few things.
Most significantly for those who choose it, the designated beneficiary relationship provides flexibility, in several ways. It allows people to opt in and
out of all sorts of legal connections and commitments, and with much
greater speed and ease than is possible with marriage—even in an era of
no-fault divorce. It also breaks down the requirement and artificial expectation that our only legal adult relationships be solely with one other person.

One needn't take a position on polygamy—I don't here—to see that, for
many people, the strict and exclusive binary status that marriage creates
and still enforces isn't sufficient. Modern family law struggles with how to
recognize multiparent situations, for example. But since the difficulty is so
closely tied to (blinded by?) marriage, a new, more flexible legal arrangement would appeal to some adults as a way of accommodating a more
complex reality. Adult siblings—such as the pair profiled in chapter 4—as
well as mutually dependent lifelong friends, and elderly parents and their
middle-aged children, to name just a few, can also find much of use in a
new status.

Will this do-it-yourself relationship model make marriage less attractive? If so, is that a risk worth taking?

It's unlikely in the extreme that marriage will wither and die just
because another option becomes available. The institution is too powerfully embedded and still seen by most people as life's most important adult
relationship.

On the other side, marriage *in fact* is in decline, leaving millions of
people without reliable legal protection. Law is supposed to solve problems, not simply stand by with Olympian detachment while the needs of

so many go unaddressed. This isn't some abstract debate. As I write this, countless families wander about in legal limbo, unable to rely on the law to protect them and their financial security. At the same time, married couples continue to enjoy a deep pool of approval, tangible rewards, and the assurance that the law will support them. Not all of this is necessary or even good public policy, though. Recognition of cohabitating couples and the creation of another legal status are sorely needed and can send a message that one size does not fit all.

In the 1970s, few were concerned about, much less involved with, the threat to the state-conferred marriage monopoly that these modest efforts at expanding relationship recognition posed. But more people should have been. Feminism and the advent of no-fault divorce had already begun to eat away at the general legal and social assumptions on which marriage critically depends for its supremacy. Despite the incremental approach taken by its originators, the domestic partnership was an early form of competition for marriage and, as we shall see through subsequent chapters, destined not to be its only challenger.

Further competition arose in part because domestic partnerships have been incomplete responses to the needs of couples. In the final chapter, I will advance a few tentative proposals for streamlining the law to achieve both consistency and desirable social ends. But domestic partnerships deserve praise for their substantial contribution to the ongoing relationship recognition project—as do their creators—and form part of the call for a more comprehensive status. Brougham and Warren were true pioneers, and their achievement should be celebrated.

1 The Dawn of the Domestic Partnership, or "We Bored Them to Death"

> When we started you couldn't have a rational conversation
> with anybody on the topic of marriage. They couldn't get
> their minds around the idea that marriage could be
> changed and should be changed. So we sort of started with
> domestic partners. We imagined that some people, some
> places, would accept a [more limited] device.
>
> Tom Brougham

Tom Brougham coined the term *domestic partnership* in the 1970s. He and his life partner, Barry Warren, then fought for more than five years to make Berkeley, California, the first place to allow two people to register for that status. Though they began with the modest aim of obtaining health benefits for couples in committed relationships, their actions were the trigger for the explosion of domestic partnership laws and benefits that now illuminate the legal and corporate landscape and exist in many forms.

The domestic partnership is the best place to start our journey through marriage alternatives, and not only because it was the first one recognized. The evolution of this creative legal status relates closely to the marriage equality movement that followed, as well as to the drive for other alternatives to marriage. And by taking a hard look at the limitations of the domestic partnership, we can soberly assess the current clutter of marriage alternatives to determine what to do next. Moreover, the debates that arose during the consideration of domestic partnerships helped to

reshape our collective ideas about what marriage means and the privilege
it enjoys over other forms of relationships.[1]

Brougham and Warren met in 1975 and have been together ever since.
Warren grew up on the shore of Lake Michigan and—like countless thousands of his closeted era—moved to San Francisco, in 1974. Brougham
didn't have as far to go, having spent most of his life with liberal parents in
the East Bay. Not surprisingly for the time and place, he became involved
in what was then referred to (and what he still calls) the gay liberation
movement: "The sky cracked open. I became very active in what we . . .
called the countergroups that grew out of the hippie movement. That's
where people started being able to talk about being gay."[2]

Suddenly, Brougham found himself "in large rooms full of gay people."
He absorbed the radical energy of the Berkeley community and went "from
repressed to having sexual fun." But not just fun—he helped to put on gay
events and stood on the legendary Telegraph Avenue disseminating information and protesting such indignities as the refusal of a gay bar to distribute the local gay paper. "We were very bold. . . . We were hassled, and
hassled right back." But because of their sheer numbers, they learned not
to be afraid. For the times, Brougham admits, he "lived a charmed life."

That kind of early confidence and youthful belief in wide possibility
would stand Brougham in good stead during the protracted effort to bring
domestic partnership to Berkeley. Over two long Skype interviews, he and
Warren discussed their relentless push for domestic partnership recognition and offered contrarian views on the now mainstream marriage equality movement.

In 1979, Brougham began working for the City of Berkeley. The previous year, Berkeley had passed one of the first antidiscrimination laws in
the country that expressly named sexual orientation as a protected class.[3]
But Brougham wasn't able to get the spousal health benefits for Warren
that married couples were entitled to. For him, that was an act of discrimination, pure and simple. "We were looking for a way of solving the problem that was immediately in front of us," he said. In so doing, Brougham
coined a new term: *domestic partnership*. "We were looking for a term
that was quasi-legalistic, nonsexual. We wanted to emphasize the humdrum arrangements that people make. . . . We wanted to bleed out anything that was sexual." Not because the couple wasn't sexual—after all,

they'd met at a bathhouse—but because it just made sense, from a strategic perspective, to highlight the commitment rather than what most would have seen as an "icky" intimacy.

Brougham and Warren were trying to perform a delicate dance. They needed to start by pointing out that the city was using marriage by different-sex couples as the basis for health benefits to the nonemployee spouse, and to use their own ineligibility to marry as the intellectual and moral scaffolding of their discrimination argument. But then they needed to pivot sharply *away* from marriage, avoiding its deeper resonances and its strong, then unchallenged association with the union of a man and a woman. In the late 1970s, even though no-fault divorce laws had begun to erode the idea of marriage as a lifelong, ironclad commitment, the connections among marriage, procreation, and child-rearing were deeply infused in the public consciousness. Marriage rates remained high, and most children were born to married couples.[4] It's true that the advent of the birth control pill, approved for contraceptive use in 1960, and the nationwide legalization of abortion through the US Supreme Court's 1973 decision in *Roe v. Wade* had begun to pry loose the traditional view of marriage as being for procreation.[5] But there was no profit in a gay couple's reminding anyone that the old world was being shaken up.

Better to emphasize what Brougham called the "humdrum" agreements that people living together often enter into, usually not even expressly. Despite their immersion in the radical, post-Stonewall culture of the time, Brougham and Warren knew that any effort to view same-sex couples as apt candidates for marriage would have fizzled spectacularly.[6]

Indeed, such challenges to the different-sex-only marriage laws had already been brought—and had failed. While the story of the fight over marriage equality typically begins in the 1990s (with a decision by the Hawaii Supreme Court, discussed in chapter 2), in fact the history is much deeper.

Before the 1970s, questioning why marriage excluded gay people was an intellectual exercise and a performative gesture. For example, a 1953 commentary in the gay-targeted magazine *One* asked why gay individuals were excluded from the sexual norms of the era. Imagining the world of 2053, in which "homosexuality [is] accepted to the point of being of no importance," E. B. Saunders asked, In that case, can gay men continue to live as sexual libertines outside the confines of marriage?[7] Saunders advanced this argument in an attempt to redirect the efforts of the Mattachine Society, an early gay rights organization, toward gaining the right to same-sex marriage and away from continuing its work to empower and make "homosexuals" more visible. The Los Angeles postmaster later declined to mail the magazine, calling it "obscene," but the Supreme Court sided with the magazine's publisher, in *One, Inc. v. Oleson*.[8]

The Postal Service needn't have worried. Saunders's idea went nowhere for almost twenty years, during which same-sex marriage efforts were largely matters of theater. One well-known, dramatic example comes from shortly after the Stonewall Riots of 1969. In 1971, members of the Gay Activists Alliance stormed the New York City Marriage Bureau with coffee and cake to stage an engagement party and to protest a public official's threat to bring legal action against a church that was performing religious "union" ceremonies, even though they had no legal effect. But the protesters didn't expect to be issued marriage licenses—and they weren't.[9] It's worth noting that the very notion that a church could be prosecuted for staging same-sex marriage ceremonies speaks to the extent of public and governmental policing of the definition of *marriage*. Today, no such ban on a purely religious ceremony could survive a challenge based on the First Amendment's guarantee of the related freedoms of speech and expressive conduct.[10]

Virtually at the same time as the New York protest, do-it-yourself litigants unleashed a mini-flurry of lawsuits seeking to upend gay-excluding marriage laws. But the results would have convinced any *practical* activist to do what Brougham and Warren did: they turned away from the judiciary and sought a narrower relational benefit—for gay and lesbian couples only. As they told me, they were not thinking about straight couples at that early stage: "Our view was that's nice, and you could do that too, if you wanted. But what we're dealing with is discrimination on the basis of sexual orientation." This thinking explains why the new domestic partnership law did not attempt to reach or protect people in other committed relationships. Why not any two adults living in a mutually supportive relationship, including, say, siblings? But that wasn't the couple's project. In a sense, Brougham and Warren were incrementalists—arguing for just as much as needed to achieve a specific goal.

Their political strategy was also careful and deliberate. They attempted to gain local public support, which they used to pressure elected officials, who needed their constituents' votes to stay in office. The political strategy was more appealing than a judicial one at that time. Indeed, the few court cases on the marriage question flopped spectacularly. A gay couple in Minnesota, a lesbian couple in Kentucky, and two gay men in Washington State (who didn't even consider themselves a couple) brought challenges to laws that denied same-sex couples the right to obtain marriage licenses. In a series of decisions issued from late 1972 through mid-1974, all three lost.[11]

The Washington plaintiffs, at least, were clear about their motivation for going after the law. One of them, John Singer, boldly proclaimed, "We would just as soon abolish marriage, but we can fight it from within, also."[12] He publicly declared the institution "wrong" and "oppressive"—as it then existed, limited to different-sex couples. His comments speak to the infusion of feminist ideology and rhetoric into the gay rights movement. But while the women's rights movement had some success in questioning and deconstructing gender roles within marriage, Singer and his contemporaries found the entrance barred. In a deep sense, the courts didn't even understand that a same-sex couple could be married: how could a court grant the plaintiffs a marriage license, a Washington appellate court wondered, when "the recognized definition of [the] relationship [is] one which may be entered into only by two persons who are members of the opposite sex"?[13] Similarly, the Kentucky Supreme Court simply defined the plaintiffs' claim out of existence, with the tautological statement that same-sex couples "are prevented from marrying ... by their own incapability of entering into a marriage as that term is defined."[14]

Worse, some of these couples suffered terrible personal consequences for even daring to broach the topic. One of the plaintiffs in the Minnesota case, James Michael McConnell, lost a job offer from the University of Minnesota, apparently because bringing a lawsuit of this kind was "not consistent with the best interests of the University." And Singer, who had been confident that his employer—the US government—would support him, also found himself without a job, because of his "immoral and notoriously disgraceful conduct."[15]

Although these judicial losses helped persuade Brougham and Warren to achieve their goals legislatively, one court case did help them construct their vision. Brougham described the 1976 California Supreme Court's decision in *Marvin v. Marvin* as "very important" to the couple's effort.[16] In a bold and unprecedented ruling from a state high court, the justices held that marriage was no longer the only chocolate in the box, so to speak. The court recognized that, if certain facts could be established, the actor Lee Marvin could be compelled to divide the property he'd acquired in his own name with Michelle Marvin, his long-time cohabitant, after the couple's relationship ended. Noting "the prevalence of non-marital relationships in modern society and the social acceptance of them," the justices looked to the *actual* relationship between two people living together and held that an express agreement between them to share property acquired during the relationship could be enforced.[17] So far, the court broke no new ground—contracts are generally enforceable, and earlier decisions had applied this logic to the domestic sphere. The court then went further, though, and found that even an *implied sharing agreement* could be enforced. Michelle alleged that she and Lee had made the same kinds of compromises that married couples make in order to maximize their collective success. In particular, she had "given up her lucrative career as an entertainer" to "devote her full time to defendant," in exchange for which he'd agreed to "provide for all of [her] financial support and needs."[18] The court was effectively recognizing a do-it-yourself domestic partnership.

Moreover, the California Supreme Court surgically separated the Marvins' domestic relationship from their sexual relationship. Michelle said she had agreed to "render her services as a companion, homemaker, housekeeper, and cook."[19] Choosing the word *companion* was sound advocacy, as it connotes deep friendship rather than sexual partnership. Indeed, the court, following earlier decisions, reaffirmed the view that no agreement between partners could be enforced if "meretricious"—a needlessly fancy word for "sexual"—services were expressly part of the deal.[20] Such an arrangement was seen as a kind of illegal prostitution.

Thus, *Marvin* provided Brougham and Warren with good source material for their effort to draw attention to the quotidian nature of what they were to call a domestic partnership: a relationship that anticipates and includes all kinds of regular labor and services but whose name pointedly diverts attention from the sexual component.

That move was necessary in the early 1980s, as a comparison of two cases—one from 1981 and the other from 1988—highlights. In the first, *Jones v. Daly*, a California appellate court refused to recognize a support claim by a gay man whose relationship with his former partner was based on services that included acting as a "lover."[21] But just seven years later, in *Whorton v. Dillingham*, a different appellate court in California severed that part of a similar agreement from consideration.[22] The 1988 decision upheld the validity of a contract between the former gay couple that rested on an extensive list of other "services that Whorton agreed to provide": "chauffeur, bodyguard, social and business secretary, partner and counselor in real estate investments[;] labor, skills, and personal services for the benefit of Dillingham's business and investment endeavors[; and] to be Dillingham's constant companion, confidant, traveling and social companion, and lover."[23] Including "lover" was no longer a deal breaker for the court—but it was still necessary to excise the offending term (and relationship) as a prelude to enforcing the agreement.

Brougham and Warren's savvy understanding of the legal and social climate led them to draft two letters to Berkeley's City Council in their quest for a marriage alternative in 1979. In the first, they asserted that Berkeley's employee policy created uneven effects and therefore violated the antidiscrimination law. The second letter proposed a new legal relationship, which they called a "domestic partnership," to solve the problem. It would have required the couple to sign an affidavit making the following set of attestations, which would significantly limit who could take advantage of the domestic partnership option: the couple were qualified to marry but for having the same sex; they were cohabitants; and the nonemployee was the sole domestic partner of the employee. Given their own needs and the difficulty of what they were trying to accomplish, the pioneering couple's strategy was not just understandable but brilliant. It followed a standard litigator's approach: ask for only what your client needs, and try to assure the court that allowing your client's case to succeed won't bring down a hail of unintended consequences. Brougham and Warren needed benefits—especially health benefits, which are typically the most valuable source of nonwage compensation employers offer. By setting the bar for entry into a domestic partnership high, they were trying to provide similar assurances. The cohabitation requirement, for instance, comes directly from *Marvin*—and was likely a necessary limitation on their attempt to gain legal relationship status absent marriage. Of course, legally married couples can live apart; some do. But cohabitation is one of the most common facts about the great majority of marriages and was used here as a proof of the kind of committed relationship that deserves legal recognition. As for the exclusivity requirement, it was probably wise for Brougham and Warren to keep more complex living arrangements—ones that might call up unwelcome images of communal (read: hippie) living or illegal, polygamous marriages—behind a thickly plastered wall.

Despite its limitations, the idea of a formal domestic partnership registry was an improvement over the ad hoc, case-specific *Marvin* approach. And since a domestic partnership, unlike the Marvins' agreement, makes financial demands on third parties, including local government, the formality and predictability of registration was absolutely necessary.

In developing their proposal in the face of resistance over the next several years, Brougham and Warren went further and agreed to a requirement that the couple show financial interdependence. So while establishing the domestic partnership was a major victory, the nature of the arrangement was more rigid than was perhaps optimal for any couple, gay or straight.

Despite what they thought to be a careful, limited, and logical approach, Brougham and Warren were greeted with polite refusals; people were just "dumbfounded" at first. But they persisted. They teamed up with Harry Britt, a member of San Francisco's Board of Supervisors, for their second attempt, in 1982. Britt was impressed by the idea of domestic partnership after hearing Brougham speak at a political meeting and brought a domestic partnership measure to the board. The measure passed. But the then mayor (and later long-serving US senator) Dianne Feinstein vetoed it.[24]

Neither their own, early defeat nor the humiliating setback in San Francisco dampened Brougham and Warren's resolve. In fact, they regarded the latter loss in a glass-half-full light, recognizing that the passage of a domestic partnership law—even though vetoed—had catalyzed awareness and discussion. While the Berkeley effort had mostly gone on in quiet frustration, San Francisco's debacle made people begin to "rage against the denial of benefits." Brougham later described the situation as "kind of neat."[25] So he and Warren got back to work.

This time, they engaged in a longer-term political strategy. They became founding members of the East Bay Lesbian/Gay Democratic Club in 1983 and leveraged its collective strength for a series of steps and actions that they believed could result in victory. Their effort began with community education and awareness campaigns about the importance of a domestic partnership law for both the practical benefits it could bring and the statement it would make about nondiscrimination (what in current political terms might be more positively called equality). They organized gay voters, recognizing their numbers as sufficient to form an identity-based voting bloc. They educated candidates for the Berkeley City Council and then got those supporters elected in November 1984.

While this was going on, Brougham and Warren were working with city council members, painstakingly researching and answering all their questions and drafting language for various documents that they demanded. (During a rare moment of ownership of the couple's work, Warren, who has a master's degree in English from the University of Chicago, stated that he had been instrumental in this aspect of the effort.) "We bored them to death" with facts, Brougham recalled with a certain well-earned satisfaction. "If they had nine questions, we answered them all." Sometimes success comes down to "not going away."

One other factor likely contributed to the success of the domestic partnership law. Between 1979 and 1984, AIDS had appeared and quickly begun to decimate the gay community. In June 1981, the Centers for Disease Control and Prevention first identified a cluster of cases in which men who had sex with men had died of unusual causes; these were soon marked as stemming from severely compromised immune systems.[26] From that date through 1984, the pace of human destruction quickened dramatically, especially in San Francisco and New York. And the disease left dramatic markers of its effects, notably the leprosy-recalling lesions of Kaposi's sarcoma and the physical wasting that reduced many victims to sepulchral, skeletal figures roaming devastated urban landscapes. The complex societal response to this tragedy has been extensively described.[27] For many, AIDS created (or intensified) a gay panic that equated homosexuality with disease and death and fed a simplistic, biblical narrative of retribution for forbidden conduct.[28]

But for many others, AIDS held a different meaning. Brougham eloquently describes how the disease created and strengthened couples, families, and communities of support—and thereby moved the needle toward
viewing gays as people. "Prior to the AIDS epidemic, it was pretty easy for
most people to see gay relationships as primarily sexual and primarily
transitory. And even if they lasted a long time, it wasn't clear to people that
gay people had as passionate a commitment. But [after AIDS], they saw
the suffering—and the commitment. They saw the passion and the work.
It was harder to dismiss it as just sex." Concurrently, AIDS made the
domestic partnership effort more critical. Health benefits were pushed
dramatically to the fore, as were complex end-of-life issues. As Brougham
stated, the disease "changed people's ideas about the significance of having
the right to control things. And to have those resources and benefits made
the issues very practical and very emotional, at the same time." Warren
pointed out that some public officials questioned whether couples might
sign up for domestic partnership status "just" to acquire health benefits
for a sick gay friend, even if the two were not a couple. His sensible
response was that the financial and emotional commitments of caregiving
were sufficiently daunting that no one would sign up for such a status
lightly, and that different-sex couples might try to game the system in
similar ways, though perhaps for different diseases.

It's possible that, had Brougham and Warren launched their campaign
after the worst of the AIDS crisis rather than before the devastation began,
they might have come up with a name other than the deliberately banal
domestic partnership. In at least one city, Philadelphia, a later bill (passed
in 1997) chose the richer term *life partnership* to describe the kind of
interconnected lives that registrants would typically share.[29] The law
expresses the requirements of this life sharing quantitatively, by mandat-
ing that the prospective life partners verify participation in at least two of
six categories, relating to joint ownership of property, cohabitation, designation of the other as a beneficiary in a number of possible contexts, and
mutual power of attorney. But the law also contains the idea of a shared
life *qualitatively*, listing among the requirements a couple's "agree[ment]
to share the common necessities of life and to be responsible for each other's common welfare." This language doesn't—and can't—mandate that

the couple be "lovers," but the simple eloquence of the phrase "responsible for each other's common welfare" betokens recognition that there is something else going on here besides the day-to-day division of labor on which the domestic partnership deliberately trained its focus. Isn't a couple's commitment to their common welfare one of the ways we define and think about marriage?[30]

When the East Bay organization's slate of candidates was elected in 1984, Brougham and Warren's relentless efforts paid off. The domestic partnership law was passed on the very day that the new council came into power. So it was that in 1984, the City of Berkeley became the first unit of government in the nation to recognize the relationships of same-sex couples. Although it would take another year for the status to include the big prize of health benefits—the reason the couple had launched their long campaign in the first place—the domestic partnership had been officially created.[31]

Other cities throughout the more liberal precincts of California quickly followed Berkeley's example. West Hollywood passed a domestic partnership law in 1985.[32] And San Francisco finally punched through a measure in 1989.[33] It was rejected by a voter referendum later that year, but a new ordinance was passed just two years later.[34] Again, the withering toll of AIDS played a role—not only in the support that the law received but also, in a foreshadowing of the variability of domestic partnership laws, in the benefits that it conferred. Chief among these were the right to hospital visitation of one's domestic partner and to bereavement leave equivalent to that afforded married couples. Health benefits, an issue that concerned insurers because of the toll of the AIDS crisis, were provided shortly thereafter.[35]

These laws soon went further than the original Berkeley proposal in one crucial respect: they typically included *different-sex* couples as eligible registrants. Indeed, even the Berkeley measure, when it finally passed, included different-sex couples. In retrospect, the law's expansion was an early sign that although marriage alternatives were necessary for gay couples, they were attractive to some straight couples too. Once the idea of unbraiding marriage from benefits was raised, there was no obvious reason to limit consideration of benefits eligibility to people who were formally excluded from marriage. Should a different-sex couple really need to marry to gain access to benefits, especially given the steady increase in cohabitation that at least some cities were beginning to acknowledge? *Marvin v. Marvin* paved the way for state and local lawmakers to consider this question seriously. While it has no easy answer, raising it invites further, sometimes uncomfortable questions about how government-conferred benefits should be allocated and distributed.

For all couples in these new domestic partnerships, the typical requirements were the same: they had to live together, share expenses, and not be married to anyone else. And domestic partnerships were easy to enter and exit: they could be registered for a small amount of money, and filing a notice of termination was enough to get the couple out of the relationship. It is clear how the simplicity of the status would appeal to different-sex couples—perhaps especially to city workers who wanted health benefits but not all the obligations that come with marriage. Likely for these reasons, San Francisco and other cities continue to offer domestic partnership status to this day—even though full marriage equality has by now come to California.[36] (In fact, as we'll see later in this chapter, *statewide* domestic partnership status remains available to same-sex couples in California.)

Not surprisingly, the disruptive potential of domestic partnerships was also clear to their opponents. One of the talking points against the original San Francisco domestic partnership law cast it as an attack on "the sanctity of marriage"; the Roman Catholic Church was particularly vocal on this issue.[37] The same strategy has been in evidence everywhere since that time: no matter how broad or narrow a proposed law granting recognition to same-sex couples, no matter how many or how few benefits it confers, determined oppositionists have sought to turn it into a referendum on whether gay and lesbian citizens have a right to marry. Sometimes the argument is cast more broadly, to include even *different-sex* domestic partnerships and other marriage alternatives, such as civil unions. They too can be portrayed as threats to marriage rather than as reasonable attempts to solve the practical problems people face. Today, of course, the argument is no longer about same-sex marriages but about the allegedly existential threat to marriage that these alternatives are posited to pose.

Until the *Obergefell* decision in 2015, states were able to push through laws and even amendments to their constitutions that banned not only same-sex marriages but all other kinds of relationship recognition for gay and lesbian couples. (Some, such as Virginia, potentially excluded private contractual agreements between same-sex partners!)[38] By folding such alternative relationships into measures that included marriage, lawmakers were able to completely fence these couples out of possible legal recognition. Sometimes these laws were successfully challenged, but courts usually upheld them.[39]

Despite these pockets of resistance, domestic partnership laws spread throughout the entire state of California and the nation. Perhaps more significant, the flowering of this once novel status was not limited to governments. For instance, in addition to applying pressure to Berkeley, Brougham and Warren pushed for the University of California to recognize their relationship, because Warren was employed by the Berkeley campus.

In the thirty-plus years since the duo's pioneering efforts bore fruit, acknowledgment of domestic partnerships has spread throughout the corporate world too. Many companies see a competitive advantage in offering benefits to the partners of gay and lesbian employees, rightly figuring that sought-after workers will choose an employer that values their relationship in a tangible way.[40] And couples can of course enter into private legally binding agreements that sometimes also go by the name of domestic partnerships.[41]

Even at the governmental level, however, because of how they were founded, domestic partnerships are an incomplete solution. Although they vary too widely to lend themselves to a simple summary, in general they provide health benefits, allow partners to visit each other in the hospital, and make couples' benefits at public facilities available to registered partners. All of these provisions are good, practical responses to real needs, but a true marriage alternative could do so much more. That's especially true because the domestic partnership alternative is beset by several problems.

The first problem is that many domestic partnership statutes and rules have been dismantled now that it is unconstitutional under the *Obergefell* decision to deprive gay couples of the right to marry. This is particularly true for those domestic partnerships that only gay couples could enter into.[42] After all, since same-sex couples now have the option to marry, allowing them the domestic partnership option can be seen as unfair to different-sex couples who have no such choice! In fact, the availability of a given status to straight couples turns out to be the biggest predictor of its continued vitality in a post-marriage-equality world. Indeed, only the state of California and certain localities in Arizona have opted to retain their domestic partnership laws. Moreover, shortly after the decision in *Obergefell* was handed down, several large corporations—including Verizon, Delta Air Lines, and Corning—informed their gay and lesbian employees that they had to marry within a certain period or lose their "spousal" benefits.[43] Maryland took a similar action for state employees: same-sex couples who had been registered as domestic partners had one year from January 1, 2013, the date marriage equality arrived in the state, to marry or lose their benefits.[44] By contrast, companies like Google and Dow Chemical, which had offered the domestic partnership option to all couples, decided to retain it.[45]

Second, domestic partnerships are maddeningly variable in the benefits associated with them, which leads to problems. For one thing, it is difficult for third parties to understand what the relationship *means* from a legal perspective. The variability may also raise uncertainties for the couple themselves. When they move from one place to another, will they need to reregister? Will one state or locality recognize a domestic partnership from another? What sense does it make to label as a domestic partnership both a local and a statewide status, as California has done? As we'll see in later chapters, the problem only multiplies when available legal relationships do. Beyond domestic partnerships lie civil unions and other statuses. With reciprocal beneficiary and designated beneficiary laws now on the books, these issues can't safely be ignored. We'll discuss how to deal with this very real, practical problem in the final chapter. The lack of uniformity also lessens the social capital of the term: whereas marriage enjoys wide (though not universal) approbation as a status to be aspired to (even among many cohabitants), domestic partnerships are often still seen as a kind of expedient arrangement—contingent, sometimes of limited utility, and definitely second best.

A third, related problem is the confusion that results from overlapping legislation. California provides a good example. Like many others, Brougham and Warren registered their relationship at the *state* level after that option became available in 1999. But that did not erase their Berkeley-conferred domestic partnership. In other words, it is now possible for couples to maintain two statuses and thereby two sets of perhaps inconsistent benefits. A local domestic partnership law will be of limited use, since localities do not provide many benefits—although those who work for a city or county will often be able to claim access to health benefits for a partner. At the state level, though, the benefits package can be much more substantial, especially as the status moves closer to marriage. In California, the domestic partnership benefits were substantially expanded in 2003 and then, through a series of subsequent amendments, eventually reached practical equivalence with those conferred by marriage, at least at the state (though not the federal) level. The problems of multiple statuses grew even more acute after same-sex marriage became available in California—and the domestic partnership law was not then repealed.[46]

Even in states that recognize domestic partnerships only at the local level, confusion abounds. Consider Arizona, which surely has the most complex system in place. There, an amendment to the state's constitution in 2008 prohibited marriages but not other forms of relationships for couples of the same sex.[47] Before the amendment was passed, several cities and other localities had enacted domestic partnership laws, and others followed after 2008. The right to visit the partner in the hospital was the most usual and sometimes the only benefit of real consequence. In a few places, like Scottsdale, the domestic partner was entitled to a city employee's health insurance benefits, but, perhaps because this meant a financial commitment, the city required substantial documentation of the couple's financial interdependence. The city didn't care whether the parties lived together but instead asked for documents in a minimum of three categories, most revolving around finances: joint mortgage, joint property tax identification, or joint tenancy on a residential lease; joint bank account; joint liabilities; joint ownership of "significant property" (such as a car, a home, or a boat); and mutual naming as primary beneficiaries in a will or a retirement account. (The law also counts conveying power of attorney from one to the other, but that would count for one of only three required documents.)[48] Sedona's law is even more generous, extending to a domestic partner whatever benefits the city provides to the legal spouses of its employees, but again requires substantial documentation.[49]

Where private companies and other nongovernmental actors are concerned, the picture is even blurrier. Domestic partnership status is generally a way for employees to have their partners named as beneficiaries of any plan or policy, such as health or life insurance, that the employer offers. Of course, each company has its own rules as to how a couple can prove a domestic partnership: while some are satisfied with a declaration of mutual interdependence (and perhaps cohabitation), others require more rigorous substantiation—such as legal domestic partnership status, where permitted, or documentation of joint accounts, a home held in common, and so on.

A fourth drawback is that eligibility is overly narrow. For example, the domestic partnership laws in both Arizona and California prevent close blood relations from entering into the arrangement. Imagine that Nancy and her sibling, Chris, are financially interdependent. In addition, they function as a mutual support system: when Nancy was sick last year, Chris took care of her. But Nancy's health has continued to decline, and Chris is worried about the financial future when she dies. That's because, although they own their home jointly, Chris might lose it through the federal and state estate taxes on Nancy's half of its value. Obviously, this exclusion of relatives has nothing to do with steering people away from domestic partnership and into the preferred institution of marriage and everything to do with viewing domestic partnership as a kind of "off-brand" marriage for limited populations.

When California legalized domestic partnerships, eligibility was quite restricted. Some lawmakers, including the then governor Gray Davis, were worried about establishing an alternative to marriage that would be too appealing to many people. Davis requested that the status be limited to same-sex couples, although many legislators wanted it to be open to all adults.[50] The compromise that was eventually reached allowed different-sex couples to choose the domestic partnership alternative only if at least one of them was at least sixty-two years of age. Why sixty-two? Because that is the minimum age for social security retirement benefit eligibility, and remarriage—but *not* entrance into a domestic partnership—would mean that an otherwise eligible claimant would no longer be able to collect retirement benefits based on their former spouse's work history.[51] This solution is not perfect. Surely there are some formerly married people younger than sixty-two who might decide not to remarry *in anticipation of* attaining that age; they too might like to take advantage of the domestic partnership. That might explain why the law was recently changed to eliminate the age requirement; now all unrelated adult couples can opt into domestic partnership status.[52]

The movement to do away with domestic partnerships stems from two related but mistaken beliefs. The first is that the status is a sort of "poor man's marriage," to be tolerated only until the real thing comes along. While some might choose to marry once that right becomes available, the experience of those cities, states, and corporations that have extended the option to straight employees who could have married shows that the *reality* of the relationship, not the legal status of marriage per se, is what needs to be supported.

This brings us to the second error: why should employers insist on marriage, or any other state-sponsored relationship, as a vehicle for the conveyance of benefits? Isn't there a right *not to marry*? Employees in living situations other than marriage have called the current situation unfair. A *New York Times* article from 2015 clearly laid out the simple, persuasive arguments of one: "'No American should be denied benefits by their employer or otherwise penalized for choosing to opt out of a religiously and societally mandated but historically problematic institution,' said Andrew Parks, who was in a committed relationship with Ashlea Halpern. 'Who is the I.R.S. or an I.C.U. nurse or an H.R. department to say that one couple . . . is more committed than another, simply because they are married?'"[53] Whatever the reason for declining to marry, people might still need or want benefits that will both make their lives more secure and—not insignificantly—provide a kind of private safety net that decreases the burden on public resources.

In short, the solution to any unfairness to straight couples with the coming of marriage equality isn't to take away domestic partnership status or benefits but to retain them—or, if such benefits were available only to same-sex couples before, to expand them to *all* couples. Although the domestic partnership has outlived its original raison d'être as a sop to same-sex couples, our continually progressing society should breathe new life into these arrangements. As Kenneth Matos of the Families and Work Institute said in that same *Times* article, "The modern family is changing. . . . As families continue to evolve, organizations are better served by supporting benefits options that can easily encompass any talented employee's family arrangements, rather than actively limiting support for uncommon family options."[54] Today it's not even accurate to say that non-marital relationships are uncommon, given that the US Bureau of Labor Statistics reported in 2014, for the first time, that more than half of those over the age of sixteen were unmarried.[55]

But what about the *cost* of such benefits? Cash-strapped cities and states and private employers looking at the bottom line might be concerned about the price of continuing to recognize domestic partnership status. So far, this fear isn't reasonable, as the cost has been minimal. Even if the price tag goes up (as will occur as more people choose not to marry), the solution isn't to continue drawing an arbitrary line at marriage but to equalize compensation to all employees. The benefits issue is explored in greater depth in chapter 5, but for now consider this solution: why not simply give each employee a lump sum for each benefit, which can be used as the employee sees fit? As things stand now, employees with spouses— and even more so, those with spouses and children—often receive more compensation than similarly situated co-workers. In the current situation, refusing to recognize domestic partnerships both privileges married couples (and those with children) and undercompensates everyone else.

Again, it seems as though the law is infected with the marriage-default virus. Even if domestic partnerships made sense as a bone thrown to same-sex couples, the governing assumption was that those who could marry should. Yet this assumption works negatively, closing off domestic partnerships to those who aren't able to marry—principally, close relatives, even if, like Nancy and Chris, they might benefit enormously from such legal recognition. What, then, is the purpose of domestic partnerships for different-sex couples? They provide only the same benefits as marriage, and only to a subset of the same people.

Well, not exactly. Take California. Although domestic partnership carries the same rights, benefits, and obligations as marriage within California, it has no value or force under federal law. That was of potential benefit to anyone old enough to take advantage of the social security retirement benefits available to married couples—not coincidentally, age sixty-two at the time the domestic partnership law was passed, as we've seen: since domestic partnership did not count as marriage under federal law, the formerly married person could continue to receive the benefits conferred by marriage even after registering for the new status.[56]

It's hard to know what to say about these other-than-marriage laws. Do they sometimes game the system? Are they weird offshoots of the fight for LGBTQ rights and recognition? Are they incomplete answers to people's actual needs? Yes, yes, and . . . well, yes, but this final *yes* requires qualification. No law is a complete answer to anything. But domestic partnership laws can be a way for two consenting adults to more easily pool their resources and gain a measure of financial and (thereby) emotional security. If that's the goal, though, then the domestic partnership laws should be more inclusive, stronger, and tied to reliance and financial need. For instance, if Nancy and Chris have interdependent finances and own a home together, then for the state to impose an estate tax on the survivor seems no fairer than it would be for the survivor of a married or domestically partnered couple. (Although California does not have an estate tax, many states do. And in any case, there is still the *federal* estate tax for large estates.)

Some domestic partnership laws and proposed laws take a more flexible approach, thus suggesting models for the future. Some localities in Arizona, for example, allow for a broader range of rights than those typically conferred by domestic partnerships. In Clarkdale and Sedona, the parties can spell out their agreements on such issues as the ownership and management of property and its disposition when one of them dies, obligations to their current or prospective children, and how they will resolve any disputes that might arise if the relationship ends. But these agreements are not filed with the locality; they are simply referred to in a series of boxes on a form that the couple does file. They can also include any other documents that establish rights or obligations they've agreed to.[57] These measures can be seen, then, as collapsing the distance between run-of-the-mill domestic partnership laws and *Marvin*'s recognition that unmarried couples sometimes wish to arrange their lives in agreed-upon ways.[58]

Several years ago, Florida legislators similarly attempted to broaden the rights afforded under domestic partnerships. Lawmakers in both the statehouse and the senate introduced bills that would have created a statewide registry to permit partners to designate each other as end-of-life decision-makers, protect their mutual estates and inheritance, and sue for the wrongful death of the other.[59] If these protections seem geared primarily toward senior citizens, no one should be surprised: the Sunshine State has the highest percentage of older Americans in the country. Yet the measures died.

In helping to establish the first domestic partnership laws, Brougham and Warren proved that marriage alternatives are possible to enact and are needed. By pushing forward the interests of LGBTQ couples first and then of others whose views of marriage fell outside the mainstream, these largely unheralded civil rights pioneers advanced the national (and, as we'll see, the international) conversation about how governments recognize, support, and value the relationships of committed couples. Once the first domestic partnership law slid into place, it was no longer possible to avoid confronting how the law advances some relationships but not others. Decades later, we can also recognize domestic partnerships as incomplete, inconsistent, and inadequate. They are the products of a riot of laws, local ordinances, and corporate largesse. They confer inconsistent sets of benefits and are not predictably portable. People can be in more than one at a time, with potentially confusing or overlapping consequences. In fact, it's not clear that someone couldn't be in a government-sanctioned domestic partnership with one person while also claiming domestic partnership status at work with someone else. The requirements for membership vary for reasons that are often not spelled out. It should be obvious that the current, scattershot situation is untenable in the long run. These are the inevitable consequences of a status that bubbled up organically from the local level.

In the next chapter, we will closely examine the civil union, which has strengths and weaknesses of its own. Doing so will lead to one conclusion: the law needs to recognize relationships other than marriage. But most of the entities that have been created so far, while responsive to their native conditions, are not easily transplanted to new locations.

2 Civil Unions

We believe strongly in family values.

Stacy Jolles, one of the plaintiffs in the Vermont marriage
equality lawsuit

Gay marriage doesn't seem like the right discussion to me.
Because it should be: "What is this institution of marriage,
and does it still need to be defined the way it has been?"

Leah Whitesel

My husband, David, looking down at our hands as we drove
out of Vermont: "Well, our rings didn't disappear."
  Me, not out loud: "Yes and no."

FROM ZERO TO ABOUT FIFTY-THREE MPH

Domestic partnerships were an important innovation. Yet because of the
way they grew up and the compromises needed to achieve them, they fall
far short of providing the protection that many couples—gay or straight,
intimate or not—need. What people "need" is a matter of debate, of course,
but because of the legal and social monopoly marriage enjoys, it was natural
for the LGBTQ rights movement to fix on marriage as the prize representing legal equality. Yet that goal would prove a bridge too far for some two
decades after domestic partnerships appeared. Something much closer to
marriage, though, arose with the turn of the millennium: the civil union.
This new legal creature was midwifed in a different way than the domestic

partnership: it was delivered in response to a judicial decision from a state supreme court. This chapter discusses the birth of the civil union and its evolution from a clever compromise designed to give gay and lesbian couples a kind of "parallel universe" marriage to an institution capacious enough to embrace different-sex couples who were looking for marriage's benefits without its baggage. As we will see, though, the subsequent victory of the marriage equality movement in *Obergefell v. Hodges* has called into question whether civil unions are still necessary. Are they the best alternative to marriage for couples—of all types—seeking legal recognition of their relationship? Probably not, because of the unique circumstances of their creation. But the history of the civil union, like that of the domestic partnership, is worth exploring as an important evolutionary step toward the recognition of a sound, workable alternative to marriage and its strictures.

In the years following the earliest domestic partnerships, the LGBTQ rights movement was perhaps most concerned with achieving legal dignity for the private lives of gay couples by repealing sodomy laws after the *Bowers v. Hardwick* decision in 1986.[1] A sharply divided Supreme Court ruled that Georgia's law prohibiting certain specified sexual acts was constitutionally permissible, and brushed aside the contention that it was enforced only against same-sex intimacy. For the court, the idea that the constitutional guarantee of liberty protected such acts was "facetious"—a conclusion underscored by Chief Justice Warren Burger in a concurring opinion.[2] In thundering biblical cadences, he noted the ancient, Judeo-Christian roots of the laws against sodomy and uncritically quoted William Blackstone, an eighteenth-century English legal scholar, on the proposition that such an act was a "deeper malignity" than rape. (Why? Because rape is procreative but sodomy is not.)[3]

The *Bowers* decision was rightly regarded as a cataclysm for a gay rights movement that had been gaining steam, as the court's holding supported a view that gays and lesbians (and certainly transgender people) were criminals.[4] As long as they were regarded as outlaws, progress on other LGBTQ issues would be stalled. So removing the sodomy laws—either by challenges in state courts or legislatively—consumed most of the oxygen in activists' war rooms.

But not all of it. In 1989, Andrew Sullivan sketched out a conservative case for gay marriage in the influential magazine *New Republic*—an argument he eloquently amplified in his 1995 book, *Virtually Normal.*[5] Sullivan made an impassioned plea for seeing gays and lesbians as fully human and then tied that humanity to the longing for family that they feel no less than others. Since the state weighs in so heavily on what counts as a family through marriage laws, to Sullivan it was unjust and, finally, inhumane to close off the possibility of marriage to committed same-sex couples.

The LGBTQ rights community didn't exactly hold parades in Sullivan's honor; in fact, he was vilified for supporting such a patriarchal institution (even though to argue for same-sex marriage was inevitably to tear away at accepted notions of gender roles) and for his assimilationist views.[6] Yet his contribution to the debate gave marriage equality an intellectual foundation and made it possible to regard the possibility as more than a joke, a fantasy, or a performance. But the movement was slow to gain traction. Indeed, initially it backfired, as a now well-known series of events then unfolded that seemed to make it less likely than ever that committed same-sex couples could ever legally wed.

These developments trace back to a case that arose in Hawaii in the early 1990s. Frustrated that they could not name each other as beneficiaries on their insurance policies, a lesbian couple, Nina Baehr and Genora Dancel, brought their complaint to Bill Woods, the founder of the Hawaii Gay and Lesbian Center.[7] He suggested that they sue the state for marriage licenses. So they did, with the local gay activist Ted Foley representing them. The trial court promptly dismissed their case, so they filed what seemed like a quixotic appeal to the state's supreme court.[8]

Then something extraordinary happened. In 1993, the Hawaii Supreme Court found that barring same-sex couples from marrying was a form of sex discrimination (expressly banned by the state constitution) and that the state therefore had a heavy burden to bear in justifying the law.[9] Through its decision in *Baehr v. Lewin*, the court sent the case back down to the trial judge to see whether that demanding standard had been met.[10]

Something like a national panic ensued. Fearful that the Hawaii courts were about to rule in favor of same-sex marriages and that out-of-state couples would then turn up in Hawaii, marry, and seek recognition of their marriages in their home states, in 1996 the US Congress quickly and overwhelmingly passed the Defense of Marriage Act, which President Bill

Clinton promptly signed into law.[11] DOMA did two things. The first was in direct response to the "threat" from Hawaii: it allowed states to refuse recognition of gay and lesbian marriages from other states.[12] Second, DOMA defined *marriage* for federal purposes as limited to the union of one man and one woman.[13] This federal nonrecognition of same-sex marriages was a major legal disability. It meant that even if and when any state (say, Hawaii) did allow same-sex couples to marry, their marriages would not entitle them to the vast panoply of rights and benefits conferred by federal law: the ability to file joint income tax returns, to receive a deceased spouse's social security benefits, or to sponsor a spouse into the country under the immigration laws, to name just a very few of the most significant.

DOMA then spread virally to the states. Like quickly falling dominoes, state after state passed laws banning same-sex marriages, often by enshrining the prohibitions within their constitutions.[14] By and large, these laws underlined the federal DOMA by announcing that their states would not recognize same-sex nuptials from other states, even though they could already refuse such recognition under DOMA and by citing their own strong "public policy" against same-sex unions.[15] (Uglier instances of such nonrecognition had occurred in the context of interracial marriages, at least until the Supreme Court declared antimiscegenation laws unconstitutional in the 1967 case *Loving v. Virginia*.[16] But the usual practice is to recognize out-of-state marriages if valid in the state of "celebration." For instance, states that don't allow marriages between first cousins will usually recognize such marriages performed in other states.[17])

Hawaii joined the antigay hysteria soon enough. The voters, through a ballot initiative that amended the state's constitution, gave the legislature the power to reserve marriage to different-sex couples.[18] The lawmakers then quickly enacted a "mini-DOMA" in 1998, thereby wiping out the lawsuit that seemed about to secure victory for the same-sex couples who'd brought it.[19] The Hawaii Supreme Court had been sitting on the case for two years by that point, likely waiting to see whether the voters would render the issue moot. Alaska too was an early adopter of a state constitutional amendment against same-sex unions. In 1998 the voters there weighed in, passing a ballot amendment that effectively overruled a trial court's decision earlier that year finding the state's gay marriage ban unconstitutional.[20] They didn't even wait to find out whether the state supreme court would have agreed with the lower court.

The Vermont residents Nina Beck and Stacy Jolles weren't unaware of the bleak legal landscape that gay and lesbian couples faced, but they signed up as plaintiffs in a lawsuit that turned out to be momentous— because personal circumstances, involving their terminally ill son, Noah, made speed necessary.[21] Using a sperm donor, Beck had given birth to Noah in 1995, when the couple lived in North Carolina. But Jolles was unable to adopt him, and difficulties arose at every turn—including when Beck suffered complications during childbirth and Jolles had trouble getting into the hospital to visit her and the couple's newborn son. So in 1996 they decided to move to Vermont, for its friendlier legal terrain. In 1993, Vermont had become the first state to legalize so-called second-parent adoption, by the nonbiological partner of a child's parent.[22] In 1997, Beck and Jolles eagerly joined two other couples in a lawsuit, *Baker v. State*, sponsored by the Vermont Freedom to Marry Task Force and helmed by the attorneys Beth Robinson and Susan Murray.[23] Like the Hawaii plaintiffs, the Vermont plaintiffs were suing for marriage licenses.

At the time, it was startling that Vermont even *had* something called a Freedom to Marry Task Force. As noted earlier, all previous attempts to legalize gay marriage had fallen with a thud, and *Bowers* and DOMA did little to fuel optimism that matters were likely to change. But Vermont was a more promising venue than other states for several reasons. First, it was notably progressive on LGBTQ issues, having passed laws protecting gays and lesbians against discrimination in employment and public accommodations, expanding the definition of "hate crime" to include antigay bias, and, most relevant, allowing second-parent adoption.[24] Second, there was no mini-DOMA law in Vermont, so nothing prevented the state's supreme court from interpreting its own constitution to require equality. And third, as the plaintiffs and their advocates knew, the Vermont Supreme Court had a reputation for issuing fair and thoughtful decisions that were often on the liberal side of issues. For example, in 1996 the court struck down a law that denied adopted children the right to inherit from siblings, finding that the measure denied them equality under the law.[25]

Perhaps more significant, activists had been developing a strategy for winning and then preserving marriage equality. The Vermont Freedom to

Marry Task Force had been created by a committee formed by the Vermont Coalition for Lesbian and Gay Rights, of which Robinson and Murray were members. Before forming the task force, the committee had spent a year discussing whether gaining the right to marry was a battle the community even wanted to fight. At that early stage, litigation was not in view—the goal was to educate the public through the kind of grassroots organizing that works only in a place like Vermont, a small state with a tradition of local democracy. That organization would turn out to be critical in the ensuing lawsuit. By 1996, the effort had paid off to the point that the hundred people at the annual Queer Town Meeting were already considering how to achieve marriage equality rather than whether the goal was worth pursuing.[26]

Nonetheless, the case didn't start well for the marriage equality forces. Just a few months after the suit was filed, the trial court dismissed it. Writing in late 1997, the court held that the exclusion of same-sex couples from marriage "rationally furthered the state's interest in promoting 'the link between procreation and child rearing.'"[27] The plaintiffs duly appealed, and oral arguments were held in late 1998. With their questions, the justices of the Vermont Supreme Court gave the couples good reason to hope for a favorable outcome. Among the highlights was Justice Denise Johnson's response to the state's argument that no other state recognized same-sex marriage: "Somebody has to be first, right?"[28]

I can still recall sitting at the kitchen table one Friday morning in late December 1999, setting out the *New York Times* (yes, in paper form) next to me as I had my morning coffee, and only then learning that the Vermont Supreme Court had decided the case the day before.[29] But the ruling was puzzling. The justices had ruled—unanimously!—that excluding gay couples from the rights and benefits of marriage violated the state's guarantee of equal protection. (In the Vermont Constitution, equality is promised through something called the common benefits clause.)[30] But the article went on to explain that the court had stopped just short of requiring the legislature to allow same-sex couples to marry.

The court's ruling became clear after I read the full decision later that day: remedying the inequity could be achieved by creating a parallel institution for same-sex couples, as long as it conferred "the same benefits and protections afforded by Vermont law to married opposite-sex couples."[31]

Using language that evinced a clearheaded understanding of stark political realities, Chief Justice Jeffrey Amestoy defended the odd decision to sever the right (to equality) from the remedy. He characterized as "significantly insulated from reality" the suggestion by Justice Johnson, who had dissented only from the court's unwillingness to grant the plaintiffs what they sought—marriage licenses—that such a remedy would have avoided "the political cauldron."[32] He called the Hawaii "example" instructive and detailed how its state supreme court had indicated a readiness to require issuance of marriage licenses to same-sex couples, only to be overruled by the people, via constitutional amendment. In other words, Amestoy feared that ordering the legislature to provide the full remedy of issuing marriage licenses to same-sex couples could have exactly the opposite effect: the passage of a state constitutional amendment against such marriages.[33]

Like most people who were following the case closely, I was surprised by the result. The expectation that the Vermont Supreme Court would become the first state supreme court to recognize its state's constitutional duty to provide marriage equality was high, but of course everyone realized that defeat was also possible. This strange, clever compromise hit our blind side.

What followed was a brief but frenzied battle throughout Vermont as citizens and legislators grappled with how to handle the court's mandate. Three positions were staked out: grant full marriage equality; amend the state's constitution to override the court's decision and give the couples nothing; or adopt the compromise position that the court had opened up and create some entirely new entity conferring the rights, benefits, and obligations of marriage but under a different name. The debate played out not only in the state legislature but in innumerable town hall meetings (a staple of the democratic process in Vermont) and, of course, in sometimes heated conversations among the citizenry.[34]

Vermonters had no truck with outsiders telling them how to govern their state. Nonresidents weren't permitted to testify at town hall meetings or before the legislature; as a result, their influence was minimal. Even those arguing for a constitutional amendment banning gay marriages rejected out-of-staters' attempts to sway the debate. Take It to the People was the organization spearheading the drive for such an amendment, but its president had this to say to an incendiary talk show host from New York who strongly opposed marriage equality: "Your political aspirations ... and your commercial radio talk show do not bring anything positive to a discussion based on Vermont's traditional values."[35]

The public debate quickly revealed that there wasn't sufficient support for amending the marriage laws to include gay and lesbian couples—that was too much, too fast. But during the three months between the court's decision and the enactment of what became the *civil unions* law, an enormous amount of public education took place, at hyperspeed. Opponents of marriage equality were confronted with countless stories of the practical consequences of second-class citizenship for their gay and lesbian fellow Vermonters, which moved many to change their position. On March 22, 2000, for instance, Nina Beck testified before the state's Senate Judiciary Committee in support of the bill: "Stacy and I have been through everything a couple can imagine. We share a deep love for each other, have shared in the joy of the birth of our two children, and the devastating grief at the loss of our firstborn. We survived that loss because of the strength of [our] bond and ... because of the vows we exchanged eight years ago."[36] On the other side, some of the attacks were so vitriolic that their effect was the opposite of what was intended, causing undecided legislators to side with proponents.[37]

Why "civil unions" and not "domestic partnerships"? Probably because of the statement by one Donna Lescoe, a lesbian who testified before the House Judiciary Committee. Whatever you do, she implored, don't use the term *domestic partner*: "It makes me feel like the domestic help."[38] *Civil* was decided on first, denoting an institution that was secular rather than religious. Then Representative Cathy Voyer, a Republican, came up with the phrase *civil union*.[39]

This was a felicitous coinage. First, it clearly separated a legal status created to deliver the comprehensive package of marital rights (by another name) from the helter-skelter, inconsistent domestic partnership.[40] Until a few localities in Arizona gummed things up in 2013 by applying the term to local packages of rights, *civil union* has held a consistent meaning as it migrated out of Vermont and into a host of other states. In every case where civil union laws have passed at the state level, they have done the same thing: conveyed the full set of rights, benefits, and obligations of marriage that the state provides to different-sex couples.[41] Second, by employing the term *civil*, the Vermont legislature was able to home in on the legal, rights-granting aspect of state-sanctioned relationships rather than the fuzzier, but powerful, amalgam of religious and social meanings with which marriage is freighted.[42]

The civil union offers many more benefits than most domestic partnership laws, especially the earlier, weaker ones. But it was a product of circumstance, leading to significant drawbacks that exist to this day.

The first has to do with the difference between marriages recognized by states and those recognized at the federal level. Usually, that's a distinction without a difference, because federal law conferring benefits on married couples simply defers to the states, which have historically been (and still are) the ones defining *marriage* and *family*.[43] Wherever a federal law uses the word *marriage* or *spouses*, it includes anyone and everyone who is legally married—by the states. But federal law nowhere makes reference to "civil unions" (or "domestic partnerships," for that matter). By passing a civil union law rather than simply issuing marriage licenses to same-sex couples, Vermont granted all the rights of marriage *that are the state's to give*. But civil unions confer none of marriage's federal rights and obligations, which are by far the more important for most people and are certainly more extensive. How, then, could the Vermont legislature plausibly claim that civil unions were the equivalent of marriage?

DOMA provides the answer. Recall that it specifically walled off same-sex couples from the federal rights that come along with marriage. So even if Vermont had used the term *married*—or *double married*, for that matter—there would still have been no federal advantage for same-sex couples. They'd be married at home but not nationally. In an odd way, DOMA gave both the Vermont Supreme Court and the state legislature the cover they needed to declare the civil union the legal equivalent of marriage, at least for gay couples. Without federal benefits either way, that was true. The trick worked until the 2013 *Windsor* decision ruled DOMA unconstitutional, more than a decade later. Once that happened, it was no longer possible to maintain that civil unions were the same as marriage.[44] A court in New Jersey, a civil union state (since 2006) that had not granted marriage rights to same-sex couples by 2013, reached exactly that conclusion, and the then governor Chris Christie did not launch an appeal, knowing it would be a sure loser.[45] (I'll have more to say about developments in New Jersey later in this chapter.)

The second problem with civil unions is deeper. The status attempted to do the impossible: grant same-sex couples all of the rights and benefits and impose the same obligations that married couples have, but without the same label. In the words of the Vermont statute, "Parties to a civil union shall have all the same benefits, protections, and responsibilities under law ... as are granted to spouses in a marriage."[46] But the civil union was pointedly *not* marriage, which, the legislators reminded us, continued to be restricted to "the legally recognized union of one man and one woman."[47]

Although many in the marriage equality movement understood the political and practical reasons for the Vermont Supreme Court's move—granting the legislature (and the court itself) political cover and giving people time to acclimate to the notion that the unions of same-sex couples were worthy of celebration, not derision—they believed, along with Justice Johnson, that the court had failed to discharge its constitutional duty to confer true equality to the couples who had come before it.[48]

That was my view at the time, sort of. Yet I recognized the huge practical benefits of the civil union to those who lived in Vermont, and I saw the symbolic benefit of even phantom legal recognition. At the very end of 2000—just a few months after the law went into effect—David and I traveled from Philadelphia to tiny Chester, Vermont, and had our civil union solemnized by Jack Coleman (now deceased), the former president of Haverford College who was then in semi-retirement and running a country inn. The weekend was snowy, beautiful, and romantic. Our union was a powerful act of commitment. It was also, legally speaking, ineffective, dissipating as we crossed from Vermont Route 7 over to New York Route 9. But, as I soon learned, the civil union left a moral trace, contributing subtly but surely to a change in the way society looked at same-sex relationships. I'm convinced, for example, that my civil union was one of the many factors that led my employer to extend full "partner" benefits to David (and to all committed same-sex partners) just a few years later. But more significantly, our friends and family treated the ceremony with which we commemorated our union as they would any marriage—mostly, anyway.

On the other hand, in a different sense the civil union can be seen as almost worse than nothing. Equality is equality. Labels matter. Granting benefits while withholding the title *marriage* leaves only pure discrimination and suggests that lawmakers knew they didn't have a good reason to keep gays and lesbians from marrying but wanted to continue to hoard the term for straight people.[49]

In hindsight and on balance, I've become convinced that equality really is a practice and a process rather than a fixed end state. Viewed that way, the civil union compromise is at least defensible. Just as the families of LGBTQ kids often need some time to absorb the newly revealed reality after their children come out, so too did Vermonters need some time to work themselves up to full equality—an equality that arrived less than ten years later, when, in April 2009, Vermont became the first state in the nation to grant same-sex couples full marriage rights, through the legislative process and without being ordered to do so by any court.[50] This move was spurred in part by the work of the Vermont Commission on Family Recognition and Protection, created by the civil union legislation passed in 2000. In a 2008 report, the commission identified many problems with civil union status, most relating to the confusion and the stigma involved in having two separate names for what was (supposed to be) the same set of legal entitlements. For instance, a woman who testified before the commission said that her employer would not recognize her civil union for employee benefit purposes and that "the CEO compared civil union couples to employees who live with their boyfriend or girlfriend."[51] Although the commission's charge prevented it from expressly calling for full marriage equality, the report closed with the next best thing: a recommendation "that Vermont take seriously the differences between civil marriage and civil union in terms of their practical and legal consequences for Vermont's civil union couples and their families."[52]

Another problem was that no other state seemed likely to recognize the Vermont civil union. This deficiency was driven home by a tragic New York case, *Langan v. St. Vincent's Hospital*, a suit brought by John Langan, the surviving member of a Vermont civil union, against a hospital for alleged malpractice leading to the death of his partner, Neil Spicehandler.[53] Even though New York was one of the few states that had not enacted a mini-DOMA law refusing to recognize same-sex marriages from other states, a New York appellate court ruled that Langan and Spicehandler's civil union was not a marriage under New York law and the men were thus not spouses. Since spousal status is required to sue for wrongful death in New York, Langan's suit was dismissed—even though he and Spicehandler were supposed to have all the rights of marriage and had taken every possible step to make that happen.

In retrospect, Chief Justice Amestoy's opinion for the court in *Baker v. State*—whatever its shortcomings as a matter of strict constitutional law—was brilliant in allowing equality to come "on little cat's feet," to borrow Professor William Eskridge's apt phrase.[54] Perhaps Vermont hadn't accelerated the rights of gay couples from zero to sixty miles per hour, but it had gotten to about fifty-three. Given that *Bowers v. Hardwick*, the 1987 Supreme Court decision blessing the states' right to criminalize the intimate conduct of same-sex couples, was still "good" law, it might be that *Baker* was the best that could have been hoped for in 1999. The Supreme Court finally overruled *Bowers* in 2003, through the decision in *Lawrence v. Texas*.[55] It's no coincidence that the first fully successful marriage equality case, *Goodridge v. Department of Public Health*, was decided just a few months after *Lawrence*—and pointedly references *Lawrence*.[56]

Part of the reason to celebrate civil unions is much more prosaic. To repeat: civil unions delivered all the rights and benefits of marriage that the state could bestow. Reading about the practical effects that the status had on couples in Vermont and considering the situation of Stacy Jolles and Nina Beck, I was struck by how much the law did to change their lives for the better. It cemented this couple's relationship to their second son, Seth, who was an infant when the law was enacted. It enabled them to stop fussing with elaborate and expensive documents to protect their finances and decision-making. In short, civil union status gave Beck and Jolles the security that different-sex married couples take for granted.

And that was what they wanted, perhaps more than the societal recognition that marriage confers. As far as they were concerned, their "real" wedding had taken place years earlier, when they had held a formal commitment ceremony. So when they civilly united, exactly nine years later, they did not feel the need to repeat the performance. They were already married but were now signing up for the benefits. For out-of-staters like us, the civil union stood as a small but important step in the slog toward equality. Jack Coleman told David and me he was glad he'd been able to see at least one state give some recognition to the relationships of gay and lesbian couples, and his words vibrated through us. I was energized for the important work of fighting for equality that still lay ahead.

From Vermont, the all-but-marriage civil union compromise began to spread. In most cases, states didn't even need courts to force the lawmakers' hands. Connecticut was first, followed by New Jersey, New Hampshire, Delaware, and Rhode Island.[57] Sometimes the move to full marriage equality was blindingly fast: most dramatically, only *two years* in Delaware, where civil unions came into force in 2011 and marriage equality arrived in 2013![58] In some states, though, this two-step process was not possible. Nevada, for instance, had a constitutional amendment limiting marriage to male-female unions; however, since the law did not mention other legal statuses, the legislature was free to go as far as "full-on" domestic partnerships, which are essentially civil unions with the messier name.[59]

CIVIL UNIONS FOR ALL

After a few states had recognized the new status of civil unions for same-sex couples, something quite different, and important, happened. Beginning with Illinois in 2011, three states soon permitted different-sex couples to enter into civil unions on the same terms as same-sex couples. Thus was created the situation in which the civil union was really two institutions in one. While same-sex couples saw the status as an important step toward full marriage equality, for different-sex couples it was a way to take a principled and perhaps even personally and economically costly stand against some of the negative associations of marriage. Most significant, for the latter civil unions were *chosen* rather than coerced by exclusion from marital status.

For many same-sex couples, however, the civil union remained an unwanted reminder of second-class citizenship, even though some, like John Kennedy of Oak Park, Illinois, regarded the inclusion of different-sex couples as a positive step—because it normalized the civil union, at least to some extent, thereby making gay and lesbian couples seem less like legal oddities.[60] One might expect that gay couples who shared Kennedy's view would convert their status to marriage at the first opportunity, as indeed he did. Yet it would be a mistake to assume that everyone in same-sex relationships is equally eager to join the marriage club. Tom Gibson of Delaware, for example, decried his state's automatic conversion of his civil union into a marriage once he gained the right to marry.[61] Even when it was the only legal recognition he could get from the state, he preferred the civil union to marriage—in part because he believes that gay and lesbian couples should not be trying to replicate straight couples in this way.

In the states that have made civil unions available to different-sex couples, there doesn't seem to be any appetite for taking away this option, at least not yet. All legal couples can still "civilly unite" in Illinois, Hawaii, and Colorado—even though marriage is now available to them all. But why on earth would any different-sex couple choose civil union over marriage? The short answer is that it is the best arrangement available for couples who do not want to marry, many because they have ideological objections to the institution.

With the helpful cooperation of the Cook County Clerk's Office in Chicago, I was able to gather some revealing information about the early numbers of straight civil union registrants and their reasons for choosing that status. Then I was placed in touch with a few couples willing to discuss their decision with me. The results—both quantitative and qualitative—were enlightening. We might use them to reach some tentative conclusions about whether the civil union is an option worth retaining as the nation moves toward full marriage equality.

In the first six months after the Illinois civil union law was enacted, only 133 of the 1,836 civil union licenses went to different-sex couples.[62] That's a small fraction, but might it portend something significant? The clerk's office was able to survey one partner from more than half (46 of 87) of the different-sex couples who had civilly united as of September 19, 2011.[63] Their reasons for entering into civil unions rather than marriage might worry traditionalists. Only four confessed to selecting this status for the same reason some couples choose domestic partnership: to preserve social security or other benefits from a previous spouse that would be lost through remarriage but not through entering into a civil union.[64] On the other hand, almost half the respondents *objected* to the institution of marriage. By more than three to one, this group agreed that "personal or religious convictions against marriage" were their reason for choosing the civil union.[65] And the most frequently proffered responses to the open-ended question "Why did you decide to obtain a civil union instead of getting married?" fell into the political/ideological category.[66] The report provides a few specifics behind that stance, including statements of "solidarity with the gay community and/or support of equality, fairness, and inclusiveness."[67] Some respondents cited commitment/label issues, such as not wanting a "husband" or a "wife" or even the "marriage" label itself.[68] And 9 percent of respondents cited religious concerns with marriage.[69] Even though religion need not be part of a marriage ceremony, for many people the two are inextricably linked. These diverse reasons reinforce one of the central themes of this book: marriage doesn't work for everyone.

The stories behind the numbers were even more revealing. Those who agreed to speak with me had clearly spent some time thinking about the meaning of marriage and decided they wanted nothing to do with it. Couples like Leah Whitesel, a nonpracticing lawyer teaching high school civics, and her partner, Justin Gates, a computer guy who comes from what he described as a conservative religious background, did not like the connotations of the word *marriage*.[70] The civil union status, Gates said, "keeps me from falling into any preconditioned behavior that I might have picked up. Calling [Whitesel] my partner, not my wife, helps me not to have any assumptions" or buy into traditional patterns.

Alex Rifman, a Moscow-born engineer, and Jennifer Tweeton, a lawyer working for the Chicago Mercantile Exchange, expressed similar feelings.[71] Their civil union ceremony, Tweeton said, "taught everyone there something" about the new law, and the couple see themselves as involved in a teaching mission in other ways. She added, "I feel like we don't value the families that choose to be families without being married. The civil union was a way to honor that ... a way to demonstrate to others" that these other family structures deserve respect too.

Both couples intended their civil unions to express solidarity with their LGBTQ friends who could not marry at the time. The fact that both were also expecting children suggested that their civil unions were meant to provide a measure of security for the families without the societal implications of marriage.

Pioneer status has its costs, though, which are familiar to many same-sex couples who will see their own experiences reflected in the stories these couples tell. Tweeton said that her family, traditional Lutherans, didn't view her union as "real" and didn't treat it like a marriage. And the couple couldn't muster the courage to come out about the civil union to Tweeton's grandmother, who was then one hundred years old and "very conservative." Even the clerk who processed their application tried to dissuade them, urging that they "should just get married" and reminding them that "the license cost was the same." In a bizarre instance of bureaucratic overreach and an inept attempt to reinforce patriarchy, the clerk also insisted that Rifman, as the male, be "Partner A," even though the license form contains no such requirement.

Another couple, whom I will call Emil Roe and Margaret Koe because they prefer to remain anonymous, had a similar experience. "Wait a minute. A civil union? This can't be right," the judge who performed their ceremony protested. Describing himself as "the world's worst wine salesman," Roe objected to what he perceived as the built-in religious aspect of marriage but added that "if push came to shove, solidarity with gays is the biggest reason" for his choosing civil union status.[72]

Since that flurry of civil union laws, several developments have changed their status for the worse. As states moved to full marriage equality, the civil union began to collapse, at least in the pioneer states that had enacted the laws as an accommodation for gay and lesbian couples only. In a few places, like Vermont, existing civil unions remained in force, but no new ones were permitted.[73] Mostly, though, they were converted, by force of law, into marriages.[74] Massachusetts remained a lonely outlier for several years after that state's supreme court commanded the issuance of marriage licenses to same-sex couples in the 2003 *Goodridge v. Department of Public Health* decision. By the end of the new millennium's first decade, though, a number of states, such as Iowa, had moved directly to marriage equality without pausing for the virtual compromise of the civil union.[75] Sometimes this goal was achieved through judicial decree, but it increasingly happened through the legislative or referendum process.[76] States even began to roll back their constitutional amendments against same-sex marriages. In Maine, for example, voters overruled the legislature to approve a same-sex ban in 2009, but in 2012 another voter referendum reversed that action and brought full marriage equality to the state.[77]

The US Supreme Court's 2013 decision in *United States v. Windsor* throwing out part of DOMA also indirectly highlighted the principal deficiency in civil union laws for gay and lesbian couples even as it afforded them greater rights. Recall that DOMA had by happenstance papered over what was a glaring problem with civil union laws: by not using the word *marriage*, they fenced gay and lesbian couples off from all the federal goodies that full "spouses" enjoy, leaving only the "skim milk" marriage decried by Justice Ginsburg.[78] But those couples would not have been entitled to those rights in any case, because, to repeat, there is no such thing as a federal civil union. It is not surprising that states that allowed only same-sex couples to civilly unite repealed those laws as soon as the veil of inequality was lifted. In states that had opened the status to different-sex couples, though, the space between "marriage" and "civil union" was in plain sight from the moment these laws were enacted, so there was little reason to repeal them.

Windsor kick-started administrative hand-wringing over whether civil unions were the same as marriage, sometimes to the different-sex registrants' detriment. Although the federal agencies responsible for the many programs and benefits that married folks enjoy could have interpreted the term *married* to include "civilly united," for the most part they did not. For instance, soon after the *Windsor* decision was handed down, the Internal Revenue Service issued a ruling declaring that all legally married same-sex couples would now be eligible to file joint tax returns but that couples in civil unions—or domestic partnerships or anything else other than marriage—would not. For many such couples, the difference amounted to thousands of dollars they could not claim—particularly since the Internal Revenue Service also allowed gay and lesbian married couples to amend their tax returns for the preceding three years.[79]

Quickly picking up on this new reality, the New Jersey trial court judge in *Garden State Equality v. Dow* held that civil unions could no longer be considered the equivalent of marriage, a compromise that the New Jersey Supreme Court had permitted back in 2006.[80] Noting that the IRS and other federal agencies (including the Department of Labor and the State Department) had determined civil unions weren't federally recognized marriages, the court brushed aside the state's argument that the new inequality was somehow not New Jersey's "fault" (since it was the federal government's interpretation of the civil union that was fencing the couples out). Per the court, "That structure [the civil union] may not have been illegal at the time it was created," but now "every day that the state does not allow same-sex couples to marry, plaintiffs are being harmed."[81]

Legislatures picked up on this new inequality in federal law between civil unions and post-DOMA marriages too, with those in Hawaii and Illinois swiftly moving from civil unions to full marriage rights for same-sex couples. And, of course, in 2015 *Obergefell v. Hodges* swamped the entire civil union compromise by eliminating its raison d'être—at least for those who had accepted civil unions as a way station on the road to full marriage equality.

Well, now what? *Obergefell* has overtaken the "solidarity with the gays" argument, but the other reasons to eschew marriage in favor of a nominally "civil" alternative still apply. Yet as the relatively small number of straight couples choosing the civil union suggests, this particular alternative does not appeal to many people—especially now that it is clear that civil unions will not be recognized for federal purposes. Why would anyone—even clever lawyers like Tweeton and Whitesel—want to navigate the complexity of a dual, state-federal system?

In fact, a later exchange with Whitesel reflects the difficulty of this reality. An email she sent me on February 6, 2014, bears extensive quoting because it shows the anguish of a true believer in alternatives who has run out of ideas and patience. Initially, she and Gates were confused about what effect, exactly, the civil union even had:

> [It] posed some problems when we were filing for our taxes. There was no guidance for how we were supposed to file—gay couples were told to file as married in Illinois and unmarried for federal, which sounds like a major pain in the butt but at least it was an answer. We found a non-binding IRS memo that suggested that hetero couples were supposed to just plain file as married, and since that sounded easy and we figured we probably wouldn't be audited and yelled at, that's what we've been doing. There are other strange labeling problems as well, like when Justin put me on his car insurance and the insurance went *up* $50 when he listed me as "unrelated adult sharing a household" or whatever but *down* $30 when he listed me as a "spouse," so "spouse" I am.

Even though the civil union was created to confer the benefits of marriage (which include a presumption that one's spouse is the surrogate decision-maker in the event of incapacity or death), that wasn't clear to their attorney, who "suggested" they "fill out medical power of attorney forms and health care advance directives."

Such problems as these, at least, should be manageable. Since Whitesel wrote me, the IRS clarified that civil unions are not marriages for federal purposes (which creates exactly the baffling situation she was in before she found that IRS memo—which turned out to not reflect the agency's official position). And presumably she can find an attorney who has taken the time to read the law and figured out that the usual spousal default rules apply to those in civil unions.

These practical concerns, though, were dwarfed for this couple by the way their civil union quickly became a weird (okay, a weirder) status once Illinois achieved marriage equality. As Whitesel told me, "Marriage equality . . . means we're truly screwed [by staying in a civil union]. I am happy that people who want to get married can have their marriage legally recognized. But this rush to marriage equality is bulldozing over our civil union." With gays and lesbians abandoning the status and with so few straight civil union pioneers, it's understandable that she felt her civil union was even less understood then than when she entered into it. She described her options, none of which she found appealing:

1. Stay in the civil union. We don't like this option because it keeps us in limbo—and we'll need to keep half-lying and either saying "yes, we're married" or "no, we're not" at our convenience, and all of the equivocation gets exhausting. There is little room for civil unions in the public discourse as it is, and that space is shrinking.

2. Get a divorce. Of course we're not going to do this, it's expensive and time-consuming. (Being non-legally tied wouldn't change our relationship, but it would lessen some anxiety. We agree on this point.)

3. Get married. . . . I've made some progress with thinking about this—I no longer start crying and/or shouting when I think about getting married. I don't want to get married. Justin doesn't want to get married. However, from our perspective, it seems like the rational choice, so we're probably going to do it at some point. Our plan is to *not tell anyone*. . . . We are not telling our parents. We are not telling our friends. We are probably not going to tell our daughter. In fact, the only person I'm telling is you.

We are also never going to use the words "husband" and "wife" (but if it's up for grabs, I prefer "husband" for myself, or maybe "hubby").

The legal and social pressure to marry, to conform, felt suffocating to Whitesel. She concluded her email with an agonized summary of her frustration:

> I feel sad and I feel betrayed. This rush to marriage equality is essentially a rush to conformity. I feel like the LGBT movement and lots of interested unaffiliated straight or passing-as-straight allies had a real moment to start actually questioning the institution of marriage—a time to figure out what it means, to deconstruct it, realize it's entirely anachronistic, oppressive, and silly, and perhaps come up with something new and awesome. Or just kick marriage out of the public sphere entirely—in my ideal world, marriage is optional if you're religious, a wedding is a party for friends and family, and the serious business of when to invite the state into a relationship and what form that will take is something else, maybe a "civil union," maybe something new. I don't see why that is so hard to understand. I am so disappointed that this conversation never took place, and when it's hinted at, it's shoved away as being "too radical" or left as an academic discussion that is inaccessible to most people.

Well, it remains too radical for most people to think about doing away with marriage and replacing it with something entirely new, and civil. The civil union was never meant as a replacement for marriage—just a strategic, perhaps beguiling, consolation prize for same-sex couples who could not otherwise marry. Legislators in the three states that allowed straight couples to civilly unite surely weren't trying to deconstruct marriage, and their political heads would have been the price for suggesting otherwise. Yet Whitesel is right to wonder why the civil union—perhaps especially the *different-sex* variety—did not trigger at least a societal discussion about marriage itself. What is it, and what is it *for*? This book is one attempt to bring that discussion forward.

Is the civil union worth retaining? That's not an easy question to answer, especially for someone who believes that the government should legally recognize relationships other than marriage, as I do. But a good start is to consider what civil union status accomplishes now that it has been severed from its origin in the marriage equality debate. There are two remaining purposes.

First, civil unions may allow couples to formalize their relationship at the state level without losing federal benefits. For instance, one woman responding (anonymously) to the Cook County survey said she needed to wait to remarry or she would lose her deceased husband's social security benefits. In another couple, both parties to the civil union would have lost benefits upon remarriage. Still another respondent candidly admitted a desire to avoid filing joint federal returns.[82]

To be blunt, these are not good reasons for retaining the civil union, which, in any event, is less effective at dodging these consequences than it used to be. In 2016, the Social Security Administration issued guidance stating that, for same-sex couples, civil unions would be equated to marriage. Oddly, the SSA did not take a hard position on *different-sex* civil unions, instead inviting couples in such arrangements to contact it directly for an opinion.[83] So it's at least unclear whether the civil union can continue to be used as a work-around for those who want the commitment of marriage without the title. Partners in a civil union (or couples in any other statewide relationship that carries the same inheritance rights as marriage) are (perhaps?) now considered married for social security purposes.

Whatever the case with social security, clever tax ploys are definitely no longer available. As we've seen, the IRS now considers those in civil unions to be married, so the dual-status game has ended there. Previously, civil unions permitted different-sex couples who understood the intricacies of the law (or had the resources to pay someone who did) to declare themselves "married" (legally speaking) by state law to obtain, say, access to a partner's employee health benefits but single when it came to financial consequences at the federal level that they wished to avoid. According to Lisa Goodman, a Delaware attorney who was involved in the enactment of that state's 2011 same-sex-couples-only civil union law, that kind of legal gamesmanship was a principal reason for the decision to restrict eligibility to the gay and lesbian couples who needed it—and who, at the time, couldn't take advantage of the two-status situation, because of the federal DOMA.[84]

The IRS decision leveled the playing field for same-sex couples in another way. When same-sex marriages were permitted by state law but prohibited at the federal level—before the Supreme Court struck down DOMA—married same-sex couples often, and rightly, complained that their dual status made life more complicated. For instance, as Whitesel mentioned, such a couple would have to file their federal tax returns as individuals but their *state* returns as married. But because the state return depends on the federal one, they would have to create a "dummy" federal return, briefly entering a parallel universe where they were married and filing jointly, to complete their state tax returns.[85]

Despite such changes, at least some couples are still entering into civil unions for the combination of benefits and responsibilities allocated between state and federal law, but eligibility for these goodies—which can disappear at any time, as these cases show—should be determined by another mechanism. In chapter 5, I sketch out some ways that the law might be revamped to achieve a more equitable and realistic support structure for the ways that families are actually living—one that tries to account for differences including class.

The second argument for retaining the civil union is more philosophical. Is this legal status worth keeping to accommodate the genuine distaste that some people have for marriage? My sense is that marriage itself could address some of their concerns, but only if certain specific steps were taken.

One step should be easy. To allay the concern about the close connection between marriage and religion, we should immediately eliminate the requirement that marriages be solemnized to have legal effect. The license should be enough, at least legally speaking, just as it is for more mundane matters, like driving and fishing. If that's too radical, simply stop allowing anyone but public officials to perform the task. It's true that a marriage already need not be *religiously* solemnized: designated public officials can and do regularly perform this function. But for some people, the connection between religion and marriage remains despite this option. As Alex Rifman said, "Marriage is too close to church for us."

A model for this secular process is already in place in other countries, such as France. There, the couple obtains a marriage license and then has it solemnized by a civil authority. They can have whatever further religious or secular ceremony they want, *if any*—but the state is left out of that step.[86] For some, this might be a sufficient remedy.

But not for all: One unnamed respondent to the Cook County survey stated that, according to the dictates of her Catholicism, she could not marry a previously divorced man, but a civil union was permissible. Others have found that family pressures relating to religion were too great to resist for long. Sheila Blackburn, who entered into a civil union in Illinois in 2012, later converted it into a marriage. As she explained to me, "My family didn't really accept the civil union. They are traditional Catholics and they frowned upon it."[87] (Rifman would smile knowingly at this statement.)

The second cluster of objections, centering on terminology that has unwanted links to an oppressive past (and perhaps, to some, an oppressive *present*), should kick-start a discussion about how to change legal language to reflect a more modern view. All references in state and federal law to "husband" and "wife" (or, in some states, "bride" and "groom") should be replaced by "spouse." The success of the marriage equality movement has already triggered this change in some places, with the marriage license forms in many states now providing the option for couples to label themselves as spouses.[88] These same forms generally allow the couple to continue calling themselves *husband* and *wife*, sometimes in response to political pressure to retain those terms, which strikes me as a reasonable way to let people make a choice similar to the marriage–or–civil union decision: to identify themselves as equal partners—whether same or different sex—or to continue using the older terms, which some prefer. The newer forms also permit both members of the couple to assign themselves the same historic role, as in two husbands or two wives. And of course they can choose to refer to each other as *partner* in everyday life, as an increasing number of married couples do.

These changes to licensing forms are important political statements. As such, they can trigger pushback. Consider the case of Kentucky. In 2016, its senate approved a bill that would have created two separate marriage licenses. The first, intended for different-sex couples, would have retained the terms "bride" and "groom," while the second, for same-sex couples and other nonconformists, would have used "first party" and "second party" instead. The legislators might as well have said "Thing 1" and "Thing 2," so evident was their distaste for marriages between two people of the same gender. Even though same-sex couples also would have been permitted to use "bride" and "groom," it would have to be both, with each assigned to one partner. This effort at official humiliation might have backfired, sparking public "drag" license-signing performances echoing the post-Stonewall "marry-in" discussed in chapter 1, but the proposed law was so clearly unconstitutional that the state's house of representatives instead followed the prevailing trend and created a single, flexible licensing form.[89] So these forms have some potential to validate the partners' chosen terms—even in a state like Kentucky, which briefly became much better known for the celebrity refusal of a local clerk to issue licenses to same-sex couples, which led to litigation and a change in the law.[90]

What about the objection of some couples to the term *marriage*? The rise of civil unions has contributed to the ongoing discussion about whether to retire this word, at least legally speaking—and *civil union* has the advantage of being a fresh and descriptively apt phrase. It is extremely unlikely, however, that *marriage* will be scoured from the law in the foreseeable future. In 2003, the Massachusetts Supreme Judicial Court subtly suggested a compromise in *Goodridge*, using "civil marriage" throughout its opinion to describe the status at issue.[91] In so doing, the justices called attention to the legal side of marriage in a (mostly unsuccessful) effort to draw down some of the heat that is generated by the ongoing struggle over the broader meaning of *marriage*. Once it is agreed that the term includes same-sex couples (legally, *Obergefell* resolved the issue; ontologically, though, it depends whom you ask), perhaps the time will be ripe for inserting the modifier *civil* before *marriage* in legal contexts. Traditionalists might howl, but most people will either not notice or just ignore the modifier and continue to describe their relationships as simply "marriage." Yet the word *civil*—even if it continues to be connected to *marriage*—might be enough to satisfy, or at least appease, those who might otherwise want to use a different label.

The civil union is an imperfect solution that has already been discontinued by those states that only ever offered it to same-sex couples. Only Vermont and New Jersey still recognize the relationship, and Vermont has not allowed new ones since opting for full marriage equality in 2009. New Jersey presents a curious case, where same-sex couples can choose civil unions or marriage but different-sex couples are limited to marriage.[92] (We await the challenge to this situation, grounded in an argument based on inequality. What's sauce for the goose . . .)

Sheila Blackburn's comments on her civil union–to–marriage were revealing for their insight into the kinds of personal and social vertigo that people presented with these choices can experience. At the start of our telephone conversation, she said, "I feel like the civil union was sort of an appeasement, not the real deal. I wanted to go the deeper level of meaning, and that was marriage." Yet a few minutes later she took a different view of why she and her partner entered into the civil union: "We had both been married and felt like we weren't ready to take that step again—we wanted a deeper level of commitment, and marriage was too much for us at the time. It turned out to be a good stepping-stone."[93]

The peculiar features of the civil union—which are tied to its justification as a clever compromise designed to help same-sex couples achieve many of the benefits of marriage while appeasing traditionalists by withholding the term *marriage* itself—seem to be losing their appeal. For no other reason, it would be best to strike the laws that established them, in favor of a new alternative that better addresses why couples today would choose a status other than marriage—an alternative more flexibly designed to meet the needs of many types of couples. There are stepping-stones (and other rocks to quarry) better than the civil union.

One final word is needed before concluding this chapter. While the abolition of the civil union might be justified, the steps some of the civil union states have taken in that direction are questionable. They have a few options once the decision is made to do away with this status. They can follow the example set by Vermont: create no additional civil unions but leave the existing ones in place. That can result in confusion—as it did when I called a clerk there to ask whether I needed to dissolve my civil union (a difficult process, since we don't live in the state) before getting married and learned that no one knew the answer to my question! This ambiguity, and a lingering civil union, could be problematic for anyone who later marries a different person in another state and is then challenged by the former civil union partner. Is the marriage valid when the civil union was never dissolved? It's unacceptable that the answer is unclear.

But that's better than what happened in Delaware and Connecticut. These states converted civil unions into marriages by operation of law. If a couple objected to this "forced marriage," their only option was to dissolve the civil union. As Professor Kaiponanea Matsumura has persuasively argued, for the state to marry someone against their will raises serious constitutional issues.[94] And it doesn't help to say that the couple has the option of avoiding marriage by dissolving the union, because that confronts them with a pair of likely unpalatable choices: either marry or be considered legal strangers to each other. In addition, psychological research shows that people are generally less likely to give up a status once they have it than to obtain it in the first place.[95] Thus, what looks like the offering of two options is in fact a skewed process that forcibly marries some couples who, in the words of Herman Melville's Bartleby the scrivener, "would prefer not to."[96]

Although the focus of this chapter is civil unions, a comparison to domestic partnership laws is instructive here. Recall from the previous chapter that in California, benefits under the state domestic partnership were stepped up gradually. They were also automatically applied to those in domestic partnerships that were far from marriage in the benefits conferred. Consider the consequences: a couple who may have wanted only a specific set of benefits under an early domestic partnership law could have found themselves, by legal default, in a status they never choose and one they could avoid finding themselves in only if one member was willing to broach the rather awkward idea that they become legal strangers. No couple should face such a situation.

Let's reintroduce Lisa Goodman. She's a lesbian who was both a driving force in the creation of civil unions and someone who entered in one in 2011, shortly after Delaware first recognized the status. Just two years later, she was able to marry her partner, Drew Fennell, as their state moved quickly from civil unions to marriage. Since they followed the "convert or (legally) die" approach, I had to ask her: why didn't the lawmakers just allow people in civil unions to remain in them?

During a telephone conversation, she did the best job possible of justifying this coercive approach.[97] Since the civil union in Delaware was designed as an accommodation only for same-sex couples, most of whom could be presumed to prefer marriage (that's especially true for civil unions but not so much for other kinds of legal relationships), few people in them would be negatively affected by the change. And the costs of allowing civil unions to continue as a legal artifact would have been steep, requiring decades of dual record keeping (including reporting statistics on marriage—but not civil union—to the federal government). There was also a concern that couples civilly united in Delaware might move out of the state and then encounter difficulty dissolving the union, a problem they wouldn't have with marriage.

These are carefully considered points. They make for a defensible, practical position. Nonetheless, forcing someone to choose between two unpalatable options isn't the best way to respect decisional autonomy. Surely the law can do better than this, even if it ends up withdrawing choices. As Vermont shows, the law already *has* done better by allowing existing civil unions to continue—despite the confusion that retaining this largely vestigial status has created. But it can do better still. Colorado has paved a clear path with its unique *designated beneficiary law*. That law is the subject of the next chapter.

3 The Designated Beneficiary Agreement Act

COLORADO'S SUCCESSFUL EXPERIMENT

We didn't want the designated beneficiary law to make the same discriminatory choices as the marriage code.

Colorado State Senator Pat Steadman, one of the principal architects and drafters of the law and a partner in a designated beneficiary agreement

The designated beneficiary agreement is a big legal step up. But there's no recognition of you as a couple to the rest of the world.

Patricia Yarrow, half of the first couple in Colorado to enter into a designated beneficiary agreement

We built a train room and put a house over it.

Marilyn McCord, half of the first couple in her Colorado county to enter into a designated beneficiary agreement

In 2009, the state of Colorado introduced a new legal creation: the Designated Beneficiary Agreement Act. Although the ideas it embodies were not spun entirely from whole cloth, this law marked an unmistakable advance from anything that preceded it. Just as the term *domestic partnership* can be traced to Tom Brougham and Barry Warren, so too can *designated beneficiary* be assigned a clear provenance: according to Pat Steadman, a Democrat and Colorado state senator, it was the Denver attorney Ted Trimpa who coined the phrase.[1] Beneath its bland nominal facade, the designated beneficiary agreement (DBA), more than any other legal entity discussed in this book, has the potential to move the nation closer to valuing all families, as any sensible legal system must do. Now the DBA just needs to expand outside Colorado, where it's been sequestered since it was invented.

A quick summary of the main provisions of this revolutionary measure will help to ground the discussion that follows. The designated beneficiary law provides a mechanism for any two competent adults to enter into an agreement that, at their option, can establish a host of mutual legal entitlements and obligations. Among these are the right to be named a beneficiary of retirement systems, pensions, and health and life insurance; the right to hospital visitation; the right to act as the other's agent for a variety of purposes (including end-of-life and other medical decisions, such as "anatomical gifts" and the disposition of the other's remains); the right to hold property jointly; the right to direct the disposition of the other's remains; the right to inherit property through intestate succession; the right to sue for wrongful death on behalf of the other beneficiary; and the right to standing for the receipt of worker's compensation benefits. Once completed and executed by the two parties, the document is filed with the county clerk's office—just like a marriage or civil union license.[2]

Many of the listed items are provided by default to married couples, and some of the same general rules and restrictions apply to DBAs. For instance, they share the age restriction that applies to marriage in most states: both parties must be at least eighteen years old.[3] More significantly, they mimic marriages (and civil unions) in following the "one at a time" rule: no one who is already married or civilly united can be in a DBA—and no one can be in more than one DBA at a time.[4] (As we'll see, there is no compelling reason for these restrictions.) Yet the DBA marks a significant departure in a couple of ways. First, it discards marriage's disqualification rules based on closeness of family relationship or the sex of the parties. Adult siblings and parents and adult children are eligible to enter into a DBA together, as are same-sex couples—and this was true even before the state had moved to full marriage equality.[5] Second and perhaps most creatively, each item in the agreement is chosen on an à la carte basis, and none need be reciprocal. So, for instance, a middle-aged man and his elderly mother want him to make end-of-life decisions for her but not the other way around. The designated beneficiary form is designed to accommodate such a possibility. For each item, there are four blank spaces: two on the left side, two on the right. Each party, A and B, decides whether to accept the legal right or protection—if yes, the party initials on the left; if no, on the right. In our hypothetical case, then, the parties might initial the document as shown in table 1 (where the son is Party A, with the initials "MAS," and the mother is Party B, with the initials "EM").

That's how the DBA process works, but how did it come to be? And to what extent does it fulfill what I see as its promise of making the law most useful for the large number of people who aren't married but still need legal protection for their relationships and expectations?

Steadman, himself openly gay, wanted to do something to protect the rights of his fellow LGBTQ Colorado citizens—and his own rights. He'd been involved in the gay (later LGBTQ) rights movement since graduating from law school and passing the Colorado bar in 1991. Soon after, in 1993, Colorado voters approved the now infamous Amendment 2 to the state constitution.[6] The measure cast the LGBTQ community as second-class citizens by effectively repealing all local ordinances prohibiting discrimination based on sexual orientation and by declaring that no similar laws could be enacted in the future.[7] At the time, Denver, Boulder, and Aspen all had such ordinances on the books.[8] Steadman worked on the unsuccessful campaign to defeat the amendment and was then involved in fighting it all the way to the US Supreme Court. In *Romer v. Evans* (1996), the court struck down Amendment 2 and declared that the Constitution "neither knows nor tolerates classes among citizens."[9]

The defeat of Amendment 2 did not quench the state legislature's thirst for doing harm to the LGBTQ community. In 2006, while he was still working as a lobbyist, Steadman became involved in two related ballot amendments. One was a measure to fortify the ban against same-sex marriage that already existed under statutory law. At the height of the mini-DOMA boom, the holy grail of disqualification was amending states' constitutions to prevent same-sex marriages, a much sturdier intervention than enacting a statute, which could be repealed or declared in violation of the state's constitution: only a subsequent amendment (much more difficult to pass than a statute) or a ruling under the US Constitution could undo such a measure. In the early 2000s, proponents of gay marriage bans

Table 1   Excerpt of a Sample Designated Beneficiary Agreement

To grant a right or protection, initial			To withhold a right or protection, initial	
PARTY A	PARTY B		PARTY A	PARTY B
——	——	The right to acquire, hold title to, own jointly, or transfer inter vivos or at death real or personal property as a joint tenant with me with right of survivorship or as a tenant in common with me;	MAS	EM
——	——	The right to be designated by me as a beneficiary, payee, or owner as a trustee named in an inter vivos or testamentary trust for the purposes of a nonprobate transfer on death;	MAS	EM
——	——	The right to be designated by me as a beneficiary and recognized as a dependent in an insurance policy for life insurance;	MAS	EM
——	——	The right to be designated by me as a beneficiary and recognized as a dependent in a health insurance policy if my employer elects to provide health insurance coverage for designated beneficiaries;	MAS	EM
——	——	The right to be designated by me as a beneficiary in a retirement or pension plan;	MAS	EM
——	EM	The right to petition for and have priority for appointment as a conservator, guardian, or personal representative for me;	MAS	——
——	EM	The right to visit me in a hospital, nursing home, hospice, or similar health care facility in which a party to a designated beneficiary agreement resides or is receiving care;	MAS	——
——	EM	The right to initiate a formal complaint regarding alleged violations of my rights as a nursing home patient as provided in section 25-1-120, Colorado Revised Statutes;	MAS	——
——	EM	The right to act as a proxy decision-maker or surrogate decision-maker to make medical care decisions for me . . .	MAS	——

were confident that progressive developments toward marriage equality were unlikely yet at the same time worried about the movement's gathering force. They were battening down the hatches in ways reminiscent of how some states had fortified their antimiscegenation laws in the twentieth century—until the Supreme Court upended that strategy in *Loving v. Virginia*, which ruled out all such laws.[10]

The strategy of marriage equality proponents was to play defense by trying to keep such amendments from even being considered by state legislatures or appearing on the ballot (in states that require voters to approve any constitutional amendment). That approach was wise, because once such amendments came up for a vote, they invariably succeeded. Steadman knew that the measure's passage was "inevitable." (He was right. It did pass, easily.)[11] But he and other progressive lawmakers tried to salvage what they could. They pushed for approval of a separate law that would have provided a limited set of rights for domestic partners. That referendum did not succeed—in part, Steadman believes, because the Democratic candidate for governor, Bill Ritter, did not advocate for it. Yet once Ritter and a Democratic legislative majority were installed in early 2007, Steadman and others were hopeful that they could get some traction for legislation that would offer at least some protection for gay and lesbian couples and families.

By the late aughts, Steadman and his fellow drafters had several models to choose from. The civil union was one way to go, but that was too close to marriage for Colorado and therefore a good bet to fail. Domestic partnerships, as we've seen, are in fact a crazy quilt of different rights and responsibilities: public or private, statewide or local, and varying wildly in the benefits and obligations they impose. Rather than dive into that murky pool, which seemed likely to extend the confusion of that polydefinitional status, Steadman and his colleagues looked to a mostly ignored model for granting rights to couples outside marriage: the *reciprocal beneficiary*.

This clumsily named status had its genesis in the first serious marriage equality battle, which began in Hawaii in the mid-1990s. It was the compromise salvaged from the ruins of *Baehr v. Lewin* and its awful aftermath—which, as discussed in chapter 2, included the passage of DOMA and an amendment to the Hawaii state constitution effectively stopping the litigation in its tracks.

Before that antiequality amendment dropped into place, the Hawaii legislature had enacted a law granting a few of the benefits of marriage to couples in a reciprocal beneficiary relationship, including hospital visitation, health care decision-making, the right to sue for wrongful death, and some property rights.[12] Importantly, though, although the impetus for this law was the recognition that gay and lesbian couples needed at least some of the same protections that were afforded to married couples, the class of those eligible for what was named "reciprocal beneficiary" status extended beyond them, encompassing other adult couples who were not legally able to marry. As a practical matter, this meant that, in addition to same-sex couples, the law covered those closely enough related to be barred from marriage by incest laws. Yet those who *could* marry were restricted to that option.[13] The reciprocal beneficiary status was much less flexible and creative than the DBA that emerged in Colorado—the list of rights was small and fixed, and the parties did not have the à la carte option—but it was an important step.

Interestingly, the reciprocal beneficiary law has evolved *away* from the gay and lesbian couples it was created to help. Since Hawaii (like all states) now recognizes the right of such couples to marry, they are thereby prohibited from entering into these agreements. Thus, only close adult relatives are currently eligible to apply for this slate of rights and protections. That Hawaii chose to retain this law even after the most significant reason for its enactment disappeared speaks to a central theme of this book. Once the issue of eligibility for marriage swam into focus, so did the real needs of not only same-sex couples but also people in relationships that the law already recognized. And, as noted earlier, laws that include folks other than same-sex couples have mostly stuck around.

Not always, though. Vermont was the only other state to enact a reciprocal beneficiary statute, but the law was a failure perhaps unmatched in the annals of legal history. At the same time that the civil union was created (in 2000), the legislature, following the Hawaii model, carved out a small set of benefits that would be available only to two people related by blood or adoption. These centered on late-in-life issues, such as the disposition of remains, advance directives, and hospital visitation.[14] In 2014, the law was repealed, for the sensible reason that *not a single reciprocal beneficiary relationship was ever created in the state.*[15]

While it's probably impossible to explain why this status didn't have any takers at all in Vermont, it was never going to be a major success. One reason may be that the civil union battle there consumed all the attention, and few even seem to have noticed the enactment of the reciprocal beneficiary law. Also, since the status was limited to those who could neither civilly unite nor marry, the class of possible applicants was small (in a small state, for that matter). The benefits were quite limited as well.

But Steadman and his fellow drafters liked some of what they saw in these laws. The Hawaii one was the best that could be forged from the ashes of *Baehr v. Lewin*, and, perhaps inspired by some of the domestic partnership measures, the legislature extended its coverage to include close relatives. In Vermont, the civil union law meant that it was *only* close relatives who otherwise had no access to defined legal benefits, so the class of possible reciprocal beneficiary registrants was small.

The drafters of the designated beneficiary law looked to these creative legal structures and created an astonishingly progressive piece of legislation that responds to several important insights. As in Hawaii, something had to be done to recognize the day-to-day reality of thousands of people in same-sex couples (including Steadman himself) who were shut out of marriage. That need was so powerful, and so centrally a part of what became the designated beneficiary law, that some legislators and lobbyists opposed it on the familiar grounds that different-sex couples had been included as a fig leaf to mask the reality that the bill was a step toward full marriage equality. For example, Bruce Hausknecht, a judicial analyst for Focus on the Family Action, said its main intention was to benefit not heterosexual couples but "another class of people entirely."[16] One did not need to guess at the "class of people" to whom he referred.

But Hausknecht, along with others such as Colorado State Senators Kevin Lundberg and Scott Renfroe, suffered from a kind of political blindness, because the drafters parted ways with the reciprocal beneficiary laws in recognizing that there was no good reason to restrict eligibility to those who couldn't otherwise marry. They understood that this new legal entity should be available to any two adults who wanted to create a life plan, as is made clear in the Legislative Declaration that precedes the law's rights-granting provisions. The lawmakers noted that people don't reliably provide for the consequences of their mortality. Many don't have wills, don't appoint anyone to make end-of-life decisions, and don't consider the possibility that they will be legally incapacitated. In such cases, the default person who holds those powers is often someone other than whom they would have wished to decide on their behalf. Even those who might recognize the need for this kind of advance planning, often simply lack the financial resources to do it. As the lawmakers further recognized, "the power of individuals to care for one another and take action to be personally responsible for themselves and their loved ones is of tremendous societal benefit, enabling self-determination and reducing reliance on public programs and services."[17]

Steadman and his fellow drafters also knew that the bundles of rights that had almost always come with recognition of any legal couple status—whether marriage, civil union, domestic partnership, or reciprocal beneficiary—were inflexible. (As discussed in chapter 2, a few of the local ordinances in Arizona are exceptions to this rule.) These statuses conveyed either many legal rights (marriage, civil unions, and some statewide domestic partnerships) or few (some forms of domestic partnership and reciprocal beneficiaries), but almost all were designed to be one size fits all, which could be avoided only by entering into side agreements—in particular, prenuptial-like contracts—that were expensive, unaffordable for many, and inconsistently enforced by courts.[18]

DBAs took an entirely different, creative approach, recognizing that different constellations of rights and benefits would suit different people at different stages of life and under different circumstances. The ingenious flexibility of these agreements is their greatest virtue. As Steadman told me, even with marriage equality now achieved nationwide, both same- and different-sex pairs continue to use the DBA. The couples I interviewed on the topic of their designated beneficiary status provide glimpses into the ways these agreements have proved useful.

We can start with Steadman himself. In an interesting oddity, he did not get to vote on the measure he had been so heavily involved in creating. The governor signed the DBA into law in April 2009, and Steadman was chosen to fill a vacant seat in the state senate the following month. When the law went into effect, on July 1, Steadman was happy to take advantage of it. To paraphrase a hoary Hair Club for Men line: He's not only the founder of the designated beneficiary law. He's also a client.

When the DBA option opened, Steadman and his partner, David Misner, signed up right away. Sadly, Misner passed away in 2012, from pancreatic cancer. The loss was as sudden and unexpected as cancer ever is: from diagnosis to death, only twelve weeks elapsed. Steadman found that the law he had so centrally helped to create worked in every respect. The agreement acted effectively in the couple's urgent health care decision-making while the illness took its brief, remorseless course. And, given the couple's "relatively simple" estate, their DBA was all the senator needed to gain the rights of intestate succession (as though he had been a legal spouse). It even functioned as a means for him to obtain trouble-free access to Misner's bank accounts. Despite what he described as "a few puzzled looks" from bank employees, Steadman reported that a call to the banks' attorneys resolved the issue quickly and easily.

For other same-sex couples, the DBA provided a bridge between the kinds of rights that contracts could secure and those guaranteed by the later-arriving civil union, and then marriage. During a long Skype interview, Patricia Yarrow and Liz Gettings provided a fascinating account of the type of legal slog that same-sex couples have often had to endure on their journey from outlaws to legally married spouses.[19] The complexity and creativity of what they did to have their relationship recognized in ways that similarly situated different-sex couples would take for granted speak powerfully to the need for full equality. But their experience also suggests the need for law to flexibly adapt to a changing society.

The two women met online in 1999 and in person in early 2000. When I spoke to them in 2014, they had concluded their long journey all the way to marriage, having accumulated and discarded several "lesser" (to them) statuses along the way. Gettings had moved to Colorado from Virginia, after leaving her marriage to a man. By early 2001, the couple had made a personal, lifetime commitment: they were inscribed as domestic partners in Denver's local registry—but the act was symbolic, because the law was created for city and county employees only, to allow their partners access to benefits. "We did it symbolically, because it was a public record," Yarrow recalled.

Gettings and Yarrow did the best they could to protect themselves legally, naming each other as beneficiaries in their wills and executing "scads of powers of attorney." "We did everything we could think of," as

Yarrow stated. This was especially smart planning in their case, since Gettings's mother, a devout Baptist, was not supportive of the couple's relationship. The legal case reporters and news accounts are stuffed with stories of surviving members of same-sex couples frozen out of decision-making and out of sharing in an estate that the late partner fully intended to pass on to them rather than to the family of origin—from whom they are, under circumstances involving challenges to the survivor's authority, often estranged. Surviving all-but-legal spouses have been kicked out of their homes, denied needed benefits, and estranged from nieces, nephews, and other family members with whom they'd once enjoyed close relationships.

But it's not just family issues that raise concerns for undocumented same-sex couples. The lack of recognition created obstacles when Gettings had health problems. In 2002, she needed major surgery and was required by her health plan to use a Catholic hospital that didn't acknowledge their relationship. As she recalled, a nurse "put her job on the line" to permit Yarrow to visit her. In 2007, Gettings developed breast cancer, and they discovered that the Family and Medical Leave Act didn't apply to them.[20] No amount of careful planning could have avoided either of these morasses.

When the DBA law was enacted in 2009, the couple signed up right away—in fact, they were the first in the state to do so. Yarrow referred to the law as "cheaper, one-stop shopping," compared to the complexities of the plan-it-yourself approach. The couple found that all of the items on the list applied to them, and they filled out and filed the document accordingly. As with Steadman, when problems arose that might otherwise have necessitated a court battle—or at least a series of time-consuming steps— the DBA came to their rescue. When Yarrow fell and broke her ankle at a bus stop, the Catholic hospital refused to allow Gettings to visit her—until the DBA cavalry arrived, in the form of the document they were able to produce. They found that the ability to designate each other as beneficiaries on life insurance policies made life easier too; before that, it was "very much a gamble whether your agent was going to recognize that you had an insurable interest in each other" (Gettings had a hard time in 2002 persuading an agent to let her name Yarrow, for instance). From the perspective of a lesbian couple who had been dealing with a system that saw them as legal strangers for so long, the DBA was almost too good to be true.

Gettings liked the DBA's flexibility and volunteered the observation that it might be useful even to "people in sharing relationships, in a neighborhood." But to both of them, the DBA was a small step that did not see them "as a couple to the rest of the world." That's not entirely true, of course, since the law does compel third parties—banks, insurance companies, hospitals, even those who negligently or intentionally cause one partner's death—to recognize such couples.[21] But in their case, the law fell far short of what they really needed and wanted: marriage. As they knew, that deeply rooted status would provide a more general societal acknowledgment and acceptance of their relationship that would be helpful in every context.

Before they could reach that goal, though, it turned out that they needed to take two more steps. The first came with the enactment of Colorado's civil union law in 2012. Again, Yarrow and Gettings were early adopters. Since the civil union was marriage in all but name—at least under state law—it materially improved their lives. For example, they could take advantage of the Colorado retirement system—an important benefit not available under the designated beneficiary law.[22]

Still determined to marry, in 2014 the couple traveled to the neighboring state of New Mexico to take their second step toward full equality. In 2013, that state's supreme court had declared that the state constitution mandated marriage equality.[23] Yarrow and Gettings wanted to take that step—and because the US Supreme Court decided the *Windsor* case that year, their marriage was entitled to federal recognition. Only one final step remained: for Colorado to complete the journey to recognizing same-sex marriage. That happened as a result of *Obergefell* in 2015 (shortly after I spoke to the couple).

"I'm pretty sure that I want to take care of Liz and she wants to take care of me," Yarrow said. Unfortunately, her willingness to care for Gettings was put into practice not long after they were finally able to complete their march to full marriage equality. Gettings died in 2017 of lung cancer, at the early age of fifty-eight. At least their private tragedy wasn't hindered by legal roadblocks. With marriage, state law helped, rather than hindered, their mutual lifelong commitment. While the DBA and the civil union have been of enormous benefit to many thousands of people who couldn't or didn't want to marry, for many gay and lesbian couples like

Yarrow and Gettings, each one of these steps was an important marker on their lives' paths but something they would have avoided if they could have. That said, in an odd and compelling way, the law's gradually eroding prohibitions allowed them to renew their mutual commitments, again and again, through deliberate actions not required of couples who could marry whenever they wished. This accidental sequence of periodic, purposeful reaffirmations might be a small but important consolation to those forced to wait for the state to catch up to their lived reality. By evolving in this way, the law provided a real-world instance of a step-by-step commitment similar to a proposal put forward by the legal scholar Jessica Feinberg: a sort of escalating, "buy-in" marriage whose partners would become more legally interdependent over time.[24]

From the start, though, Steadman's legislative masterpiece attracted a larger following than the same-sex couples who were its most obvious beneficiaries. While Yarrow and Gettings were filing their DBA, Marilyn McCord and Don Anderson were queuing up to do the same thing in another county. At the time, McCord was sixty-eight and Anderson seventy. When I spoke to McCord five years later, Anderson had died and the DBA had done just what it was supposed to do: made dealing with their finances and end-of-life decisions unproblematic.[25]

Although McCord freely admitted that part of the decision to enter into a DBA rather than marry had to do with avoiding the loss of social security benefits from her deceased second husband, her story provides a window onto the complex reasons that many couples might have for choosing a status other than marriage.

Speaking from her home in the resort community of Vallecito, McCord told me that her property, in an old mining town, abuts the state's largest wilderness area. It keeps her in good aerobic shape, as the town sits eight thousand feet above sea level. The adventurous septuagenarian described a full life, rich with experiences including obtaining a pilot's license at age fifty-five and then flying to New Mexico and back. It wasn't surprising to learn that she was willing to take a flier on the new law too.

McCord described Anderson as her "late partner," and the satisfying life they shared revealed a couple secure in their personal relations and canny about their personal finances. In 1997, McCord had been a widow for five years. Anderson moved into the house next door, and within a short time they moved in together—McCord remembers April 27, 1997, as the exact date, her "half-birthday." She called their pre-DBA relationship a common-law marriage, but she was using the term in a nonlegal sense. Although Colorado is one of the few remaining states to recognize that status, she seems to have been saying that the couple was openly cohabitating. As she noted, a remarriage (including a common-law marriage, which has the same legal effects as a "regular," ceremonial one) would have ended her social security benefits, but it doesn't appear that the couple met any of the requirements for common-law marital status. They don't seem to have "held themselves out" as married, and there was no evidence of a clear intent to be married. Rather, they were legal do-it-yourselfers: they shared resources but had separate bank accounts; withdrew more of his long-term assets than hers when he became ill, as he had a steady income stream from a public pension; and sold both of their houses and built one together. A priority in that endeavor was constructing a train room to accommodate Anderson's passion for model railroads. The trains themselves had enough value that McCord described them, at least semi-seriously, as an "insurance policy."

When the DBA option presented itself, McCord and Anderson cherry-picked the features they liked and needed and used separate agreements to achieve a more detailed plan. For instance, they accepted the "intestate succession" provision but later drafted a pour-over will and trust so that there would be no probate of Anderson's estate after his death.[26] (McCord was the trustee, and all the assets passed to her when he died. She then carried out their informal agreement to distribute a small sum of money to each of his nieces and nephews.) The DBA turned out to be useful in the stressful, decision-making process at the end of Anderson's life too.

Unlike Yarrow and Gettings or Steadman and Misner, McCord and Anderson neither expected nor intended to marry. They were older. Their DBA worked. And they didn't need a marriage to protect any children;: McCord's were long grown, and Anderson had never wanted to be a father.

In short, the couple had all kinds of reasons—not just the obvious, economic ones—for keeping things as they were. "We pretty much did the things a married couple would do anyway," McCord told me. "And people are more accepting of folks living together without marriage these days."

The DBA let this couple share their lives together without the worry that their documents might be ambiguous, challenged, or even contradictory.

They might have been, in McCord's words, "a whole different animal" from the LGBTQ families that inspired the statute's drafting, but their creative, successful use of the status shows how the law can grow to meet actual needs. Steadman and his colleagues may have included couples like Anderson and McCord in its scope primarily for strategic reasons, but it's clear they also had a bolder, broader vision in mind. In 2014, Steadman told me that, over the past several years, all kinds of people in Colorado had taken advantage of the law. But, as we'll see, recent data from the Denver County Office of the Clerk and Recorder suggests that it is losing rather than gaining favor.

The DBA is a brilliant, problem-solving piece of legislation. The à la carte flexibility it provides is legal innovation at its best, and the decision not to exclude any class of adult couple *whether or not* they are able to marry is a clear recognition that people in all kinds of relationships need, and deserve, the law's protections. Yet more must be done for the designated beneficiary law to work as effectively as it could. Chapter 5 offers a set of recommendations for how it might evolve to account for a changing society, but a few suggestions are appropriate here, in the context of these personal narratives.

First, there is no reason to restrict DBAs to those who are neither married nor in a civil union. This exclusion was presumably the result of a couple of factors. Despite its visionary inclusion of many kinds of couples, the DBA law was primarily a compromise for same-sex couples, and the state at that point did not want to encourage people who could wed to choose some "lesser" status. Marriage continued as sovereign, as it still does. A more compelling concern is the complexity of record keeping across multiple relationships and the fear that a court might need to resolve competing claims to authority or to the right to property. This is a misguided worry, though. Such conflicts already arise. For instance, a person's death can trigger a dispute between their surviving spouse and their other family members who might have claims under a will or based on something less clear—informal writings, oral promises, and so on. Marriage has default rules, but the married couple remains free to make other arrangements. The DBA just provides a handy way to collect such arrangements in one place and with great simplicity. It offers a clear indication of the decedent's intent for the areas it covers—and so specifically that it's likely to be quite helpful in resolving disputes. Of course, there would have to be some mechanism for establishing priorities in certain cases. But the law already has ways of resolving this issue, which would likely be less common or messy if a DBA were in place. Knowledgeable folks like Jennifer Tweeton and Alex Rifman and the other couples profiled in chapter 2 can easily deal with creating more than one legal relationship.

The second area for improvement is the seemingly sensible rule that a person can be in only one DBA at a time. The solution here is similar to the one suggested above. Consider the current situation and how allowing multiple DBAs might ameliorate rather than increase confusion. Imagine an older couple like Marilyn McCord and Don Anderson, in which the woman believes her younger brother rather than her partner is the best person to direct the disposition of her remains (say, for religious reasons). Currently, the way to arrange that is for her to withhold that right from her partner in their DBA and to execute a separate agreement with her brother. This is of course possible, but it would be better for sister and brother to create a separate DBA—meaning that she would have two such agreements—declining all rights and benefits except for this one narrow grant of authority.

Allowing a second DBA would be better than requiring an independent agreement, for a couple of reasons. First, it's likely to be cheaper to use this standard form than to hire an attorney for such a purpose. And there is no reason to drag a lawyer into the proceedings for something so straightforward. Second, the possibility of inconsistency should be easier to eliminate in the case of multiple DBAs than in the case of a DBA and a different class of document, which one of the parties might not even know about.[27] The DBA registry, housed in an electronic format, could link each individual's documents in such a way as to trigger the rejection of an inconsistent agreement. So, if the woman in our hypothetical had already granted her partner the right to deal with the disposition of her remains, the system would flag her attempt to allow her brother to do that through a subsequent DBA and link it back to the original declaration. Then she could decide whether to amend or stick with the earlier DBA. Not so hard to do.

Colorado today leads the nation in legal options for couples. Patricia Yarrow and Liz Gettings went through every formal one of them, in ascending order, but they might have stopped at any point. They registered as domestic partners under local Denver law. They used contracts and other mutual legal agreements to try to protect their relationship. They took advantage of the designated beneficiary law until the civil union became possible, at which time they chose that status. When marriage equality arrived in a neighboring state, they made that final commitment—albeit one that Colorado acknowledged only later. As each new status was created, Colorado retained the previous ones. The state has provided a range of options that others ought to look to (concerns about the continuing wisdom of the civil union aside) in thinking about ways to serve all of their increasingly diverse residents. Within the rich diversity of options Colorado offers, none is so forward thinking or innovative as the DBA. Other states should consider adopting such a law, taking into account the suggested modifications discussed above.

Yet Colorado's experience also provides a sobering picture of how difficult the adoption of such a forward-looking option might be. Although Steadman told me that the DBA was "catching on" as more and more people became aware of it, in fact the opposite seems true, at least recently. Denver County, which is the most populous in the state, suggests that interest in the designated beneficiary law has waned as the marriage equality movement has succeeded. From the law's enactment in 2009 through the middle of 2016 (shortly after the *Obergefell* decision), a total of 460 DBAs had been entered into.[28] Of these, the vast majority (415) were for same-sex couples, while only 42 were for different-sex couples. (The forms do not specify gender, so I had to rely on educated guesses based on first names; in three cases, it was impossible even to hazard such a guess.) For both same- and different-sex couples, the greatest number of these agreements were created in 2009, presumably because of a combination of pent-up demand and the initial publicity that surrounded the law's enactment. Both groups have seen drop-offs since then, however.

It appears that, since 2010, the DBA has been chosen no more than six(!) and as few as two times per year by different-sex couples; it recently stabilized at a paltry *four* before dropping yet further in 2018 (see table 2). The year 2020 saw an uptick, but when the numbers are so small, the takeaway is that the DBA is generating only low-level interest, however useful the status might be for at least a few people.

What about same-sex couples? In table 3, the time line is a bit more detailed, to account for the dates of significant events in the marriage

Table 2   Designated Beneficiary Agreements
between Different-Sex Denver County Couples

Year	New DBAs
2009	14
2010	3
2011	6
2012	6
2013	2
2014	4
2015	4
2016	4
2017	4
2018	2
2019	2
2020	6

equality movement. The numbers paint a sharp picture. "The DBA Show" opened with great fanfare and to rave reviews, but, with each advance in the marriage equality movement attendance has dwindled, as same-sex partners acquired more and possibly better options. Civil unions had a dramatic effect, and full marriage equality has all but killed the move toward alternative statuses, at least for now. Indeed, civil unions too have taken a hit now that same-sex couples can marry. The numbers have gone down for everyone, but in Denver at least, since 2015 more *different-sex* than same-sex couples have chosen this option (see table 4).

As discussed in the preceding chapter, there are good reasons to question whether the civil union should continue to exist. But the DBA is so obviously a good idea that it's hard to see why it has failed to gain traction and why interest in it has instead dramatically decelerated since its inception. Surely, marriage is not the best fit for every couple, straight or gay. But the law's attempt to value all families can succeed only if people take advantage of such problem-solving legal statuses.

Despite the dismal numbers, we should remain bullish on the DBA. Its disappointing failure to gain a stronger purchase among Colorado

Table 3 Designated Beneficiary Agreements between
Same-Sex Denver County Couples

Year	New DBAs
2009	171
2010	83
2011	55
2012	54
2013	26
	(Civil union law went into effect on May 1)
2014	18
2015	7
	(*Obergefell* decision brought nationwide marriage equality on June 26)
2016	2
2017	4
2018	3
2019	2
2020	1

Table 4 Civil Unions in Denver County

Year	Same-Sex Civil Unions	Different-Sex Civil Unions	Unknown-Sex Civil Unions	Total Civil Unions
2013	726	14	11	751
2014	199	10	4	213
2015	6	10	0	16
2016	4	16	2	22
2017	5	17	0	22
2018	3	7	1	11
2019	2	11	0	13
2020	2	6	0	8

The records of these civil unions do not specify the sex of the parties, so "same-sex" and "different-sex" reflect educated guesses based on first names and "unknown-sex" indicates too low a degree of certainty to allow for a guess.

residents may have something to do with the fact that, no matter the attempt to convince the public otherwise, it was closely associated with the marriage equality movement and therefore not likely considered by people who might have benefited from it. Remember that McCord described her relationship with Anderson as "a whole different animal"— because the "animals" the law was trying to satisfy were same-sex couples fenced out of marriage. For the same reason, the DBA law is also linked to the civil union law in many people's minds, being viewed as a similarly inferior alternative to marriage rather than as a potentially dynamic and creative vehicle for structuring adult relationships. Consider as well the very real possibility that attorneys may not have an incentive to push clients in the direction of the DBA, because the device's simplicity threatens to cut into the lucrative business of estate planning. Or perhaps they don't understand the law well, or they fear that a DBA won't work as intended.

The DBA law's failure to ignite widespread interest is unfortunate but need not be its ultimate fate. The Colorado bar should get behind the initiative, emphasizing its fit for many people in need of legal protection— people who will not otherwise do estate planning and for whom marriage is not the best option (or even a possibility). Folks for whom a DBA has worked, like McCord, might help to spread the word. At some point, it might reach a critical mass and gain the kind of acceptance that marriage alternatives in other countries have received. Here, France's *pacte civil de solidarité* (discussed in greater detail in chapter 5) is instructive. It's a kind of "marriage lite" that has attained widespread popularity among different-sex couples, even though it too was machined with gay and lesbian couples in mind. But not even the *pacte civil* boasts the kind of do-it-yourself creativity that makes the DBA such a brilliant innovation. I believe that the day will yet come when Pat Steadman sees his brainchild gain a strong foothold in Colorado—and, I hope, in every other state.

4 What Is Marriage, Anyway?

(AND WHAT ISN'T MARRIAGE?)

Why is the government playing Cupid?

May Doe

Economically, we benefited by being different genders.

Anne Quinn

Marriage . . . solved certain legal issues for us, but what we
didn't anticipate was that marriage was going to change the
fundamental nature of our relationship, . . . that suddenly
we were looking at each other as committed to one another
in a way that I never conceived of. . . . There is a feeling of a
deeper commitment, a deeper attachment, a deeper
bond. . . . It's almost magical.

John Hunter

SQUARE PEGS, ROUND HOLES, AND LATECOMERS: THREE MORE RELATIONSHIP STORIES

The discussion over the past few chapters about legally recognized relationships has focused primarily on two groups of people. The first are the
gay and lesbian couples who did not have the option to marry and sought
another form of legal protection for their relationships. Tom Brougham
and Barry Warren didn't want marriage, but plenty of others—like Patricia
Yarrow and Liz Gittings—did and instead had to settle for *something* not-
quite-marriage. The second are the different-sex couples who *could* marry

but found, for a host of sometimes overlapping reasons, that marriage wasn't the best fit for them. The thoughtful Chicago couples I interviewed spoke eloquently of their problems with the institution of marriage that led them to choose the civil union status (see chapter 2), while others— like Marilyn McCord from Colorado (see chapter 3)—were motivated at least in part by the loss of benefits that remarriage would have caused but also by a sense that they needed something other than marriage at that stage of their life.

Now we will consider a few other situations. The first involves people who legally could have married but did not, simply because they were unable to establish relationship with suitable partners. In such cases, we might expect the affected people to find someone to support them in a way that might look something like marriage. The second is about a couple, their children, and a third adult, for whom marriage assumed a complicated and unsuitable place. The third account is about a gay couple who married once the law allowed them to. Their story, and how it reflects a changing view of marriage for both straight and gay couples, will lead nicely into our broader discussion: What is marriage? What *should* marriage be in the current century? And what other legal relationship statuses should the law create and recognize?

The first two accounts will show that some valuable human relationships do not fit comfortably within marriage—even under its current, broad definition. They remind us that this status is still barricaded against close family relationships and those involving more than two people, which will naturally draw us into consideration of how the law might serve the needs of real people without doing violence to the institution of marriage itself. The marriage equality battle teaches that legal advances are possible even if marriage remains elusive for some (whether for justifiable reasons or not). More broadly, there are people who are in all kinds of human relationships that bear little resemblance to marriage but whose interests and mutual reliance the law should protect.

Two Armenian American Sisters

I met May and April Doe (these are pseudonyms, at their request) in the office of a financial planning company of which they are clients.[1] The two have lived together for their entire lives and have supported each other throughout adulthood. That's not surprising, because they are sisters. The compelling story they recounted convinced me that the law needs to do a better job of recognizing relationships like theirs. Basic fairness requires no less.

The sisters were born in the mid-1930s, four years apart. Their parents were Armenian immigrants, whose values and social realities posed challenges for their daughters. From an early age, the sisters lived in relative isolation: even after their parents moved the family from an Armenian American community in West Philadelphia to the neighboring suburb of Upper Darby (the birthplace of notables Tina Fey and Hall of Fame catcher Mike Scioscia), their circle remained small. Their mother stringently restricted what they were permitted to do. No dancing, no movies, no card playing, no makeup. "Well, where does that leave you?" April wondered, rhetorically. Their father was not as religious but had a great fear of mishap. So the kids weren't allowed to ride bikes or use roller skates either.

When it came time for them to start dating, obstacles were everywhere. Socially, they had been purposely protected from the broader society by their parents. Their father even commissioned a woman fluent in Armenian cuisine to teach his wife how to cook in that style. Then there was the expectation that the sisters would marry men within the Armenian American community, which gave them a small dating pool in which to swim. They recounted how their father would worry to the point of walking up and down the sidewalk in front of their home when they were out late.

Nonetheless, the sisters remembered him fairly. He provided for their needs. He never laid a hand on them. And it was obvious that, in his own way, he cared about them and their happiness. But his controlling version of what that happiness might look like precluded it from ever happening—at least when it came to finding a spouse.

As the girls became women, they eventually put their feet down. April, the younger of the two, won a scholarship to the University of Pennsylvania, where she studied education. May took secretarial courses but had to turn down an offer with Sun Oil because her father worried about the safety of "the El" (Philadelphia-speak for one of the city's subway lines, describing the route's "elevated" portion) and the distance between Upper Darby and the downtown Philadelphia office. And when she did find what she calls "a stupid job" closer to home, her father offered strong advice about how she should spend her own money. The final indignity came when May was on the phone with a woman who was trying to offer her a job as a vocalist with a church. With her father standing next to her, she had to turn it down.

Shortly after that—with the sisters by then in their late twenties—they left home for good, to their father's horror: "You're moving out of the house and you're not married!" he cried. Their mother, however, supported their independence, recognizing how unhealthy the family situation had become. They thus began what would turn out to be a long period of deep adult interdependence.

Since that time—and with the exception of a nine-month period when April took a sabbatical in Argentina, where the family had relatives—the sisters have lived together. April retired from teaching Latin and English at the suburban Springfield High School after twenty-one years, and May, who eventually did land a great job at Sun Oil, worked there for some fifteen years before downsizing compelled her to take a retirement package in her fifties. They are completely financially interdependent. All of their accounts are held jointly—except for their retirement accounts, which will not go to the surviving sister once the holder dies.

Their father and then their mother passed away within a few years of each other. When their mother died, they came into a nice inheritance—the lifelong frugality of their immigrant parents did have its benefits. But now they worry about what is going to happen once the first of them dies, because the survivor may have to pay a federal tax levied on the value of the decedent's estate and will surely be hit with state inheritance taxes, which in Pennsylvania are charged against what the decedent's named beneficiary is entitled to take.[2] Surviving spouses pay nothing in either case, while siblings get no exemption under federal law and only a small reduction on their Pennsylvania inheritance tax rate (from 15 down to 12 percent).[3]

Because of these expected tax burdens, the sisters fret that the survivor will become a "bag lady" who will have to rely "on food stamps" to survive. In fact, they both said that their concerns about what will happen when the first of them dies are the principal animation of their conversations with the financial planner every year.

From what I can determine, a dire outcome is extremely unlikely. The sisters inherited their parents' frugality, and even though they regularly used to go to Argentina, they told me they no longer want to travel. Their assets might be sufficient to allow the survivor to remain in the home they now share, even if the taxes are substantial. But that's not likely: when I interviewed them, the federal estate tax applied to amounts only in excess of $5 million, and with the enactment of the Tax Cuts and Jobs Act of 2017 the exemption rose to $10 million per taxpayer.[4] The sisters, who are well heeled enough to have a financial planner, are not going to end up in the streets. But their concerns raise larger questions.

Is the legal system fair? Is the law treating these two the same as it would other couples in a similar situation?

To understand the sisters' financial concerns and their broader perspective on the law, it's helpful to revisit Edie Windsor. Recall that she was legally married to Thea Spyer, although the federal government did not recognize them as married because of DOMA. The practical consequence was that, when Spyer died, Windsor was hit with a federal estate tax bill for a whopping $363,000. Had she been married to a man, the usual exemption for spouses would have applied, reducing her obligation to . . . zero. When the Supreme Court struck down DOMA, it protected Windsor's right to inherit Spyer's estate without having to pay the tax.

The Doe sisters followed Windsor's case with interest and were impressed by her willingness to challenge the law to gain fair treatment. But what about *them*? Perhaps it was the fact that now the government was recognizing the importance of allowing *two women* to protect themselves under the law that made them see their own situation as unfair. Windsor didn't have to pay the estate tax, and they believe that they too should have the ability to protect their assets in some way—even if, as for some of the couples profiled in earlier chapters, *marriage* isn't the right word to describe their strong relationship.

During our conversation, they were crisp and clear in their arguments against treating Windsor differently from them, at least as far as government benefits go:

- The government is "playing Cupid" in deciding that only romantic relationships are deserving of protection.

- That's especially true where procreation isn't involved, as in both the *Windsor* case and their own situation.
- If sexual intimacy is what marriage is about, consider that some spouses "never even touch each other."

These arguments have weight, although they miss something vital. Consider that if these sisters had instead been first cousins, they would have been able to marry in some states—even if they had grown up in the same household, as sometimes happens in extended families. And here's a nugget that's perhaps even more telling: in some states, like Indiana, first cousins are permitted to marry *only* if they are unable to procreate![5] (That's because, historically, one of the chief objections to marriages between closely related people has been that their children would have a high rate of disabilities. If procreation is not a possibility, that objection disappears.)

So if marriage isn't always about intimacy or procreation, what *is* it about? For these sisters, it's interdependence. And that they've got—more than most couples, married or otherwise. They movingly described the feelings of bereavement they'll experience when the other dies and then wondered why the government is doubling their pain by mistreating them.

But they're not asking to be married. Nor, I submit, should the law permit them to enter that relationship. Although the sisters adroitly deconstructed marriage, the taboo against intimate family relations—incest, to use the incendiary term—has strong roots in both criminal and family law. The ancient genetic argument against the union of close family members still informs laws such as the Indiana statute mentioned above, even if it doesn't sit well with a modern bioethical approach to family decision-making. In an age when many kinds of genetic anomalies can be tested for, there's still no suggestion that nonrelated couples who are at high risk for bearing a child with very serious diseases be barred from doing so. As Professor Courtney Cahill has noted, "Even when there is a strong likelihood that each parent carries a recessive trait, as in the case of Tay-Sachs disease in the Ashkenazi Jewish community, the law does not require parents to undergo genetic testing prior to having children to determine whether the child or children will be born with a genetic abnormality."[6]

These laws are justified on other grounds, though. It's a natural, and salutary, part of human development to leave one's family of origin and to create new relationships outside that structure. If children grew up in a society that treated their relatives—siblings, but especially *parents*—as potential life partners, the goal of developing a rich, diverse nation would be seriously compromised. Citing research from the fields of anthropology and sociology, one court explained the incest taboo as a way to force people "to go outside their families to find sexual partners, requiring people to pursue relationships . . . that help form important economic and political alliances," and as an indispensable tool in "protecting young family members from exploitation by older [ones] in positions of authority and [in] reducing competition and jealous friction among family members."[7] Marriage has long been the legal and social lubricant for that movement from the family into the broader society.

Yet not all people find an intimate partner, and there are plenty of stories of siblings who stick together throughout their lives. Surely, the law can do better than to ignore them. The Doe sisters want their close life-long relationship to be recognized as some kind of "civil union," at least in a general sense—for the law to treat like cases alike. As far as their economic interdependency, at least, they are not too different from Spyer and Windsor. The most we can say is that the sisters' relationship looks like marriage in some ways but not in others. It's also fair to say that most people would think these sisters should not be able to marry but that the law should recognize their mutual reliance in some way. As we'll see, the DBA, suitably modified, is ideally suited to their situation.

A Gay Man and a Lesbian Walk into a Marriage . . .

Our second story is about one of the married couples the sisters might have been referring to when they mentioned that the law imposes no requirement of intimacy. It's the tale of a gay man and a lesbian who found that marriage was, at least for a time, the best legal option available to them—but one that still fell far short of what their complex family situation needed.

Terry McKeon and Anne Quinn met in 1986, when both were working for a community health project in New Jersey.[8] Perhaps atypically for the time, they were out to each other in short order: McKeon was a gay man, Quinn a lesbian. They became friendly, and by 1988 they had expressed the desire to start a family with both of them as biological parents. Quinn recalls that it was on McKeon's birthday, in September of that year, that they began to "put things in motion" to achieve their mutual goal.

Originally, they had resolved to have and raise their biological children in separate households. But by the time Quinn became pregnant in 1989, McKeon decided he did not want to live as a single parent, so the two moved in together. Within a few years they had three children—their oldest daughter, Emma, and the twins, Jordan and Kate, who are two years younger. Although he was the biological dad, McKeon was concerned that, if the relationship ended, he could be fenced out of being their parent. (DNA testing was available at the time, but it did not become virtually foolproof until the 1990s.)[9] As Quinn recalls, the lawyer they consulted to make sure McKeon was recognized as the father was taken aback—mostly, she had dealt with men "trying to keep from having their paternity acknowledged." But Quinn had every intention of recognizing McKeon's paternity, no matter what happened between them, and the children's birth certificates confirm that reality.

In their liberal enclave of Montclair, New Jersey, a gay man and a lesbian living together in the 1990s wasn't the deliberate misdirection it might have been in earlier times, when such arrangements were often unions of convenience. Yet while the pair were open and comfortable in their roles as parents, they didn't consider themselves husband and wife. Indeed, using those labels at the beginning would have been legally inaccurate, because they were both single then. But in 1992, they did marry.

Why didn't they do this sooner? Had they been married at the time of their first child's birth, McKeon wouldn't have needed to worry about being acknowledged as the father, because the law in every state contains a presumption of paternity, which holds that any man married to a woman when she gives birth is the father, absent unusual circumstances.[10] But because Quinn and McKeon didn't think of themselves in that way—and didn't want the outside world, including potential romantic partners, to do so either—they chose a harder route to have McKeon recognized as the dad.

But they didn't have a nonmarriage workaround for another need: as Quinn recalled, "We got married because of McKeon's health insurance. I had a set of twins and wasn't working full-time." As discussed in chapter 5, the idea that health benefits should be tied to marriage has outlived whatever usefulness, or tether to reality, it may once have had. But marriage was what McKeon's employer required for Quinn to qualify for benefits, so marriage it was. "Economically, we benefited by being different genders," as Quinn put it.

Both McKeon and Quinn told me that, if the civil union option had been available in New Jersey then, they would have taken it. McKeon remembers how confused and in denial his original family was about his and Quinn's nontraditional living arrangement and how some of them dealt with their discomfort by simply pretending that the couple was straight. Just like straight couples, they were living and raising children together. The optics supported this fantasy—and once Quinn and McKeon married, those same family members were more convinced than ever that the two were really straight, whatever their protestations to the contrary. On the other hand, McKeon told me, his gay friends weren't all supportive of his life decisions, and some questioned whether he was "really" gay.

During our long Skype conversation, McKeon and I discussed in great detail the arrangement that he and Quinn had forged. "We decided that either of us could enter a [romantic] relationship but that the other would have a veto over whether the new adult would be permitted to move in with the family," he said.

That day soon came—not for McKeon, but for Quinn. In 1992—the same year the twins were born—she met Joyce Weeg, who was painting a nearby house. The two fell in love, and soon thereafter, Weeg moved in, with McKeon's approval. There she remained for many years, becoming a third parent to the kids—not legally, but as a practical matter.

But the law didn't—and mostly still doesn't—recognize three parents, whatever the actual circumstances. So even though Weeg, a schoolteacher with a schedule most similar to the children's, did a good deal of the day-to-day parenting, the family had to rely on the goodwill and progressive attitudes of school officials, doctors, and dentists for her to exercise parental authority. And when Weeg traveled with the children by herself, Quinn and McKeon drew up papers giving her emergency legal authority to act in the children's behalf until the "real" parents could get there.

These three adults are hardly the only ones who have had to deal with the legal complication of having only two members of their group recognized as parents. For instance, stepparents have no legal say over what happens to the kids they are in fact raising unless a biological parent of those children voluntarily gives up his or her rights.[11] The uniqueness of the McKeon-Quinn-Weeg situation just dramatically underscores the limitations of the current legal landscape.

Recently, there have been some incursions into this limit. Most significantly, California enacted a law in 2013 that permits a child to have more than two parents.[12] Through judicial decisions, other states have occasionally recognized third parents—sometimes fully, but more often only to the extent of granting visitation rights or imposing support obligations.[13] Although I once opposed (and still harbor reservations about) the legal recognition of more than two parents, in some cases this might be the best way to protect the child's interests.[14] There should have been some way for Weeg to have been recognized as a parent of Emma, Jordan, and Kate, at least to the extent of giving her authority to act in certain cases.

This point is underscored by what happened some years later. When it became legally possible for Weeg and Quinn to wed (although not in New Jersey, their state of residence), they did so, in 2010. For that to happen, of course, Quinn and McKeon needed to divorce. By that time, their marriage of economic convenience was no longer necessary, and the women's marriage best reflected the family's reality—given the limited options the law recognizes, because no provision is made for multiple spouses or for "mixed-use" types of relationships.

Sadly, Quinn's second marriage ended very shortly after it began. Weeg left her for another woman, and so that union too culminated in divorce—leaving McKeon and Quinn where they started: at last check, they were still living under the same roof—even though the kids are all now well into adulthood. And McKeon has not settled into a long-term relationship with another man.

What should the law do about a family like this? What is the optimal set of legally recognized relationships here? There's no perfect answer, but it seems that the first marriage (between McKeon and Quinn) was not the best option for them and that some other legal status—and an acknowledgment of their reality by McKeon's employer, who could have provided

Quinn's health insurance even without marriage—would have been preferable. The trio's parenting situation might have been recognized more flexibly too, along the lines discussed above. As we'll see in chapter 5, an expanded version of the DBA could accommodate the complex web of relationships among three—or even more—adults without the government having to take a position on polygamous marriages. Although McKeon, Quinn, and Weeg weren't in a polyamorous relationship, a not too different trio might be. The law needs tools for each situation. This Montclair family proves the point.

Let's consider one more story before we tidy up this messy bundle of laws and lives and move to some kind of synthesis and recommendations. Chapter 1 profiled the same-sex couple who created, and still abide in, a domestic partnership. We finish with another gay couple, who decided, once they were able, to engage in that ultimate act of assimilation: marriage. The course of their lives and their changing views of an institution that long defined itself in opposition to them provide a useful way to think about marriage more generally—and then to disassemble it into its many component pieces.

Some Things Are Worth Waiting For

John Hunter and Harold "Hal" Kooden are seventysomethings who married in New York City in 2011, right after that option opened up to them.[15] The long, strange journey of their lives holds valuable clues about what marriage means. Sometimes it's easier to see an institution clearly when you have been excluded from it for decades, as the couple's insightful observations show.

Hunter is an artist who has also been an art history educator and administrator. After completing a PhD in art history at the University of Michigan, in 1983 he began teaching at Cleveland State University, where he remained until his retirement some twenty years later—at which point he moved to New York City to live with Kooden. Since then, he has become a painter, acquired a studio, and held several studio shows.

Kooden is a clinical psychologist with a PhD from the University of Chicago. He's also long been involved in social justice movements and was a founder and board member of the National Gay and Lesbian Health

Foundation, a board member of the New York State Martin Luther King Jr. Institute for Nonviolence, and a national cochair for Psychologists for Social Action.

So here are two highly educated gay men, in an interracial marriage, who have lived in an ever-changing world and community. Their somewhat different backgrounds and perspectives open fascinating windows onto marriage, family, and commitment—and not just for same-sex couples.

Both came of age at a time when marriage was still defined in traditional ways. As Kooden recalls, at seventeen years old (in the early 1950s), he was talking with a group of gay men and women, and "the discussion was very clear: if you wanted children, it meant [having] to get heterosexually married, and if you didn't want children then you could live a gay lifestyle, as clandestine as it would be. . . . Marriage was only a means to have children."

Defined that way—and excluding all but the most closeted gay men and lesbians—marriage was not seen by Kooden and those in his politically liberal circles as something to be aspired to. It didn't help that several members of his extended family, including his parents and grandparents, had divorced before doing so was common; as he told me, for him marriage contained "so much dissension." And then his feminist leanings led him to question the very definition of marriage he and his friends had agreed to earlier—a definition built around children and bound up in patriarchal ideas of roles that any self-respecting gay man would reject. That skeptical view of marriage "was pretty much my thinking for a while," he said, "and also thinking about not wanting to be like 'non-gays.' Not wanting to model ourselves in that way—we were creating a new world."

Ideologically, Kooden and his fellows had more in common with the early radicals of the 1970s discussed in chapter 1—the brave souls who stormed the New York City Marriage Bureau to performatively deconstruct marriage—than with Tom Brougham and Barry Warren, who pursued an incremental, cautious approach. But Kooden had no part of the former group's particular stream of activism.

Hunter, by contrast, describes himself as coming from "marrying folk." In his family, that's what you did—and, by and large, you didn't divorce either. That's what he would have done too—ceremonially at least, with his former partner who died in 1999 of complications from AIDS. (Kooden also had a partner who died of AIDS-related complications, a few years earlier.) But, as Hunter recalled, he never got beyond broaching the subject of marriage with his late partner: "He wasn't willing to talk about it, or maybe it didn't seem really important to him." Perhaps that is because the union would not have been legal—but perhaps not. As the stories throughout this book make crystal clear, marriage was and still is not a goal of everyone—whatever their sexual identity.

So when Hunter and Kooden met in 2001, it was probably inevitable that the issue of marriage was going to come up—especially after 2003, when Hunter retired and moved to New York. ("Hal wasn't going to budge," he recalls.) For them to realize that step, though, two things had to happen: Kooden needed to get on board with the idea of marriage, and it had to be possible in New York State.

Kooden described his process of getting to marriage as "evolutionary." Like Jennifer Tweeton, Alex Rifman, and others who preferred the civil union, he first had to separate marriage's religious and civil aspects. His insights on the topic are among the most developed you'll find and bear extensive quotation:

> John read a book . . . around the idea of marriage and what the social ritual meant: that it was just not about two people coming together, but it was the community-based support and the affirmation of the community. Since part of my background was in anthropology/sociology and [that's] the way I think about things, all of that made perfect sense and fit into my thinking, and I realized it was more than just duplicating the heterosexual patriarchy. It was something else that was being evolved, and I began to become more persuaded towards that aspect of marriage—that it wasn't duplicating what I didn't like, but rather it was bringing something to my life that I had always lacked.

The importance of community had a spatial dimension for Kooden too: he wanted his marriage ceremony to be performed in the garden of his own home—as it eventually was. In fact, Hunter disagreed with him about the importance of waiting until marriage was possible in New York. Although their state didn't enact its law allowing same-sex marriages until 2011, it had been recognizing same-sex marriages from other states since 2008—the result of a court decision and an order by the then governor

David Patterson—even if the couple resided in New York and left the state just to marry.[16]

But Kooden refused to be treated as a second-class citizen. Having lived through a complex personal and sexual history, including an arrest for gay cruising as a teenager (an entrapment) and early rejection from his family, he wasn't about to settle for an out-of-state, left-handed recognition of the union that he had at long last come to embrace. Hunter, on the other hand, worried that they would not live to see marriage equality come to New York and was willing to go to Canada or Connecticut to wed. But since Kooden was determined to wait, that's what they did.

When they finally did marry—some ten years after they'd met—Hunter found the experience transformative, and he described the "deeper commitment, deeper attachment, and deeper bond" that he now feels with Kooden. He also understood the importance of legal equality and got into a heated argument with another gay man during a Gay Pride march: "I said, 'You have to understand what it was like to be African American before civil rights and realize the inequality of treatment and how that affects everything in your life.' . . . Marriage to me is an extension of that very same experience." Hunter is correct. While the civil rights movement worked to gain basic rights such as voting and freedom from discrimination in civic life for Blacks, marriage occupied a similar place in the LGBTQ rights movement. Along with exclusion from military service, the marriage ban came to represent the government's fencing out of the gay community—and Hunter would have been more personally attuned than younger, white gay men and lesbians to this parallel.[17]

Kooden characterized his initial reaction to obtaining a marriage license as "intellectual," but then he experienced a profound emotional resonance: "The most gut feeling I had was when we were walking down through that huge room [where marriage licenses were issued] . . . and I was looking at nongay couples that were . . . waiting, and [there was this] feeling of 'I have as much of a right to be here as they do.' . . . When you don't have a sense of entitlement, you don't realize what other people have." Being suddenly faced with that missing entitlement, Kooden explains, "was the first time . . . I had a sense of what it must be like to just feel 'that's the way the world is' and not that I am the outsider or less than them."

The story that Kooden and Hunter tell is one of triumph, of enjoying the fruits of an ongoing transformation of marriage that the success of the marriage equality movement signals but does not fully capture. Today, what marriage means and what it is expected to do are very much contested.

We have focused on couples—and, in one case, a family headed by three adults—who have been excluded from marriage, found it not suitable to their needs, or only recently been permitted to join the club. Yet their stories, and countless others like them, provide a useful perspective from which to view marriage.

WHAT DOES MARRIAGE MEAN, AND WHO IS IT FOR?

Had marriage not so many meanings and so much value—both to those eligible and to those excluded—the marriage equality battle would not have gobbled up so much time, energy, and passion. As detailed in chapter 2, Vermont would have moved directly to full marriage equality rather than hitting the civil union "pause button." The California activists who supported Proposition 8, which stripped gay and lesbian couples of the right to marry but left the full domestic partnership law (with all the same benefits) in place, would not have worked so hard to get it approved.[18] Neither Congress nor the states would have passed acts "defending" marriage. And, as detailed in chapter 3, Colorado would not have moved in such a deliberate, three-step fashion, from permitting DBAs through enacting a full civil union law to (admittedly, only when compelled) recognizing marriage.

It would be a mistake to think the battle is over, though. Since the Supreme Court handed down its marriage equality holding in *Obergefell* in 2015, there has been a raft of political pronouncements condemning it, threats of constitutional amendment to undo the decision, intransigence and defiance by a few courts, and state laws privileging religious freedom over the civil right of marriage. Gay and lesbian couples have been turned away by companies that offer wedding services and have sued under anti-discrimination laws (which don't apply to sexual orientation in about half the states).[19] States have passed laws making it even easier for businesses to avoid dealing with the LGBTQ community.[20] County clerks, on the basis of their own religious views, have claimed the right to decline to issue marriage licenses to same-sex couples.[21] States have refused to list the names of nonbiological parents on birth certificates.[22] Most recently, the Supreme Court has "blessed" the right of a religiously affiliated foster care agency to not work with gay and lesbian couples, even if they are married.[23] Some of these battles have already been resolved, while others continue. In any case, the list of antiequality actions keeps expanding and, like the snow in that famous holiday song, doesn't show signs of stopping.

But what is really at issue here? The pitched battle over same-sex unions and the flowering of other legal statuses as a surprising by-product of that battle have illuminated the complexity of marriage and its deep resonance for all—not just partisans invested in the issue. Although its meaning and entitlements are always contested, questions about the institution are drawn in sharp relief at certain times—like now. The stories told throughout this book highlight these issues, and we can use them to talk about the many dimensions and understandings of marriage.

Once that terrain has been mapped, the final chapter of this book will offer some tentative suggestions on how the law might evolve in two related ways. Namely, we should think about how to support couples and families (and possibly other groupings) in real and productive relationships that the law currently does not "see." We should also consider what changes might be made to marriage itself to reduce its vast distance from other relationships that the law does (or should) recognize, while recognizing that marriage retains deep meaning for many, both as a kind of social glue and as a powerful mechanism for announcing, recognizing, and enforcing a strong commitment between two consenting adults.

So, what is marriage, and what does it do? Many scholars have thoughtfully addressed this question, but perhaps none has captured the institution's kaleidoscopic, shifting nature as well as the journalist and writer E. J. Graff, the author of *What Is Marriage For?* In a memorable metaphor, she describes it as "a kind of Jerusalem," a "site on which the present is constantly building over the past, letting history's many layers twist and tilt into today's walls and floors." Also like that biblical city, marriage is "a battleground, owned and defined" by succeeding groups. Both the city and the institution have retained their "ancient name[s]," but in each case "very little else has . . . remained the same . . . except the fact that it is inhabited by human beings."[24]

The more detailed discussion that follows is indebted to Graff's description of marriage and to her insight that no account of it can ever be complete: like any other complex institution, it has both private and public dimensions and is ever evolving. I have tried to integrate the insights developed by many thoughtful scholars and observers of marriage—and by those interviewed for this book—into broad thematic discussions. But even a necessarily imperfect account can usefully foreground the recommendations that follow—especially since they flow from the realities I encountered while writing this book.

With that backdrop in place, let's take a look at marriage as it's been variously defined and described, and at what it includes and excludes. Each of the purposes that follow is necessarily a simplification, and most people would likely say that marriage is for some combination of them, not just any *one*. Nonetheless, this is a useful way to tease out the different conceptions of what marriage is *for*.

> Most traditionally, marriage is for uniting a man and a woman within an institution that contains certain expectations and requirements— generally including permanence and the raising of children.

Marriage was long imagined as a forever thing—and that understanding still infuses newlyweds with optimism. The law enforced that societal expectation until very recently. Divorce was quite rare in the United States until the 1970s, because the understanding and legal rules allowed a couple to end their relationship only when one party was seriously at fault. Adultery, cruelty, and abandonment were the most typical grounds for divorce for centuries.[25] The at-fault spouse was penalized in decisions regarding both the distribution of property and alimony awards.[26]

Change arrived with the advent of no-fault divorce, which is today the law throughout the United States. But a mini-movement in the other direction arose in the early 2000s, when a few states began to permit couples to enter into so-called *covenant marriage*. Those who choose this option are signing up for a marriage that is tougher to terminate. These laws require counseling before that can happen and in effect allow people to return to the era of fault-based divorce.[27] That these laws have proved unpopular and not spread beyond the states that first adopted them speaks to the stubbornness of a transformation in the way people think about marriage.[28] Or perhaps it reveals a cognitive dissonance between couples' optimism that they're entering into a permanent union and their knowledge that reality often differs from the ideal.

Historically, the consequences of divorce also supported the notion that marriage is expected to be permanent. Divorce brings about an equitable and final division of property acquired during the marriage, and alimony has been an another important marker of the assumption that marriage should be lifelong. Until quite recently, such payments were almost always directed from the ex-husband to the ex-wife, reflecting both economic reality and societal expectations about the breadwinner's identity. But the move away from alimony with no limit on duration—now more often called "support"—signals the weakening of this view of marriage.[29]

Another important facet of the traditionally understood marriage is the expectation that the parties will have conjugal relations and (if possible) children. Once upon a time, a spouse's inability to reproduce was grounds for annulment.[30] Although incapacity of that sort no longer suffices, traces of the norm persist: even today, courts will support a petition for annulment by a person who can show that their spouse refused to engage in sexual relations or misrepresented the ability to bear children.[31] But these cases are rare and depend on a finding of fraud—that one party lied to the other about something deemed essential to marriage. And, of course, older couples have always been permitted to marry, even when it is unlikely or impossible that they will have children together. As the Supreme Court stated in *Obergefell v. Hodges*, "An ability, desire, or promise to procreate is not and has not been a prerequisite for a valid marriage in any State.[32]

Harold Kooden's conversation with his gay friends on the connection between marriage and children took place decades ago, but something like the traditional definition and expectations still weigh heavily on both the meaning of marriage to many couples and the public discourse around it. The marriage equality battle reanimated this discussion, pushing partisans on both sides to more deeply consider and argue for their positions. Those defending the more traditional view included academics like Robert George, public intellectuals like Maggie Gallagher, and politicians like

Rick Santorum, whose arguments in fact reflected deep concerns about marriage itself. For George, the very definition of marriage is the union of a man and a woman.[33] As noted in the introduction, Gallagher's practical argument was that, because they decouple marriage from procreation and its weighty responsibilities, same-sex marriages would accelerate the flight of men from the responsibilities of marriage and child raising.[34] Santorum gave political voice to a version of Catholicism that hearkens back to earlier beliefs: sexual relations should take place only within marriage and should be dedicated to the project of procreation. So for him, contraception was also ruled out—to the extent that he once stated that government funding for contraception, not just abortion, should be eliminated.[35] (This is absurd. Most sex, whether within the bonds of marriage or not, isn't about procreation.)[36] Of course, the proponents of marriage equality upended the notion that marriage is a way of supporting children: gay and lesbian couples raise children too—and, as Justice Kennedy memorably noted in both *Windsor* and *Obergefell*, those children benefit from their parents' marriages.[37]

While the battle for marriage equality ended in legal victory for gay and lesbian couples—and their children—the traditional view still holds powerful sway over many people, whether they are married or not. Some have had difficulty reconciling this conception of marriage with the reality of families headed by same-sex couples. In any case, while marriage neither is defined by nor requires child-rearing, the stability that it offers over less formal relationships (such as cohabitation) does benefit children.[38]

> Marriage is primarily about the companionship and intimacy of
> two people.

The traditional view of marriage has taken sustained fire for decades. Couples now have small families or don't procreate at all.[39] No-fault divorce and the ensuing high divorce rate have put the lie to the notion of marriage as permanent, since more than half of all marriages currently end in divorce.[40] Prenuptial agreements allow couples to change the financial and other rules that have traditionally governed marriage and, more significant, the dissolution of that relationship. Most vividly, the success of the marriage equality movement has upended the view that marriage is necessarily limited to the union of a man and a woman, thereby defeating the notion that the institution is in place only to support and channel the procreative impulses of men and women in what natural law adherents call "biological complementarity."[41] Recent challenges to antipolygamy laws have further eroded the older view.[42]

Thus, while the traditional view still has some purchase, it has receded in favor of one that focuses on the emotional health and well-being of the couple. There are many, complex reasons for the ascendancy of this newer understanding of marriage, but the achievements of feminism deserve special emphasis. Beginning with the publication in 1963 of Betty Friedan's book *The Feminine Mystique*, women—and some men—began to openly look critically at women's still subordinate role within marriage. Over the ensuing decades, increasing numbers of people have come to value personal fulfillment and equal partnership between spouses as the primary—or essential—goods of marriage.

Note that this view of marriage does not necessarily include children. Indeed, the US birthrate began a dramatic decline in the 1960s and is now about half of what it was a century ago.[43] This phenomenon can't be pinned exclusively on the more recent, companionate view of marriage, but that view is closely tied to developments that have combined to reduce the number of children born in the United States. Of particular significance has been women's increasing ability to make their own choices about reproduction, thanks to the availability of contraception[44] (and, more controversially, abortion)[45] and a stronger social and economic position than before.[46] Smaller families are also more common because of women's increasing participation in the labor market, which has, among other results, led many to begin families later. (In fact, the birthrate among women over the age of forty, though still a tiny percentage of all births, is the only one that's growing.)[47] So while it's often mentioned that about four in ten children are born out of wedlock today, it's also true that there are just fewer children being born, period.[48] (The continued population growth in the United States is attributable to immigrants.)[49]

The dominance of the companionate view of marriage was extremely useful to the proponents of marriage equality. Once the institution is primarily seen as a means of recognizing and solidifying the committed relationship of two adults, little reason remains to exclude same-sex couples.

But that's not the only effect of the companionate conception of marriage, as the lifelong close relationship of the Doe sisters shows. In ways they themselves likely don't realize, these siblings have absorbed this perspective, at least in part. While they're not arguing that they should be permitted to marry, exactly, the modern view of marriage—severed from its unquestioned tether to procreation and available to any two unrelated adults (such as Edie Windsor and Thea Spyer)—powerfully grounds their argument for equal treatment under the law.

The sisters are onto something similar when they emphasize their financial concerns. Married people are usually more economically interdependent than what the law requires, and their financial melding becomes more powerful as the marriage increases in duration.[50] Marriage is about economic sharing; in this respect, the Doe sisters *do* look married—certainly more than many married couples.

> Marriage is a means for couples to express their commitment and to communicate that commitment to the larger community.

These benefits of marriage aren't financial or measurable in the same ways as those discussed above but are nonetheless extremely important to many, if not most, people who choose to marry—even those who profess adherence to the traditional view. For John Hunter and Hal Kooden, for Liz Gettings and Patricia Yarrow, and for countless others, marrying is both a powerful affirmation of the idea of marriage as a permanent union and an expression of the personal commitment that supports that goal of permanence. When David and I were finally able to marry, in 2013, we recited Shakespeare's Sonnet 116 to each other:

> Let me not to the marriage of true minds
> Admit impediments. . . .
> . . . .
> Love alters not with his brief hours and weeks,
> But bears it out even to the edge of doom.

Focusing on the commitment that marriage entails helps to explain why the civil union compromise, while an important part of equality practice, was never going to be the movement's final destination. Similarly, no one would have thought that the decision in *Loving v. Virginia*—the 1967 case where the Supreme Court threw out laws banning interracial marriage—sufficed had the court simply required the state to grant Richard Loving and Mildred Jeter the benefits of marriage without the valued status of marriage itself. Marriage signals a level of commitment that no other relationship can yet aspire to.

That commitment extends far beyond the couple. Marriage sends a strong message to family and close friends that the couple are united and are to be treated (in some ways, at least) as a single entity. Through law and ritual, it also signals their commitment to the broader community. This vital dimension of the law was captured by Georg Hegel, the early nineteenth-century German philosopher. He saw marriage as a kind of status mediating between the individual and society. By marrying (and creating a family), couples form a microcosm of the nation in which they abide and are thereby better able to navigate the broader world. In *The Philosophy of History*, Hegel noted that marrying couples "in uniting to form a state bring with them that sound basis of a political edifice—the capacity of feeling one with a Whole."[51] Perhaps those who react so emotionally to state recognition of their right to wed are underscoring the point Hegel made centuries ago—the individual selves, their families, and the nation to which they belong are finally, fully integrated. It's important, in this regard, that marriage equality, when it arrived, followed years of gay and lesbian people being out—both individually and as halves of committed couples. Only then could robust social acceptance be achieved and celebrated.

This leads to the related point that, at least for those gay and lesbian couples formally excluded from the institution, the commitment entailed by marriage is also a political statement. In this sense, no particular person (or couple) should feel compelled to marry, but the state must provide adults with the right to do so unless there's a powerful justification for excluding them from making such a defining personal and political commitment. The Supreme Court established the right to marriage in a series of rulings before marriage equality ever appeared on the horizon, finding that both prisoners and child support debtors could not be denied the right to marry. As Justice Sandra Day O'Connor stated in her majority opinion in *Turner v. Safley*, "Inmate marriages, like others, are expressions of emotional support and public commitment."[52] More important for the marriage equality forces, the *Loving* decision anchored the right of interracial couples to marry in principles of both equality and liberty ("due process," constitutionally speaking). Finally, *Obergefell* represents the triumph of a movement that has convinced the court and the public that gay and lesbian couples are no less entitled to recognition than the rest of society.

For some, the personal and the political become inextricably bound up, so that marrying gains an extra dimension of significance. Like Kooden and Hunter and like Yarrow and Gettings, many other gay and lesbian couples have recounted the joy they felt when they married—a euphoria they attributed, in part at least, to the fact that the state now recognized them as "legitimate." Similarly, Sheila Blackburn found that her initial satisfaction with a civil union waned—both because she did not see the status as reflecting the deepest level of commitment and because her family felt the same way. Given that even some people who were not excluded from marriage understood its social superiority over other legal relationships, it is natural that being eligible to marry would assume outsize significance for those who were not allowed to do so. The state's willingness to see gay and lesbian couples as united in the same way as their straight counterparts was the final step in a long journey toward equality. For some people, of course, marriage is far more instrumental and practical—a patriarchal relic to be tolerated just for the benefits, say. Speaking of benefits . . .

> Marriage is primarily a way of delivering a set of benefits to (and imposing obligations on) a committed couple.

The unfairness of denying marriage-associated benefits to same-sex couples was an important argument of marriage equality proponents. This was a clever and effective strategy, because marriage today does carry a significant package of perks and rights that are otherwise unavailable or accessible only with great effort. The same strategy was used, although less directly, by folks like Tom Brougham and Barry Warren, who understood that focusing on specific benefits that were tied to marriage (even if, like health benefits, they weren't directly conferred by it) was a way for the unmarried to gain them.[53] Yet that strategy was self-limiting, at least in the short run: once the benefits were evened out between straight and gay couples, the argument for full marriage recognition was weaker. The civil union decisions by state supreme courts in Vermont and New Jersey underscored that point. But how important should marriage be to gaining access to these substantial financial advantages?

It's useful to separate two broad classes of economic preferences that married couples enjoy: those that are provided under state law, and those that arise under federal law. Generally speaking, the state law preferences should remain attached to marriage, as default rules that most closely mirror a couple's mutual reliance and expectations as to fairness and security when the union dissolves—whether by divorce or death. As we will see, the federal benefits that have glommed on to marriage should largely be rethought.

Under state law, marital benefits include the rights arising under intestacy—rights of ancient provenance that protect the family's assets and strengthen kinship—and the right to the division of property (and sometimes support) when the marriage ends in divorce.[54] The advent of no-fault divorce has increased the importance of property division, while the growth of women's economic power (and the more philosophical commitment to sex equality) has reduced the incidence of alimony payments.[55] Indeed, what are today often referred to as "support payments" are rarely for life, because the usual assumption is that the receiving party will be able to become self-sustaining within a reasonable period. The underlying value here is marriage's function as a kind of private welfare system, with the parties taking on mutual responsibilities that survive the death or incapacity of one of them and, to a lesser extent, even the union's voluntary dissolution.

These postmarriage obligations are just the tail end of a related benefit of marriage: channeling people into a relationship that privatizes dependency, with gains to the couple and to the society in which they abide. A rich, though contested, vein of social science research suggests that marriage serves broad interests in physical and mental health, income security, and wealth accumulation.[56] Generally speaking, married folks do better than their unmarried counterparts, whether cohabiting or single. These advantages may be attributable in part to selection bias—a greater percentage of people who are healthier in the first place may be choosing marriage[57]—but the prevailing and likely best supported view is that being married, in and of itself, conveys at least some advantage to the couple and thereby reduces society's responsibility for caring for dependent people. To the extent that this societal benefit is real, recognition and support of other forms of relationships should lead to similar gains, though it is impossible to say how significant those might be, especially given the small number of people who have chosen such relationships to date. This is not to diminish the role that marriage plays in shaping these benefits, because the institution creates and enforces them as a default assumption.

All of the state-conferred advantages—direct and indirect—were made available to same-sex couples through one simple step, the civil union. Indeed, as the Vermont law shows, this ingenious compromise measure was a fusion of the benefits and companionate views of marriage—and, by continuing to wall same-sex couples off from marriage, a way of respecting traditionalists as well. The Legislative Findings accompanying the law's catalogue of rights and benefits affirms the definition of marriage as "a union between a man and a woman" but then pivots to an articulation of the state's interests in marriage, primary among which are that it "encourage close and caring families" and be the "exclusive source of numerous benefits, responsibilities and protections." The findings go on to say that, without access to marriage, "same-sex couples suffer numerous obstacles and hardships," which the "system of civil unions" is designed to redress, although without "bestow[ing] the status of civil marriage."[58] If any law were ever designed to reflect a changing, contested view of marriage, the Vermont civil union law is Exhibit A. Reading it induces a kind of whiplash, as it darts back and forth between the traditional and modern ideas of what this institution should be and encompass. Although the civil union pointedly continued to fence same-sex couples out of marriage, many, like Nina Beck and Stacey Jolles, jumped at the chance to gain the benefits of marriage that different-sex couples had long enjoyed. (For David and me, our civil union was mostly a symbolic affirmation of our mutual commitment.)

Federal benefits, though, are a more recent consequence of wedlock and, as will be explored more fully in the next chapter, are not tied to marriage as compellingly. The legal scholar Kerry Abrams has thoroughly dissected marriage's rising importance within the growing federal administrative state.[59] From preferential immigration rules to social security advantages, military housing, and tax treatment, the federal benefits that have accrued to it beginning around the time of the New Deal have infused marriage with a practical importance—and therefore, in a way, *meaning*—that it didn't have before. And with that abundance of goodies dumped on the marriage platter, LGBTQ rights activists had a more than plausible basis for claiming that exclusion constituted discrimination. Thus, the decision in *United States v. Windsor* and, as a kind of inevitable next step, the moral claims of people like May and April Doe.

Private parties also confer substantial financial advantages on the basis of marriage. Marriage has long served as the indispensable signal to employers that an employee is entitled to benefits for a second person (and perhaps for children too). They have latched on to the status as a reflection of traditional values and thus a way of identifying good employees. The inextricable linking of "traditional values" to marriage can occasionally lead to anomalous results, as when Terry McKeon and Anne Quinn married primarily so she could gain access to his health coverage. This association also poses problems for recognized alternative relationships, as the current move to do away with domestic partnership benefits at some major corporations attests—the new rule is "If you can marry, do it, or lose your benefits."

      •   •   •   •   •

Marriage, then, is a complex beast, with multiple meanings and dimensions. We might distill the discussion above into a few elements that define this institution:

- It unites men and women and encourages "responsible procreation."
- It expresses a mutual bilateral commitment.
- It provides a strong setting for the raising of children.
- It serves to protect couples' expectations.
- It encourages companionship between two adults.
- It establishes eligibility for state-conferred benefits.
- Often, it makes one eligible for private benefits.
- It serves an expressive function.
- It reaffirms a civil right, which is especially important to groups previously excluded from it.

- It privatizes dependency, creating a mutually supportive unit that can relieve the government of some burdens.

Depending on the reader's views, experiences, and biases, the items in this list will seem relevant, quaint, vital, marginal, or—perhaps—just plain stupid. But that's sort of the point. One person's marriage essential is another's filigree or flotsam. That's what we'd expect of any institution with such a thick, messy set of meanings.

To quote Abrams, "We are asking marriage to do too much."[60] While it's inevitable and even healthy that the deep meaning of marriage be contested, its continued tie to so many benefits is no longer justified, if it ever was. As the stories told throughout this book have made clear, marriage is not the best vehicle for transmitting financial rewards. On the one hand, it's hard to justify the glut of stuff that married couples enjoy no matter their financial or personal circumstances. On the other hand, it's equally hard to defend a system that so poorly cares for those whose life circumstances aren't accommodated by the institution of marriage—either because they aren't eligible or because they're ill suited to it. Just ask McKeon and Quinn.

The expressive view of marriage, and the societal privilege that attends the institution—even apart from the benefits—is a double-edged sword too. Because it has been invested with so much power, those who find themselves outside marriage may share the Doe sisters' sense that they've been dealt an unfair hand. As they said to me: Married people have all the social advantages. Why do they need economic ones too? It's hard not to hear the bitterness of exclusion in these comments. While this very real problem of social exclusion is hard to address directly, recognizing other legal relationships and tying benefits to needs is likely to have the collateral effect of knocking marriage down to size—at least enough for those on the outside not to look on with such longing, envy, or anger.

The task, then, is (1) to allow marriage to continue to do what it does well, (2) to remove (or at least question) the benefits that aren't tied to marriage in some intrinsically important sense, and (3) to provide legal support for those in other kinds of relationships. Only once that is done can the law reflect the lives people are actually living. In a sense, any recommendations made here will be inadequate. That's not only because it is impossible to imagine every way the law might be changed but also because of the nature of law itself. Statutes and legal rules and presumptions are always attempts to solve problems for the greatest number of people; they are always making proxy judgments, so the question is whether the proxy is a good one. Even the best laws won't work for everyone. That doesn't mean the effort to ameliorate things shouldn't be made. To that task I now turn.

5 Matching Relationship Law to Reality

> After marriage equality is finally achieved, we will also need
> to work toward a society that can imagine family and social
> organization beyond the wedded couple, as we've known
> for a long time now that that model is in dire need of
> updating.
>
> J. Bryan Lowder

The birth and expansion of marriage alternatives—domestic partnerships, civil unions, DBAs, and others—may have been a response to the needs of gay and lesbian couples, but, as we've seen, these clever creations quickly overran their original justification. The growing recognition of same-sex relationships was made possible in part because social norms had begun to change, as underscored by *Marvin v. Marvin*, making marriage no longer the only kind of acceptable two-adult committed relationship. That's why it was inevitable that these marriage alternatives quickly grew to embrace straight couples as well. For good or ill, marriage is no longer the only game in town.

But until recently, the marriage alternative movement had stalled.[1] That is not surprising, because the focus on marriage equality led many people—notably, state legislators—to declare the issue settled once that goal had been achieved and to move on. That understandable impulse, though, begs the question of what the "issue" actually is. As the stories of the couples profiled in the earlier chapters highlight, the law should do more to protect and nurture adult relationships beyond marriage. For many people, such as May and April Doe, and Terry McKeon and Anne Quinn, marriage is not what they need. There have been many thoughtful and creative suggestions about how best to support nonmarital relationships, some of which will be discussed in this chapter. The best approach, though, requires beginning with a consideration of how marriage *itself* should be changed, in ways that allow it to accomplish its core goals while bailing out the excess water the institution has taken on. That exercise enables critical thinking about how the law should support couples—and people in relationships with more than two members—whether they are married or not.

The solution turns out to involve three parts. First, continue to recognize marriage—but only in a streamlined form that retains what is useful about it without creating unfair benefit categories that leave out others in need of support. In sum, marriage should help couples (and their children, if any) flourish and should protect the reliance that each spouse has on the other. Second, make the rules for recognizing informal cohabitation relationships much clearer. And third, expand one of the existing marriage alternatives in a couple of ways, enabling it to better capture the web of adult connections that the law should support. That alternative is the DBA. My not so modest proposal is that the law underlying it, now enacted only in Colorado, should be expanded and then exported to every other state.

RETHINKING MARRIAGE, BENEFITS, AND RELIANCE

Marriage isn't going anywhere. The abolition impulse may have some appeal, but it's not tied to reality. The institution is so firmly rooted in law, society, and the popular imagination—even in an era when only about half the adult population is married—that campaigning for its demise is quixotic in the extreme.[2]

It's not just practical political considerations that counsel against the abolition of marriage either. As noted throughout this book, marriage anchors expectations and allows couples to plan and direct their lives' projects in relation to each other and to their children (if any). That feature of marriage, typically enforced through state law rules on property distribution upon the dissolution of marriage or the death of a spouse, should be retained—whatever the admittedly checkered history of the institution. Could this goal be achieved through other means, such as con-tracts, recognition of other cohabitation relationships, or something like the other legal statuses discussed throughout this book? Yes, but probably not to the same extent, because the default rules of marriage (if operating properly, which is not a given) will likely work better, on average, for the economically more vulnerable spouse at death or divorce, as they were expressly designed for that purpose. Then there's the strong cultural and symbolic meaning of marriage, discussed in chapter 4. Whatever one may think of the institution's patriarchal past (and, to a lesser extent, present), it's undeniable that, for many people, marriage *itself* shapes behavior and expectations in ways that alternative legal statuses do not. Here's what Linda McClain, a leading family law scholar, had to say on the subject: "At least one dimension of marriage might be lost if we adopted [the] pro-posal [to substitute some other legal status]: The symbolic significance of marriage. . . . All appear to agree that marriage has public significance. It signals peoples' aspirations for commitment, love, mutual responsibility, interdependence, and family. And even though marriage has evolved over the centuries, its very durability as an institution allows those who marry to, as it were, tap into reservoirs of meaning."[3]

Yet marriage and the laws concerning all adult relationships are both in need of serious, thoughtful reform. Marriage enjoys *too much* privilege. Valorizing it to such an extent implicitly devalues other relationships and in any case isn't necessary to the achievement of its central goods.[4] It's past time to consider how to shrink the distance between marriage and other relationships and to reflect on exactly what the law is encouraging and protecting—and *why*. Granting legal status to currently unrecognized relationships will lead to social advantage, given the law's important expressive and teaching functions.

We can begin by stripping from marriage any features that aren't prop-erly tied to it. The most obvious candidate is the substantial benefit pack-age that comes with it.[5] I can see two possible justifications for ladling financial goodies on married couples and *only* on those couples. Neither one convinces me, at least not as a reason to retain the benefits as they're currently distributed. While some—mostly those conferred by *states*, not at the federal level—properly support the couple's expectations (and reli-ance on each other in shaping a life together), others attach somewhat clumsily to the status of marriage. These should be questioned and possibly diminished or even rescinded.

Let's start with the argument that the benefits of marriage are an incentive to wed.[6] But—McKeon and Quinn notwithstanding—most people do not decide to marry for that reason. If the benefits were intended in this way, we would expect the law to be more consistent in privileging married couples. In fact, it sometimes *discourages* marriage. As any couple with two high-wage earners knows, they will pay a higher federal income tax if they marry than if they remain single. Such disincentives appear at other points on the economic spectrum too. A recent report by the Institute for Family Studies and the American Enterprise Institute suggests that, at least for couples at the higher end of the lower middle class, the prospect of losing Medicaid and food stamps discourages marriage in a small but discernible percentage of cases.[7]

Even if the aim is to encourage or reward marriage, skewing the incentives in this way isn't sound policy, because it leads to people marrying for exigent financial reasons rather than any of the intrinsic reasons discussed above: companionship, sharing a life together (including relying on each other as part of an economic unit), raising children. Unless we value the benefits over its other goods, tying marriage to them so closely makes little sense. One obvious reason is the same one that makes enforcement of prenuptial agreements so controversial: the time factor. When a couple decides to marry for benefits or enters into a prenuptial agreement, it's impossible to know how a shared life in marriage over a period of years is going to affect—well, *everything*. This explains why some courts look at whether a prenuptial agreement is fair at the time of the marriage's dissolution rather than when it was entered into. So if we assume that people will take into account financial benefits accruing to marriage, the effect might be this paradox: the more generous the package, the likelier it will be to skew a couple's decision-making away from the vital issue of whether they are compatible and good candidates for the commitment of marriage.

The second reason for tying benefits to marriage better explains why the law makes this connection: marriage, cohabitation, and financial connection were formerly inextricably linked. When the federal benefit outlays exploded during the first half of the twentieth century, to live with an intimate companion was usually to be married to that person.[8] Indeed, the law strictly enforced this norm. Adultery and fornication were illegal, as well as socially frowned upon, which meant that different-sex couples could not live together outside marriage—at least not openly.[9] So to the extent that the government wanted to reach entire households for the purpose of distributing benefits, marriage (along with kinship) was an excellent proxy.[10]

But that simply hasn't been true for some time and is becoming ever less so as we move deeper into the twenty-first century. People now live together in all sorts of arrangements—intimate and otherwise—with far less social opprobrium attached to their choices. Laws against such arrangements either have been abolished or are largely unenforced. Scholars and policy makers debate both the causes and the desirability of these changes, but there's no denying them.[11] In short, whatever justification there might once have been for the marriage-benefits connection is gone—and its persistence exacts a toll on every kind of relationship that doesn't bear the talismanic *marriage* label. This is an argument not for doing away with the benefits entirely but for tying them more closely to reality. The hard question is how to fine-tune them to better reflect any adult couple's reasonable reliance on each other—and then how that reliance might be exported to other adult relationships. Some of these relationships will be between sexual intimates, but some will not.

A few examples will illustrate the comprehensive ways the law ties benefits to marriage. Social security provides the best vehicle for understanding both how it attempts to protect the expectations of both members of the couple and how it falls short of that goal in the twenty-first century. For married couples, the principal benefits kick in upon the retirement or death of one of the spouses. The eligibility requirements have affected the construction of the other legal statuses discussed throughout this book, as we've seen, so it's worth exploring how these pieces of social security fit together—and how they fall short.

Enacted in 1935, the Social Security Act represented a national commitment to provide basic income for those who had reached what was considered a reasonable retirement age and faced poverty during the Great Depression without financial security for their old age.[12] When the law was passed, only those who had participated in market labor were eligible for its benefits, which became available at age sixty-two.[13] Although social security payments—then as now—furnish not much more than subsistence income, they do provide a floor for the many millions who have little or no other source of money in their old age.

In 1939, the act was amended to provide an additional way of calculating benefits for married couples. Instead of receiving benefits based on their own work history, each spouse could now elect up to half of those that the other spouse was eligible for.[14] Thus, the couple could receive 150 percent of the retirement benefit of the higher-income spouse. This option made eminent sense at the time, given that most adults in intimate relationships were legally married and women often did not work outside the home.[15] By allowing (primarily) women to receive one-half of their husband's retirement benefit, the law supported the prevailing social structure and expectations: couples would marry, stay married—divorce was difficult and frowned on—and women would be at home to raise their children. This spousal benefit has continued, with some modifications regarding the age of eligibility, to this day.[16]

The other relevant class of social security benefits for our purposes is for surviving spouses. As the name denotes, these are made available when one spouse dies, and, like retirement benefits, they are tied to what the deceased spouse was receiving.[17] Currently, the survivor can receive anywhere from just over 70 to 100 percent of that amount.[18] The payment is based in part on the notion that the stay-at-home spouse not only forwent market income during the couple's married life but also did not acquire or keep current with the skills needed to earn a living.

To further cement and enforce the expectations of *married* couples, the law includes disincentives to divorce and remarriage, although these vary according to the benefit. At first, those who divorced were not eligible for any spousal benefits unless they had been married for at least twenty years to the person whose benefits they were using to calculate their own. This statutory requirement was later shortened to ten years, where it remains today.[19] Remarriage, on the other hand, has different consequences between our two benefit categories. In the case of survivor benefits, the key issue is age: as long as the surviving spouse is at least sixty (or fifty, if legally disabled) at the time, remarriage will not affect these benefits.[20] Retirement benefits tied to the income of the former spouse, on the other hand, screech to a halt upon remarriage.[21] In this way, the rules mirror state divorce laws, which, with very few exceptions, cut off alimony to former spouses who remarry.[22]

Note the assumptions embedded in these rules relating to divorce and death. By requiring marriages to last at least ten years for spousal benefit eligibility, the law reflects the view that marriages of short duration do not create substantial interdependence or reliance interests. By cutting off people who remarry from spousal retirement benefits, the law shifts the burden for providing for the wife (typically) to the new husband. The same is true of widows and widowers who remarry, except that the law takes pity on older people, sparing them, after age sixty, the choice of whether to lose benefits or forgo the chance to spend their remaining years in the favored relationship of marriage.

These rules about getting, keeping, and losing benefits do not sync up well with modern realities, in two ways.

First, by depriving those who remarry of retirement benefits tied to their ex-spouses, the law overlooks the reality that many such people face financial hardship. Given that half of those over fifty-five have no savings and that more than half have no private pension coverage, even a modest social security income (the average benefit was estimated to be only $1,539.68 per month in 2022) is absolutely necessary for many millions of senior citizens.[23] It is fantasy to think that a second marriage will reliably protect those in financial need. And the analogy to alimony payments that end upon remarriage isn't persuasive, because those come from a private source—the ex-spouse—while social security is a public benefit.

These realities help explain why states created domestic partnership registries for those age sixty-two and older.[24] Doing so provided cover for those who wanted some measure of legal protection for their current relationship but did not wish to forfeit retirement benefits tied to their ex-spouse. The evolution of what the SSA terms "non-marital legal relationships" has occasioned a shift in its policy, though—so that now some of them may be considered the same as marriage and might thereby risk the same loss of benefits.[25] This move by the SSA avoids treating similar relationships differently but does not solve the problem of how best to protect retirees who depend on the spousal benefit.

Second, a sharp legal distinction between married and unmarried couples makes little sense today, especially when the relationships of many long-term cohabitating couples closely mirror marriage.[26] To the extent that the benefits of marriage are meant to protect couples' expectations in a shared life, they are no less necessary when the couple is unmarried. Currently, about one-half of all US adults are unmarried, and many in that category are in relationships of mutual dependence.

Although state law generally does better than federal law at tying the benefits of marriage to the parties' reasonable mutual reliance and expectations, here too the Maginot Line separating marriage from relationships that look similar can lead to results that privilege the former over the latter without good reason. Wrongful death laws and entitlement to accede to the substantial benefits of rent control law—to name just two—tie benefits to marriage while fencing them off from people in other long-term committed relationships. When someone's negligence causes another person's death, only spouses and other close relations, by blood or in law, can sue for wrongful death.[27] And when a tenant who enjoys a cheap, rent-controlled lease passes away, the law generally requires their landlord to extend the valuable benefit of rent-controlled increases only to the spouse or a family member of the tenant. A few courts have been able to sidestep these restrictions via creative interpretations of the law, but such agility would not be necessary if the laws simply caught up to the reality that human relationships can't be so easily boxed.[28]

The problem, of course, is that once we move beyond the easy equivalence of marriage and benefits, deciding how best to distribute government largesse gets complicated, fast. For instance, it doesn't make sense to allow a couple who met a week ago and then moved in together to gain the half-benefit social security option currently restricted to spouses, nor to sue for wrongful death or accede to the substantial benefits of rent control. Some workable rules would need to be established if marriage were no longer the touchstone for benefits.

Where government is supplying the benefits, the first move should be to connect them to need, at least in a broad sense. As the humorist Dave Barry once reportedly suggested, some elderly couples are able to use their social security payments entirely for purchasing sun hats for their polo ponies. Some kind of maximum wealth or income might be established for social security (and other) benefits, which would be given on a proportionate basis to those below the threshold—up to full benefits for people under a certain level. Changing policy in this way would require gradual implementation—given that couples have arranged their retirement finances around the expectation that the current rules or substantially similar ones will remain in place—and public education on the justification for social security, perhaps focusing on the meaning of the words *social* and *security* themselves: the program is meant as *security* against the risk that we will not be able to provide for ourselves if we grow old, disabled, or economically vulnerable because of the death of a breadwinning spouse and recognizes that because this risk is faced throughout society, its cost should be similarly distributed—just the sort of *social* risk that supports creating such a program in the first place.[29] Understood this way, social security is similar to the excise tax–funded National Vaccine Injury Compensation Program, which recognizes that we should all be willing to share the costs of the rare health problems caused by vaccination—by compensating those injured—to gain the benefits of an immunized population.[30]

As for the central question of what kinds of relationships in addition to marriage should qualify for benefits, the answer depends on whether it makes sense to tie those benefits to relationships in the first place. If so, then substantial interdependency is crucial. Perhaps for this reason, marriage itself isn't *quite* enough to trigger eligibility for social security spousal benefits, because the parties need to be married for at least one year before the application will be processed.[31] This rule seems to stem from a concern about marriage fraud but might also be seen as recognition that financial interdependence doesn't happen immediately. Creating legal statuses that are less "all in" than marriage but tie the couple together, especially financially, is a similar way to ensure that some level of interdependence is established in order for these spousal-type benefits to be received. That may explain why the SSA now considers civil unions and "marriage-like" domestic partnerships as the equivalent of marriages. But this is a helpful step only if the rules on marriage, divorce, and remarriage of beneficiaries are changed. How might that be accomplished?

Again: government-conferred benefits should be means tested and not dispensed simply because a couple happens to be married. Legally recognized "not-marriage" statuses and cohabitation sturdy enough to meet certain criteria should also trigger the entitlement, subject to the same needs testing. Interdependence, not a specific status, should be the guide. In any case, a household income or asset ceiling on benefits should be considered, as discussed above.[32]

Another approach to government-provided benefits is to untether them from relationships. We might simply give each retiree a flat benefit regardless of work history; a variation on that theme would be a progressive benefit, phased out for those with other sources of income but ensuring that everyone else gets something even if they have no work history at all.[33] This would neatly end the problem of cutting off benefits because of remarriage. Another option, splitting the difference between individual and relationship-based eligibility, would be to modify the current benefit structure so that an insured worker could, at the age of retirement, take a solo benefit or a lower, joint benefit that would also be payable to a survivor of his or her choice—including spouses, unmarried partners, siblings, and children. In that case, some provision would need to be made for spouses and other long-term partners who reasonably relied on the income of the deceased. Note that some of these potential reforms look to the relationship, while others do not—reinforcing the point that, whatever policy changes are made, there is no warrant for continuing to give marriage such a place of privilege.

A similar approach that considers actual relationships rather than formal status could work for a host of other federal and state-conferred rights and benefits. Couples in many kinds of relationships rely and depend on each other, often in ways that the law should protect. To return to the example of wrongful death law: since these statutes aim to compensate the surviving family members for the financial support they would have received had their relative not died, anyone who can prove financial dependence on the person who was killed through the defendant's negligence should be eligible for compensation—whether the law otherwise recognizes their relationship or not. But the wrongful death laws don't work that way. In almost all states, an unmarried long-term cohabitant will typically be unable even to pass through the courthouse doors to lodge a claim of financial loss because of the death of an intimate partner. Michigan has taken a significant step in the right direction by allowing anyone named in the decedent's will the chance to prove their loss, but of course many people do not have wills or are unaware of this law.[34]

Private benefits should similarly be decoupled from marriage. Even though this change will be a matter for corporations and other nongovernmental actors to implement, federal and state laws can make things easier in a couple of ways. Consider employer-subsidized health care, which is often the most significant source of emolument other than wages. As noted in chapter 1, some private companies that once offered such benefits to their employees' domestic partners have retrenched and now require marriage for eligibility. Others, though—like IBM—on reflection decided not to change their qualification criteria. This is a sound move, both from a business perspective and as a matter of fairness: employers can offer benefits to a wider range of people, thereby attracting and retaining good workers who have other employment options. But doing so creates its own headaches. For one thing, the tax exclusion that employees receive for the value of benefits the corporation pays on behalf of spouses doesn't apply to domestic partners or other cohabitants—and creates an accounting complication for employers, who also need to settle on a never perfect set of requirements to signal a relationship sufficiently close to trigger entitlement to benefits.[35] If the state or locality where the employees live recognizes formal relationships other than marriage, those statuses will typically qualify—but most places do not offer such options.

Perhaps the day will come when employers no longer provide health benefits and instead increase wages to allow employees to make their own insurance decisions. Or maybe—wishing for a unicorn here—we will one day move to a single-payer health care system.[36] Until then, though, there is no reason to discriminate among members of a workforce by effectively compensating them at different rates according to their family structure. A single person with no dependents is often undercompensated compared to coworkers with families, whose spouses and children receive substantial employer contributions toward their health care. While family-friendly workplaces are in the national interest, the way to achieve that goal isn't by creating unfair disparities among employees. Employers should stake each employee to a certain benefit subsidy, which the employee can decide how to spend—on anyone, related or not. Anything beyond that amount would come from the employee's paycheck. I realize that this change would increase the burden on some large families, but that problem could be solved with government subsidies for low-income employees—a policy initiative that would more fairly spread the cost across the entire population rather than just one employer's workforce.

Separating benefits from marriage is important and should be a priority. Of course, as the example above shows, this move would need to be carefully implemented and phased in over time, because of the substantial reliance many people have placed on their ability to access these benefits.

This discussion has established that there are two important goals. The first is to recognize that government-provided benefits should be means tested. The second is to tie financial security to the reality of couples' interdependent lives rather than to marital status. Binding the law too tightly to formal marriage excludes too many people in other relationships who rely on each other and make decisions based on that reliance.

At the state level, there are other financial advantages to being legally married. While we don't typically think of these as benefits, they are no less important. For instance, built into marriage are dissolution rules recognizing the importance of honoring and protecting the commitments that have been made and protecting the spouse who has forgone paid market labor for unpaid domestic work. These laws come into play when the couple divorces or when one spouse dies. If the divorce (and intestacy) laws did not protect the financially disadvantaged spouse, there really would be a disincentive to marry. Today courts in every state treat most of the property acquired by both spouses during marriage as fair game for division when the union dissolves.[37] A few states go even further and consider *all* of their property fair game for distribution—even things that were acquired by one of the spouses before marriage.[38] Moreover, the courts are supposed to equitably distribute the entire value of the marital estate and ensure that a spouse's unpaid contributions to the family— raising children, work around the house, behind-the-scenes support of the wage earner's career—are valued at the point of dissolution.[39]

As many thoughtful scholars and commentators—including Professor Alicia Kelly—have pointed out, the reality is often different, because judges too often continue to undervalue the contributions of the non-market-employed spouse (usually still the wife in a male-female marriage).[40] But to the extent that courts continue to value market work over other contributions, they are missing the essential point that marriage is a partnership that reaches across economic, personal, and often spiritual boundaries.

Unless courts respect that partnership—in all its dimensions—people will be less likely to choose nonpaying labor, because they will be left to shift for themselves if the marriage fails.

Similarly, some outside financial protections reflect the insight that people in committed relationships structure their lives with this partnership model in mind. The wage-starved spouse can opt for one-half of the other spouse's social security retirement benefit, since the government recognizes that this person might have stayed out of the labor market because of the couple's decision about what was best for *both* of them, not just *one* of them. The wrongful death defendant has to pay the surviving spouse because the negligent act deprived that person of an income stream. The estate tax exemption protects the surviving spouse's ability to remain in the home the couple created together. Again, it makes sense to means-test government-provided benefits (not wrongful death recovery, which of course comes from private funds), but they are a necessary protection for people in committed relationships, which society does and should value.

But if these laws and policies make sense when a married couple divorces, what should be done when couples who aren't married—including those in domestic partnerships, discussed earlier, and those who are cohabitating—separate? A thoughtful family law system ought to account for the expectations of people in these groups too—although it will of necessity do so imperfectly.

RECOGNIZING DE FACTO RELATIONSHIPS

Cohabitation has become firmly entrenched over the past several decades. As of 2016, eighteen million Americans were cohabitating without marriage.[41] Setting aside for the moment the lively debate about the social costs of this phenomenon, one thing is clear: any system that does not account for this large a population is obviously deficient. To the objection that such recognition would boost an unwelcome competitor to the "preferred" institution of marriage, it perhaps suffices to note that broad economic forces are at work that make wedlock unrealistic for many people. As June Carbone and Naomi Cahn have persuasively shown, a dearth of economically and educationally "eligible" partners for women partly explains the decline of marriage.[42]

But deciding what legal rules should be applied to these couples is complex, because when it comes to cohabitation, one size pointedly does *not* fit all. People cohabitate for all sorts of reasons, at every age, and with or without the intent of eventually marrying.[43] Some are not even in intimate relationships yet are interdependent. Some have children together, while some do not. Of course, people marry for all sorts of reasons too, but *on average* there is greater economic sharing in marriage—in part because of the way the law protects the parties' expectations (and thus shapes their behaviors), but not only because of that.[44] But if married couples want to avoid the default rules, they can enter into prenuptial agreements that vary their financial relationship (usually by treating them as separate property owners at the marriage's dissolution).[45] Such contracts further collapse the boundary between marriage and cohabitation.

Despite the daunting obstacles confronting any attempt to determine when cohabitation should be treated like marriage, two notable authorities have tried to align the expectations of parties in such relationships more precisely with reality. The *Principles of the Law of Family Dissolution,* a publication of the American Law Institute (ALI), assimilates the consequences of the dissolution of certain cohabitation relationships to those of divorce but has not been adopted by any US state.[46] In Australia, a similar approach has been in effect throughout the country since 2009.[47] Cases reflect the effort that Australian judges have been willing to expend in making the difficult decision of whether the members of all kinds of relationships meet the definition of "de facto couple." If so, when they break up, either person can petition the court for a determination that their assets should be divided and support payments made as though they had been legally married.[48]

A brief discussion of these two approaches to cohabitation will do two things: show how the law can protect the reality of couples' lives even when they have chosen no formal legal status, and foreground the benefits of recognizing relationship statuses other than marriage.

The official commentary accompanying the ALI's suggested rules on cohabitation begins by noting both the explosion in the number of cohabitating couples and how courts have been searching for creative ways to recognize and safeguard the expectations of the people in these relation-ships.[49] Some will protect the weaker party only if there is an express con-tract (which usually need not be in writing) between the two. Some, like the California Supreme Court in the *Marvin* case, will "imply" a contract based on the parties' conduct, but there's no consistent pattern to these decisions; some are looking for a relationship that is similar to marriage and others are not. As the ALI notes, the results "flow more from the court's sense of fairness than from any mutual intentions inferable from the parties' conduct."[50] Indeed, courts sometimes go beyond the idea of agreement and base entitlement to sharing on equitable doctrines with fancy Latin names, such as *quantum meruit*—which means, in essence, that a party who has provided services is compensated for their value even if there is no contract.[51] *Marvin v. Marvin* has cast a long shadow over the law, for good and ill. It's time for a more systematic approach, one that leads to fairer and more predictable outcomes.

The ALI admirably blares a horn through this fog and tries to identify circumstances where a court's sense of fairness might lead it to allow cou-ples who cohabitate to have claims against each other when the relation-ship dissolves. Under the ALI's terminology, satisfying such requirements would make them domestic partners, eligible for marriagelike treatment and protection. The presumption is that domestic partners would want to treat each other fairly, at least when they were *in the relationship*. (At the point of dissolution, the parties often don't want to treat each other fairly, of course. That's why the law steps in to protect the expectations that shaped the *intact* relationship.)

A great deal of consideration is apparent in the ALI's complex approach. In sum, it's this: Each state should set a specific period of cohabitation for couples, after which the law will presume that they are domestic partners. A smaller amount of time can be chosen if they have a "common child" (one who is legally theirs or should be factually recognized as such). If the relationship doesn't reach the state's threshold, the couple will still be con-sidered domestically partnered if the party seeking to establish that status can prove that they lived together and "shared a life together."[52]

Where the minimum time requirement isn't met, the devil is in the details. The ALI lists a long series of factors that a court can use in deter-mining whether a couple has shared their lives. Many of these look like the kinds of implicit deals and expectations married couples often make and have. For instance, intermingling finances and "fostering economic inter- dependence" are on the list, as are the extent to which the parties changed their lives and behavior in "furtherance of their life together." Naming each other as beneficiaries of different types of plans can also be relevant, as can a number of purely qualitative things: emotional and physical inti- macy, the couple's reputation as such in the community, and whether the parties recognized their relationship as "qualitatively distinct" from one either of them might have with another person. Having or adopting kids together is also a consideration.[53] Note that this approach eliminates the need to separate intimate relationships from others—intimacy is a factor in determining only whether the couple has been sharing their lives.

The final item on the above list leads directly from this domestic- partnership-through- conduct approach into the second topic: formal domestic partnership. The ALI counts "the parties' participation in a commitment ceremony or registration as a domestic partnership" as fur- ther evidence of a domestic partnership that can be "operationalized" into a marriage for dissolution purposes.[54] (It would have been better for the ALI to use some term other than *domestic partners* to describe these cou- ples, because that label leads to confusion between the ALI's recognition through factual analysis and the formal status granted by governments and even private sector employers. "De facto relationship," used in Australia, both avoids the confusion and better describes what courts are actually doing.)

The ALI also tries to account for variation. If the couple has been together long enough for the general presumption of domestic partner- ship to apply but one of them doesn't agree that it should, that party can introduce evidence that they did not in fact share a life together.[55] For relationships that don't meet the time threshold, as mentioned above, the onus is on the party trying to establish the relationship. In either case, both parties are free to contract around the marital presumption that arises.[56]

The drafters of the ALI proposal realized, of course, that such a fact- dependent inquiry would lead to many uncertainties and attempted to pro- vide guidance by including some illustrative cases and stating whether the parties would be considered domestic partners or not. They're instructive and could help instruct courts in difficult, close cases. Unfortunately, not a single US state has seen fit to adopt these guidelines.[57]

To see how the ALI's approach (or something like it) might be implemented in practice, it's instructive to look at how courts in Australia have handled the issue. Under the Australian Family Law Act, de facto couple status is recognized for any relationship that was dissolved after March 1, 2009. Moreover, many of the factors that the courts are called on to consider in making the determination of whether the couple qualifies as de facto bear a striking (eerie?) resemblance to those recommended by the ALI, to wit: the duration of the relationship, whether the parties share a common residence, whether they have a sexual relationship, the degree of their financial interdependence and commitment to support each other, the way property is held between them, whether the couple has been caring for and supporting children, and how others view the relationship. Another factor is the couple's mutual commitment to a shared life, which the ALI regards as the conclusion rather than a consideration. Finally, Australian law also considers, like the ALI, whether the relationship is registered in places where that's possible.[58]

This law applies to all unmarried unrelated adult couples, gay or straight, and courts have shown remarkable attention to detail in assessing whether particular duos meet the "de facto couple" standard. Consider *Crowley & Pappas*, a 2013 decision by the Family Court of Australia.[59] There, two men had been in a relationship from 1987 through the end of 2005 and then separated. The issue was whether, when they resumed cohabitation in 2006, their "de facto" relationship continued. If so, the 2009 law would apply, since the cohabitation then lasted until early 2011.

For the court, the central inquiry was "the degree to which parties have merged their lives into one."[60] There was evidence on both sides. To an outsider, it would likely appear that the men remained a couple. For the most part, they lived only with each other. "They socialized jointly at their home, enjoying drinks [and] meals . . . with mutual friends. Each contributed equally to the expenses associated with the home."[61] Against this the court weighed competing evidence about the partners' intimacy. They disagreed about how often they had shared the same bed, with Pappas also claiming he had done so only under coercion, and whether they'd had sexual relations—Pappas denied Crowley's assertion that they had, but the court found the evidence of a continued sexual relationship more credible.[62]

Moving beyond physical and emotional intimacy, the court noted that the men had continued to run a retail business together but begun to separate their finances and purchases—in particular, Pappas had closed the parties' joint account and bought property on his own. But they owned a car together. In the court's view, Pappas had taken steps toward "keeping his options open to 'escape' the relationship, if things went badly, but also to continue [it otherwise]."[63] For this judge, hedging bets in this way was consistent with a de facto relationship.

Two final factors broke in favor of Crowley. First, Pappas had been in a close parental relationship with Crowley's son. Second, the parties' families and friends testified, consistently, that they all believed the men were in a de facto relationship until 2011—including one friend who was a family law attorney and seemed to the court to reject "as complete and utter nonsense" any suggestion that the two were not a couple.[64]

On balance, the court concluded that the couple met the requirements of a de facto relationship and thereby qualified for property division and an order of support.[65]

Reading through even a synopsis of this complex case—and the reader's patience is appreciated—reveals the difficulty in deciding whether a couple is "marital enough" to warrant the law's protection, especially after the relationship has dissolved. It's therefore not surprising that the ALI's approach hasn't gotten traction in the United States. Moreover, part of the reluctance in the United States to grant property and support rights in the wake of the dissolution of a de facto relationship is the country's strong pro-marriage culture. Indeed, the ALI drafters sustained heavy criticism for their approach, much of it from traditionalists who feared that recognizing such relationships would reduce the incentive for people to marry.[66] Addressing this possibility head on, the ALI took exception to that conclusion: "On the contrary, to the extent that some individuals avoid marriage in order to avoid responsibilities to a partner, this Chapter reduces the incentive to avoid marriage because it diminishes the effectiveness of that strategy."[67]

Possibly. On the other hand, perhaps some parties would, over time, come to see marriage as a needless formality given that the consequences of a long-term relationship would be similar. (That determination could of course be affected by the availability of other benefits, as discussed above.)

Whatever the problems and concerns engendered by the ALI and Australian approaches, though, they are both reasonable responses to today's realities.[68] And notwithstanding the incentives to marry, because of the availability of some of the remedies usually associated with marriage, it's time to end the complete separation of married folks from couples in similar relationships.

To the extent that benefits—including favorable tax treatment and couple-targeted eligibility for programs such as social security—continue to be awarded to married people, other couples should also be able to establish eligibility for them, but only by convincing a court (or perhaps an agency designed to handle such claims) that their relationship bears the hallmarks of a de facto relationship. Consider the Family and Medical Leave Act, the federal law that permits certain employees of middle to large companies to take unpaid leave to care for family members—but only if those family members are on an exclusive list.[69] Neither unmarried cohabitants nor adult siblings qualify as caregivers by this definition, no matter the strength or duration of their relationship. If May Doe had fallen sick, her sister April would not have been able to take the time off work needed to care for her. But who better to do so?

A more reality-based approach is evident in Australia. In *Attiwill & Secretary, Department of Education, Employment and Workplace Relations*, for instance, an administrator had to decide whether an applicant whose relationship had dissolved had been in a de facto couple, thereby making her eligible for a certain kind of government payment (called a "newstart allowance").[70] Although the case was concededly close, the administrator found that the couple had indeed dissolved their relationship and that their continued financial interdependence was born of necessity. That same necessity was related to why the applicant required the allowance in the first place, however, and the administrator used discretion in reaching a finding that landed on the fairest result.[71]

The ALI approach is better in at least one way. Unlike Australian law, it does not exclude blood relations from the de facto relationship category: although those related by blood or adoption cannot avail themselves of the presumption of domestic partnership status, they can claim that status by demonstrating a shared life together.[72] This would help couples like the Armenian American sisters in the previous chapter only if the ALI rules were extended to apply to cases of death (not just dissolution of the relationship) and if the surviving member were afforded the same benefits, including estate tax advantages, available to surviving spouses. With the huge asterisk discussed above—that benefits should be means tested— these changes should be implemented. After all, May and April Doe's interdependence is as strong as that of many, and likely most, married couples. Of course, these benefits can be extended only through separate legislation—at both the state and the federal level.

Let's recap the discussion so far. Marriage is being called on to do many things all at once. Because of the various meanings and benefits that have been affixed to it, those on the outside rightly complain of their exclusion from the institution, or at least from its benefits. So the first step is to strip away what we might call the *external benefits*, leaving only those legal protections that deserve to flow from the couple's reasonable expectations and from the societal interest in supporting marriages, by giving the party in the weaker economic position some assurance of fair treatment when the relationship ends. Those same protections should also apply to couples in de facto relationships, which the parties should be able to establish in some way, perhaps along the lines suggested by the ALI and actually in force in Australia.

But something else is needed. The Australian cases show the extreme difficulty and consumption of judicial resources that stem from looking back in time to determine whether a cohabiting relationship qualifies as a de facto marriage, supporting the conclusion that some other kind of formal relationship ought to be recognized. As one perceptive commentator stated, "Cohabitation is nothing more than a precarious union which does not automatically presuppose its legal stability."[73]

Thus, the law should recognize some *third thing*: something that is neither marriage nor cohabitation but a formal institution which acknowledges that many adults in relationships need a legal status that reliably supports them and provides a structure that can be recognized by both the state and third parties.

This third thing is a legal chameleon, shifting color depending on the particular circumstances of actual people. While some of the couples described in this book have found relationships such as domestic partnerships and civil unions suitable to their needs, others—particularly Anne Quinn and Terry McKeon—would likely have decided that a more creative option was the best fit.

The relationships discussed throughout this book provide some useful clues as to what this legal status should look like.

CREATING A NEW LEGAL STATUS

Marriage doesn't satisfy the needs of many, many people, for different reasons.[74] Some couples in intimate relationships simply don't want the form-fit and (still presumed) lifelong commitment. For them, judicial recognition of their de facto relationship might be desirable—but maybe not. They might prefer a more flexible structure, into which they could pour whatever agreed-upon content they chose. For other adults in different kinds of nonintimate, personal, contractual, and professional relationships, marriage isn't even close to what they need. May and April Doe complained about the unfairness of their not being allowed to enter into something like marriage, but their true beef is that the law doesn't provide a simple, effective way to organize their affairs together and guarantee the survivor a measure of financial security. They discussed marriage, it seems, because that currently stands as the only real way to accomplish these goals. But it doesn't have to be: the law must do better. Fortunately, there is a legal relationship model hiding in plain sight that could dramatically improve the lives of millions of couples nationwide were it to be expanded. What would its basic requirements be?

For a start, *the relationship has to be recognized across state lines.* France's *pacte civil de solidarité,* to take one example, is a nationwide status that confers some of the protections and responsibilities of marriage (see sidebar). An obstacle in the United States is federalism—the separation of powers between the federal government and the states—so the nationalization of a new status would have to be achieved one state at a time. This task will be easier if there is a model law to work from; even then, however, developing a nationwide alternative to marriage will probably take years, possibly decades. Other proposed uniform approaches to

THE FRENCH EVOLUTION: *PACTE CIVIL DE SOLIDARITÉ*

As noted earlier, this book mostly concerns the development of marriage alternatives in the United States. That decision is based in part on the observation that most of those in Europe (as well as Australia and New Zealand) don't amount to substantial variations on the legal structures presented here.[a] But one does deserve a place of privilege: the French *pacte civil de solidarité* (usually shortened to *pacte civil* or *PACS*). Like the designated beneficiary law, the pacte civil is a particularly important innovation. Enacted into law in 1999 after a long struggle, it was expressly designed to occupy a middle space between marriage and what the French call *concubinage* ("cohabitation" to Americans).[b] French reformers and progressive legislators recognized that the concubinage law was an insufficient vehicle for the protection of cohabitants' expectations, even though the consequences of such a relationship were assimilated to those of marriage—if a decision-maker agreed that the facts supported a finding of cohabitation. The Australian examples remind us that cases can be close and judges have their own biases. And the French high court had made crystal clear that same-sex couples were not eligible for the benefits of cohabitation, ruling in a series of cases that only couples who could legally marry—pointedly, *not* gay and lesbian couples—could qualify for a relationship with quasi-marital status.[c]

With the passage of the pacte civil law, opposite-sex couples had three legal options for relationship recognition (in addition to contracts, which were not predictably enforced): marriage, pacte civil, or concubinage. Same-sex couples now had two, because the new law expressly declared them eligible for concubinage status. The pacte has proved immensely popular: their number has steadily increased, and among opposite-sex couples, statistics show that there are about two issued for every three marriages.[d] It was to be expected, then, that when same-sex couples finally won the right to marry, in 2013, there was not the slightest impulse to throw out the pacte civil law.

The pacte civil is designed only for two people we might traditionally think of as a couple. It's not available to closely related people or to those in what we might think of as long-term roommate situations.[e] As its first provision notes, the law is intended to offer some protection to those who wish to "organize their life in common" but do not want (or at the time of its passage were not allowed) to marry.[f]

Like most domestic partnerships, the PACS is easy to get into and easy to exit.[g] To enter one, the couple simply registers their agreement with the local government clerk, who publishes the fact of the union. To get out of the deal, one or both parties similarly notify the clerk (and the other party, if this is done unilaterally), who registers and publishes notice of the dissolution. The parties are encouraged to settle the rights and obligations arising from their union, but judges are standing by to do so if they can't agree. Areas of disagreement might involve property or child custody.

What are the rights and obligations arising from the pacte civil? They differ somewhat from the default rules for marriage, although, as with marriage, the couple can choose whatever regime of property ownership best suits them. The law initially presumed joint ownership of assets, but reforms enacted in 2006 included a shift to a presumption of separate ownership. This can be rebutted, however, through the parties' agreement, which, unlike a prenuptial agreement in the United States, is part of the pacte civil itself and not a separate variance that a court must later interpret.[h]

The law further provides that debts incurred by either member of the couple "for the needs of daily life" are the responsibility of both, but the Conseil constitutionnel has held that either will be compensated for a financial loss that is the fault of the other.[i]

The parties are also expected to assist each other, and not just in ways that law can quantify. Consider this provision, which makes clearer than any other the serious nature of the commitment expected: The partners "commit to *a life in common* and to material aid and to *reciprocal assistance*. If the partners do not provide otherwise, material aid is proportionate to their respective means" (emphasis added).[j] The italicized phrases make clear that the legislators were keen to encourage the kind of mutual commitment that comports with a modern understanding of one of the key goods of marriage. The emphasis on reciprocity and sharing a life in common owes much to two related views discussed earlier: marriage as commitment and marriage as companionship.

Once thought unlikely to gain much traction beyond the gay and lesbian couples it was primarily designed to help, the PACS was quickly embraced by straight couples too: they have consistently been in the majority of couples entering these unions. It is of course true that there are far more straight than gay couples overall, but the huge success of the law caught even its most optimistic proponents off guard.

With some time for reflection, it's easy to see why the pacte civil has been such a hit. France is a heavily Catholic country, which means that divorce continues to impose a high social and personal cost for many couples.[k] Marriages are still supposed to be for life. Yet most people today are savvy enough to realize that many of them fail—and remain hard to get out of. Shorn of marriage's woolly religious coat, the pacte civil thus commends itself to practical couples—especially the young. Yet for all the powerful religious associations marriage carries, there's this paradox: officially, at least, French marriage is entirely civil. A couple can choose to have a religious ceremony, of course, but it is only the civil ceremony that makes the union legal.[l] In other words, the French are already accustomed to marriage as a civil union—making the pacte civil a not entirely unfamiliar creature. It's just a less bossy one.

Marriage of one or both of the parties or the death of one ends the pacte civil.[m]

a. For a recent, comprehensive account of the past, present, and future of "registered partnerships" (a different umbrella term for *marriage alternatives*) in Europe, Australia, and New Zealand, see Jens M. Scherpe & Andy Hayward (eds.), *The Future of Registered Partnerships: Family Recognition beyond Marriage* (Intersentia, 2017).

b. Du pacte civil de solidarité et du concubinage, Loi n° 99/944 du 15 novembre 1999 (since amended), https://www.legifrance.gouv.fr/jorf/id/JORFTEXT000000761717. The discussion in this sidebar relies principally on the recent, comprehensive accounts of the history and evolution and the summary of the law by Laurence Francoz Terminal, "Registered Partnerships in France," in *The Future of Registered Partnerships: Family Recognition beyond Marriage*, 153 (Jens M. Scherpe & Andy Hayward eds., Intersentia, 2017), and Ji Hyun Kim,

Scott A. Oliver, & Margaret Ryznar, "The Rise of PACS: A New Type of Commitment from the City of Love," 56 *Washburn L. Rev.* 69 (2017).

c. "It became apparent that the legal definition of cohabitation, as settled by the Cour de cassation [France's highest court], which referred to a relationship akin to marriage, which was exclusively of opposite-sex nature at that time, was excluding any possibility for same-sex cohabitants to benefit from any form of . . . social welfare benefit, health insurance or housing rights." Francoz Terminal, "Registered Partnerships in France," 155, citing Cass. Civ. 3, Dec. 17, 1997, no. 95-20779 (refusal to allow claim for lease transfer of home to surviving same-sex cohabitant); Cass. Soc., July 11, 1989, no. 86-10665 (refusal to extend health insurance benefits to same-sex partner). For a brief historical account of the emerging recognition of cohabitating relationships in France before enactment of the PACS, see Kim, Oliver, & Ryznar, "Rise of PACS," 81–83.

d. A rich set of statistics (though not as up to date as one might wish) is found in Francoz Terminal, "Registered Partnerships in France," 164–67. In 2013, the most recent year for which Francoz Terminal provides full data, 231,225 different-sex couples married and 162,072 entered into PACS. That was also the first year during which same-sex couples could legally marry, and their numbers were much closer: 7,367 marriages, 6,064 PACS.

e. As Francoz Terminal notes, the exclusion of relatives was based on "the fear that the incest taboo would be raised in an already harsh discussion." Id., 158.

f. French Civil Code, Art. 515-1 (Titre XIII: Du pacte civil de solidarité et du concubinage). For a fuller discussion, including analysis of the Conseil constitutionnel's interpretation of the exclusion of siblings and other nonintimate couples, see Kim, Oliver, & Ryznar, "Rise of PACS," 83–84. Although the sibling exclusion seems simple to enforce, there's reason to question whether the effort to exclude couples in platonic relationships has been successful. For an early expression of skepticism on that point, see David Orgon Coolidge & William C. Duncan, "Reaffirming Marriage: A Presidential Priority," 24 *Harv. J. L. & Pub. Pol'y* 623, 642 n.74 (2001).

g. The process for entering and exiting the pacte civil is ably described, with relevant civil code sections cited, in Francoz Terminal, "Registered Partnerships in France," 167–68.

h. Id., 169–71. Even if the parties opt for joint ownership of assets, certain items will be excluded (just as they would be for married couples, although the French exclusions differ somewhat from those typical in the United States) unless the parties further specify that even those will be treated as jointly owned.

i. Id., 171, citing Conseil constitutionnel, Décision no. 99-419 DC, Nov. 9, 1999.

j. French Civil Code, Art. 515-4 al. 1; translation from David Gruning et al., *Traduction du Code civil français en anglais version bilingue* (2015),

halshs-01385107, https://halshs.archives-ouvertes.fr/halshs-01385107
/document.
k. As of 2014, about two-thirds of the French populace was Christian, of whom
more than 80 percent identified as Catholic. Benjamin Elisha Sawe, "Religious
Demographics of France," WorldAtlas, March 13, 2018, https://www.worldatlas
.com/articles/religious-demographics-of-france.html.
l. France in the United States, Embassy of France in Washington, D.C.,
"Marriage in France," Ministère de l'Europe et des affaires étrangères, Nov. 13,
2007, https://franceintheus.org/spip.php?article387.
m. French Civil Code, Art. 515-7 al. 1.

family law have mostly resulted in different states choosing different
paths, but there are a few exceptions. Notably, most have now moved from
the broad discretion that used to be standard to a formulaic method of
determining child support. Congress helped the process along by tying
federal funds for child welfare to the passage of laws compatible with the
Adoption and Safe Families Act.[75] This law shifts the emphasis in dealing
with dependent children from reunification with birth parents to quicker
permanent placement.

The importance of uniformity is underlined by current difficulties in
dissolving state-specific relationships such as domestic partnerships and
civil unions. When David and I decided to marry in 2013, we were still in
a Vermont civil union. Had we wanted to get out of it, we would have had
two bad choices: move to Vermont for six months(!) to establish residency
before being allowed to end the union, or go through the expensive, time-
consuming, and uncertain process of trying to dissolve it in our home
state of Pennsylvania—which did not recognize our civil union in the first
place. In the end, we did neither. Instead, we followed the informal advice
of a clerk in Vermont (offered over the telephone, at that): ignore the civil
union and just get married. Of course, for couples who really do want to
get *out* of their relationship, a lingering civil union could present enormous difficulties. A state that doesn't recognize a civil union or domestic
partnership might not let the couple dissolve it. What happens, then, to
the property they might be fighting over? How will child custody decisions

be affected? And can either person then marry someone else? It wouldn't exactly be bigamy (since there was no first *marriage*), but complications could nonetheless ensue. In sum, uniformity is vital.

Next, as this also illustrates, *the relationship should be easy to exit.* If another status is to be recognized, this quick exit feature is vital. This agility is a key feature and draw of the French pacte civil. Similar flexibility marks many domestic partnership laws. A couple might want a formalization of their relationship but justifiably fear that getting out of it will be difficult, time consuming, and stressful. No-fault divorce laws have gone some way toward improving the situation for marriage, but the process remains challenging for most, and many states still require that a couple live "separate and apart" for a specified period of time before filing.[76] Less formally, the lifelong commitment that marriage entails, at least from social and rhetorical perspectives, exacerbates the difficulty of extrication. An easy off-ramp would encourage greater participation in a new legal institution.

Finally, *the institution should be designed with maximum flexibility to suit individual circumstances.* Marriage and even the ALI's approach fail in this respect. Marriage has default rules, and so, in effect, does the ALI's de facto relationship once a couple is determined to meet its requirements. Yes, couples can contract around these rules in either case, but that's not a realistic solution for most people. Entering into such contracts can be expensive, and those in de facto "marriages" might not even understand that they need a superseding agreement. As the legion of prenuptial contract cases populating family law texts illustrates, the economically weaker party often feels compelled to accept terms they might not find fair, as well as (in the case of marriage) pressure to go through with the union even if the wisdom of doing so is called into question by the prenuptial agreement or the circumstances of its execution.[77] These barriers explain the low rate of these contracts, especially in first marriages.[78] Courts enforce them inconsistently too. Some states require that the agreement be fair to both sides—an inherently subjective test that makes the outcome uncertain and might therefore be affecting the rate at which couples enter into them.[79]

By contrast, an *inherently* adaptable agreement would anticipate and build in the needed flexibility. More than twenty years ago, the Law

Commission of Canada issued a report suggesting such an approach, but its recommendation did not generate much interest. It is time to revisit the issue, now with the wisdom gained from experience since that report came out.[80]

A NEW AND IMPROVED DESIGNATED BENEFICIARY AGREEMENT LAW

When I began researching and thinking about how the law should protect the great, wonderful diversity of families and variety of other relationships, I believed that several statuses besides marriage should be recognized. After all, the couples in domestic partnerships, DBAs, and even civil unions were benefiting from them in certain ways. Why not just improve on those? Several scholars agree with this position. Jessica Feinberg, for instance, a law professor who has written extensively on these new legal statuses, has forcefully argued for a set of rules under which nonmarital relationships from one state would be recognized by other states and the federal government.[81] Her approach would keep in place the various statuses that have been discussed throughout this book. William Eskridge's "Family Law Pluralism," as the title implies, supports a creative menu of legal options that include civil unions as well as reciprocal and designated beneficiary statuses.[82]

Reflection has brought me to a different place, for a few reasons. I now think it best that just one marriage alternative requiring registration survive. The first reason is practical. It's not going to be easy to get any new relationship status recognized, and one law will be easier to push through skeptical legislatures than two or more. In fact, there's reason to believe that the confusion inherent in the availability of multiple legally recognized relationships is part of the reason why they are losing traction in the wake of the marriage equality victory.

We shouldn't need more than one new status anyway. The adaptability of DBAs reveals the flexibility that can be built into a law that tries to recognize couples' actual shared lives. In effect, one statute can contain the ingredients for the kind of variety that would otherwise be available only through a multiplicity of laws. Why not capture them all under one roof?

But how should such a law be constructed? What elements should it contain?

The suggestions that follow are intended only to ignite a debate about how the law can move to formal, consistent recognition of many of the relationships that couples live in today. I am under not the slightest illusion that these recommendations will be enacted in their present form, nor that they can't be improved. Consider them a down payment on a long overdue bill. Their inspiration comes from two kinds of sources.

First are legal examples, which include the myriad domestic partnership statutes, ordinances, and corporate policies; the DBA law; and the French pacte civil, a compromise measure on the road to full marriage equality in its nation, but a law that quickly gained traction and then wide acceptance among different-sex as well as same-sex couples.

The second source of inspiration, of course, is the couples whose stories anchor and fill this book—and the many millions more families who live without legal protections that would measurably improve their lives.

The law for which I advocate might be thought of as creating a sort of turbocharged DBA, where couples in various kinds of relationships—with different practical needs—can set forth their desired legal connections by opting in or out of various benefits and obligations. Constructed with sufficient imagination and breadth, it might serve couples who need to cement their relationships for all sorts of reasons: siblings like May and April Doe, who demand a firm legal foundation for their interdependency; coparents like Anne Quinn and Terry McKeon, whose relationship isn't best captured by marriage but who needed legal protections for themselves and their children (more about children in a moment)—and, significantly, for Anne's partner Joyce, who required some of the powers that parents traditionally enjoy to make decisions affecting their children; couples like Jennifer Tweeton and Alex Rifton, who want the protections of marriage— but maybe not all of them—without the name and would like an easier exit from their obligations if the relationship sours; and perhaps even couples like Tom Brougham and Barry Warren, who might have found the new law more convivially adaptable to their do-it-yourself approach than the domestic partnership law, with all of the strictures it imposes.

The building blocks for such a law are largely in place already, peering out at us from the extensive lists in the designated beneficiary law, the chameleon-like domestic partnership laws, and the "marriage lite" approach of the French pacte civil de solidarité.

THE PROPOSAL: RECOGNIZING REALITIES

Here's how the proposed law draws from the various legal entities discussed in this book: From the domestic partnership, we borrow the do-it-yourself activism and the early recognition that the legal system can and should do something to protect couples who either cannot or do not wish to marry. We also steal the flexibility that resulted from the nationwide eruption, in cities, counties, states, and the private sector, of domestic partnership laws and policies: while each one had its own strict set of benefits and obligations, together they served as a kind of laboratory for the creation of many different legal entities. From the civil union comes the insight that some people want and need protections similar to those of marriage but without its procrustean presumptions. From the French pacte civil we borrow the idea that, for some, easy entry and exit from a relationship status are desirable. And from the DBA, we get . . . well, everything else.

What follows is a list of items and options that the proposed law might include. Nothing here is new, exactly, but the legislation's recombinant character and the plea for national uniformity are the most novel features at the heart of the proposal.

> Establish a statewide registry for what we will continue to call *designated beneficiary agreements*.
>
>> This name best suits the flexibility of both the relationship type and the benefits that the Colorado law allows. It is apt and should be adopted.
>
> Retain most of the options and other features of Colorado's Designated Beneficiary Agreement Act.
>
>> The law is quite clear and useful on many issues, including end-of-life and other proxy decisions, tort remedies, and the ability to name another person as a beneficiary in various contexts. The "one-stop shopping" the law contemplates and enables is a time and money saver.

Bring clarity to the joint ownership of property.

Among the less satisfying aspects of the Colorado law is its relative lack of clarity about co-ownership of property. Depending on the state, there are two or three possible legal forms available to married couples. The new law should allow the same flexibility to other couples, as long as creditors' interests are properly protected.

Allow couples to gradually integrate their property interests over time.

When a couple's marriage dissolves, the law generally treats most of their property as fair game for division (no matter who earned it or whose name it's in), but a few kinds of assets—like gifts to one spouse or property that one of the spouses owned before marriage—are considered separate and indivisible. The ALI has suggested a third approach: "recharacterization" of separate property as joint property as a marriage progresses. The idea is that, in long marriages, the couple comes to intermingle their assets to such an extent that a court's sorting out of who owns what is both too hard and unlikely to reflect their actual views of ownership.[83]

But this is all too directive. Why not let the couple decide how they want to divide their assets? The law could even include an option for recharacterization according to a schedule that would be set out in plain English.[84] This approach might make choices more deliberative while avoiding the expense and (to an extent) the inequality of prenuptial agreements.

The law should be drafted with the idea that the couples who choose the status it offers are not trying to mimic marriage. It should allow for multi-party arrangements set forth in multiple DBAs.

Those who want to marry will continue to do so. But others will choose the new status because, as siblings or nonintimate friends, they either can't marry but want to protect their assets and their relationship with the other beneficiary or need a more modular, à la carte approach to their situation. Some will find more desirable a combination of marriage and another arrangement dealing with specific legal issues. For this reason, people should be able to be in a marriage *and* a DBA—just not with the same person and not in a way that puts the two statuses in conflict. They should also be able to enter into multiple DBAs at the same time.

This is the proposal's most radical aspect. But it is embedded in the very DNA of the DBA approach, which envisions opting in and out of various agreements with another person, so there are rights and obligations that might need to be secured with multiple documents. Let, say, an elderly person give medical decision-making power to a daughter and control over certain property in the event of disability to another person—through a separate DBA. The law already allows this, in a way. Currently, even married people can designate someone other than a spouse as a health care proxy decision-maker, for example. The expanded DBA could contain this sort of arrangement and others. A cross-referenced electronic database would help take care of duplications and inconsistencies, flagging and disallowing them.

Any kind of multiperson arrangement leads naturally to a debate about polygamous marriage.[85] But that issue is *en dehors* of this proposal. The expanded DBA isn't about marriage at all but about an evolution in the law to have it reflect the rich, sometimes messy complexity of people's lives. Once we move away from marriage—with all its baggage—it should be easier to see that adults often end up in fundamentally important relationships with more than one person at a time. For example, consider Terry McKeon, Anne Quinn, and Joyce Weeg. Why shouldn't McKeon and Quinn have been able to give Weeg at least some legal authority over their children, since doing so would have served everyone's interests—importantly, including the children's—and provided both clarity and legal immunity for anyone, like a school official or doctor, who needed a handy way of recognizing that authority? The new law could help courts resolve issues that now seem intractable, and would be blind to whatever intimacies those in DBAs enjoy outside these agreements.

This is a very basic sketch of what the proposed law would look like. It has the virtue of covering those who don't want to marry as well as people in relationships that currently don't provide reliable or consistent protection. Recent scholarly interest has insightfully focused on the law's quite limited recognition of *friendships* as relationships sometimes in need of legal protection.[86] By entering into a DBA, friends who wish to share certain responsibilities and benefits can move the discussion in a positive direction.

But how is any of this going to help May and April avoid their tax problem? In fact, *should* they be helped? We can end with them, since my experience in discussing the stories that fill this book has shown that their case inspires much interest. It calls us to think about relationships in all their myriad, wonderful, messy variety. And it returns us to the themes developed throughout this book.

Importantly, we should look at *means*. The estate tax exemption lives on a kind of line between two benefit categories discussed earlier in this chapter. First, there are benefits distributed to couples just because they're married, in a windfall that depends not on need but on an antiquated view of how people organize their lives and relationships. Second, there are legal protections that exist to safeguard parties' reasonable expectations; these generally derive from the way a couple organizes their lives together.

The Doe sisters have done everything that law and creative financial planning allow. Their expectations are no different, really, from those of any married couple: when one of them dies, life will generally get harder for the survivor—and the law recognizes that in a variety of ways, including the estate tax exemption.

To the extent that exemptions like this are needed to avoid hardship, the Does should be able to take advantage of them. The expanded designated beneficiary law proposed here should be sufficient to protect the sisters' expectations *if* they choose forms of joint ownership that tie their assets together in imitation of the typical status of property in marriage. The tax law should be amended to recognize this kind of interdependency.

But where the exemption perpetuates inequality, it should be amended—for all couples, married or otherwise. Federal law sets a high floor for estates subject to the tax: $11,580,000 for 2020.[87] It should probably be much lower, and in any case it isn't going to result in anyone becoming homeless. The current law isn't fair to the Doe sisters. But it also isn't fair to those at the bottom of the economic pile, who enjoy none of the benefits that similarly situated married couples have.

It is perhaps a sign of the times that the Does think it unfair that they are excluded from marriage—or, perhaps more precisely, from something like it. Because what they're really complaining about is not just the denial of that institution's benefits but the fact that their lifelong commitment is still seen as a bit odd and not worthy of celebration or emulation. This grievance springs from twenty-first-century developments in the understanding and definition of marriage and dramatically shows how healthy the national conversation about it has been. Today the institution is increasingly seen as a vehicle for expressing commitment rather than as a required structure for having and raising children. But it's also a way of delivering benefits to a privileged class.

This newer understanding of marriage is more in step with today's realities. It's an understanding that allows us to continue to talk up marriage as a time-tested way of encouraging stability and predictability for couples and their children while embracing and supporting other relationships. If marriage were to shed some of its excess baggage, the committed elderly siblings of this world would likely feel less like unwanted outliers. They'd have an option that *sees them* and their relationship as worthy of the law's protection.

The proposals advanced in this chapter are an attempt to approach that goal: establish a uniform registration system for those who wish to opt into something more creatively flexible than marriage, and recognize unregistered partners who are cohabitating.

Is there anything, at last, that unites the various, complex ways that people understand and navigate their lives together? Maybe it's as simple as this: "A chaotic world can be made sensible, and the cruelties of entropy can be resisted, through that most unpredictable and yet stabilizing of things: love."[88]

It's well past time for the law to recognize that love and human relationships take many forms.

Notes

Epigraphs. Obergefell v. Hodges, 576 U.S. 644, 666 (2015); Michael Warner, *The Trouble with Normal: Sex, Politics, and the Ethics of Queer Life,* 115–16 (Free Press, 1999). Warner's book is a relentless, often effective attack on what the author sees as the limited and dangerously normative aims of the marriage equality movement. Although the issue has been decided (as a legal matter, anyway), Warner's concerns about the fence between marriage and other relationships have lost none of their salience.

1. Of course, some couples in committed relationships will continue to structure their lives together outside of the legal system's protections, even after the new and more compatible designated beneficiary agreement alternative is in place. In chapter 5, I argue that courts should more consistently enforce obligations of couples in de facto relationships, even if they decline to formalize their relationships. Yet the intensive judicial fact-finding that is often necessary in these cases makes them a decidedly second-best alternative to the legal registration regime I propose.

2. 576 U.S. 644.

3. In Pidgeon v. Turner, 538 S.W.3d 73 (Tex. 2017), the Texas Supreme Court held that, despite the clear directive of *Obergefell* that gay and lesbian couples are entitled to marry on the same footing as their straight counterparts, the City of Houston was not necessarily compelled to provide government employees in

same-sex marriages with the benefits other married couples enjoy. The case is appalling for several reasons, not least of which is that the Texas Supreme Court initially—and quite properly—declined to hear an appeal from a lower court that had found the unequal treatment unconstitutional, but later cowered and capitulated to political pressure to "reconsider" that decision. Upon that reconsideration, the entire, all-Republican court issued its absurd ruling and sent the case back to the lower court for further consideration. See Amita Kelly, "Texas Supreme Court Rules against Benefits for Same-Sex Couples," NPR, June 30, 2017, https://www.npr.org/2017/06/30/535021154/texas-supreme-court-rules-against-benefits-for-same-sex-couples. After those challenging the issuance of benefits lost again at the trial court level, an appeal was taken to the Texas Court of Appeals. Finally, more than seven years after the case was initially filed, the Texas Appellate Court upheld the dismissal of the claim against the city and the mayor for a whole host of reasons relating to jurisdiction, the failure to prove an injury to any party from the equalization of benefits to same-sex spouses, and governmental immunity. Pidgeon v. Turner, 538 S.W.3d 73 (Tex. Ct. App. 2021).

4. I have addressed this question in John G. Culhane, "The Right to Say, but Not to Do: Balancing First Amendment Freedom of Expression with the Anti-discrimination Imperative," 24 *Widener L. Rev.* 235 (2018), and "The Most Important Cake in America," *Politico*, December 4, 2017, https://www.politico.com/magazine/story/2017/12/04/cake-supreme-court-case-gay-marriage-216006. The issue of how best to accommodate these competing interests remains unresolved as of this writing. See Culhane, "The Supreme Court Punts on Cakes for Same-Sex Couples," *Politico*, June 4, 2018, https://www.politico.com/magazine/story/2018/06/04/the-supreme-court-punts-on-cakes-for-same-sex-couples-218591; Culhane, "The Cake Controversy That Just Won't Go Away," *Politico*, August 16, 2018, https://www.politico.com/magazine/story/2018/08/16/masterpiece-cakeshop-controversy-219365.

5. With right-tilting Supreme Court justices now holding a clear 6–3 majority, this confidence comes with an asterisk. At least two of them have expressed continued disagreement with the *Obergefell* ruling. See Davis v. Ermold, 141 S. Ct. 3, 4 (2020), statement of Justices Clarence Thomas and Samuel Alito respecting the denial of cert.: "In *Obergefell v. Hodges*, the Court read a right to same-sex marriage into the Fourteenth Amendment, even though that right is found nowhere in the text. . . . By choosing to privilege a novel constitutional right over the religious liberty interests explicitly protected in the First Amendment, and by doing so undemocratically, the Court has created a problem that only it can fix" (citations omitted). The recent decision in Dobbs v. Jackson Women's Health Org., 142 S. Ct. 2228 (2022), raised the decibel level of the alarm. In overruling Roe v. Wade, 410 U.S. 113 (1973), and Planned Parenthood v. Casey, 505 U.S. 833 (1992), which had established and then affirmed that women had a constitutional right to terminate their pregnancies, the court employed a mode of his-

torical analysis that left other fundamental rights on shaky ground. See 142 S. Ct. at 2319 (joint dissent of Justices Stephen Breyer, Sonia Sotomayor, and Elena Kagan): "No one should be confident that this majority is done with its work. The right *Roe* and *Casey* recognized does not stand alone. To the contrary, the Court has linked it for decades to other settled freedoms involving bodily integrity, familial relationships, and procreation."

6. Melissa Murray, "*Obergefell v. Hodges* and Nonmarriage Inequality," 104 *Calif. L. Rev.* 1207, 1240 (2016).

7. The 2013 figures are based on data taken from the Census and the Bureau of Labor Statistics. Richard Florida offers a good summary: "Singles Now Make Up More Than Half the U.S. Adult Population. Here's Where They Live," Bloomberg, CityLab, Sept. 15, 2014, https://www.citylab.com/equity/2014/09/singles -now-make-up-more-than-half-the-us-adult-population-heres-where-they-all-live /380137/. Since then, the numbers for both have continued to hover around the 50 percent mark.

8. This topic is explored in depth in an influential work by two legal scholars: June Carbone & Naomi Cahn, *Marriage Markets: How Inequality Is Remaking the American Family* (Oxford University Press, 2014). The authors argue that widening economic inequality has made marriage a rational choice for those at the higher end of the economic pile but an often poor choice for those whose economic stability and possibilities are less healthy. For a clear summary of the statistical evidence, see Linda McClain, "The Other Marriage Equality Problem," 93 *B.U.L. Rev.* 921, 960 (2013). The data are reported at Pew Research Center, "The Decline of Marriage and Rise of New Families," Nov. 18, 2010, http://www .pewresearch.org/social-trends/2010/11/18/the-decline-of-marriage-and-rise-of -new-families/.

9. Pew Research Center, "Decline of Marriage and Rise of New Families" at "II. Overview": "Blacks (32%) are much less likely than whites (56%) to be married, and this gap has increased significantly over time."

10. United States v. Windsor, 570 U.S. 744 (2013). The case is discussed in more detail in chapter 2.

11. Defense of Marriage Act, 110 Stat. 2419 (1996). The statute contained two operative provisions. The first (section 2) declared that any state could refuse to recognize a same-sex marriage entered into in any other state. *Windsor* was a successful challenge to the other provision (section 3), which, as the text explains, declared that same-sex marriages legally entered into in any state would nonetheless not be recognized for any purposes at the federal level.

12. 570 U.S. at 774.

13. Edie Windsor was the subject of a detailed and sympathetic profile in the *New Yorker*: Ariel Levy, "The Perfect Wife," *New Yorker*, Sept. 30, 2013, http:// www.newyorker.com/magazine/2013/09/30/the-perfect-wife. Windsor herself died in 2017. Robert D. McFadden, "Edie Windsor, Whose Same-Sex Marriage

Fight Led to Landmark Ruling, Dies at 88," *N.Y. Times*, Sept. 12, 2017, https://www.nytimes.com/2017/09/12/us/edith-windsor-dead-same-sex-marriage -doma.html.

14. "For the Federal Government then to come in to say no joint return, no marital deduction, no Social Security benefits; your spouse is very sick but you can't get leave—one might well ask, what kind of marriage is this? [The Defense of Marriage Act creates] two kinds of marriage—the full marriage, and then this sort of skim milk marriage." Supreme Court Justice Ruth Bader Ginsburg, during oral argument on *United States v. Windsor* (Mar. 27, 2013). The transcript and audio recording are available through the Oyez Project, https://www.oyez .org/cases/2012/12-307.

15. US Government Accountability Office, "Defense of Marriage Act," GAO-04-353R, Jan. 23, 2004.

16. Federal income tax law creates separate filing categories for married and unmarried couples, with significant financial consequences attaching to the appropriate status. 26 U.S.C.S. § 1 (2021). Federal estate tax law exempts surviving spouses but not cohabitants—even in relationships of long standing. 26 U.S.C. § 2056 (2021). Social security law recognizes the financial interdependency of married couples in several ways, by providing benefits to surviving spouses, by allowing the economically weaker spouse to choose to receive retirement benefits based on the other spouse's employment history rather than his or her own, and by letting benefits continue to flow to the surviving spouse after the primary wage earner's death. 42 U.S.C. § 402 (2021). (As will be discussed in chapter 5, the law has recently been changed to permit people in certain kinds of other relationships these same survivor benefits.) The valuable immigration preference is spelled out in 8 U.S.C.A. § 1153 (a)(2) (2021). As the GAO estimate indicates (see previous note), there are countless other rights, benefits, and obligations that inure to married couples only.

17. See, e.g., Goodridge v. Department of Public Health, 798 N.E.2d 941 (Mass. 2003) (listing these and other marriage-connected benefits under Massachusetts state law). Other states confer similar benefits, though the details vary.

18. Two recent books provide vivid detail of the struggle for marriage equality: William N. Eskridge Jr. & Christopher R. Riano, *Marriage Equality: From Outlaws to In-Laws* (Yale University Press, 2020); Sasha Issenberg, *The Engagement: America's Quarter-Century Struggle over Same-Sex Marriage* (Pantheon, 2021).

19. 798 N.E.2d 941.

20. 576 U.S. at 658–59.

21. Id. at 740 (Alito, J., dissenting).

22. Id. at 738.

23. This position has been most forcefully articulated by Robert George and his colleagues. See Sherif Girgis, Robert George, & Ryan T. Anderson, "What Is Marriage?," 34 *Harv. J. L. & Public Policy* 245 (2010).

24. Maggie Gallagher, "What Is Marriage For? The Public Purposes of Marriage Law," 62 *La. L. Rev.* 773, 779–81 (2002).

25. 1999 Vt. Acts & Resolves 91 (creating civil unions in Vermont); 15 Vt. Stat. Ann. § 1201 et seq. In 2009, Vermont passed a marriage equality law, after which no new civil unions could be formed. Existing civil unions remain in place, however. The legislature also took steps to make dissolution easier. 15 Vt. Stat. Ann. § 1206.

26. Colo. Rev. Stat. § 14-15-104 (2013); Haw. Rev. Stat. Ann. § 572B-1 (LexisNexis, 2011); 750 Ill. Comp. Stat. Ann. § 75/10 (LexisNexis, 2011) (dates of enactment).

27. Haw. Rev. Stat. Ann. § 572C (2021); 15 Vt. Stat. Ann. § 1301 (2000) (repealed 2013). Both came about in response to judicial decisions on marriage equality. Vermont repealed its reciprocal beneficiary law in 2013. Colorado's Designated Beneficiary Agreement Act was enacted in 2009 and to date remains the only such law. Colo. Rev. Stat. § 15-22-101 (2022). It is discussed in detail in chapter 3.

28. Although this is true of the marriage equality movement generally, there were those who questioned the focus on marriage—and who continue to do so. Among the most prominent and effective of these is Nancy Polikoff, whose *Beyond (Straight and Gay) Marriage: Valuing All Families under the Law* (Beacon, 2008) is still the most compelling work available on the need for law to take a much broader perspective, one that recognizes and supports the rich diversity of actual relationships. More than any other, Professor Polikoff has inspired me in the creation and development of this book.

CHAPTER 1. THE DAWN OF THE DOMESTIC PARTNERSHIP

1. As Douglas NeJaime has persuasively argued, the LGBTQ community, through its advocacy for the rights of its members, has transformed our general understanding of marriage and parenthood. NeJaime, "Before Marriage: The Unexplored History of Nonmarital Recognition and Its Relationship to Marriage," 102 *Calif. L. Rev.* 87 (2014); NeJaime, "Marriage Equality and the New Parenthood," 129 *Harv. L. Rev.* 1185 (2016).

2. Quotations from Tom Brougham and Barry Warren are drawn from two long Skype interviews with them in Sept. 2011.

3. Berkeley, Calif., Mun. Code, chapter 13.28, Discrimination on the Basis of Sexual Orientation, https://berkeley.municipal.codes/BMC/13.28, last visited Mar. 9, 2022. The law prohibits discrimination in employment, housing, and "business accommodations." Today, such ordinances number in the hundreds, and there are also statewide protections available in about half the states. An

accurate count is difficult to come by, as these laws change frequently, cover different forms of discrimination, and vary as to whether they apply based only on sexual orientation or also on gender identity. The Movement Advancement Project keeps an up-to-date list of states, cities, and counties with antidiscrimination laws in one form or another: see "Local Nondiscrimination Ordinances," last visited Mar. 9, 2022, http://www.lgbtmap.org/equality-maps/non_discrimination_ordinances/policies.

4. Ana Swanson, "144 Years of Marriage and Divorce in the United States, in One Chart," *Washington Post*, June 23, 2015, https://www.washingtonpost.com/news/wonk/wp/2015/06/23/144-years-of-marriage-and-divorce-in-the-united-states-in-one-chart/.

5. Roe v. Wade, 410 U.S. 113 (1973); *Time*, "A Brief History of Birth Control: From Early Contraception to the Birth of the Pill," May 3, 2010, http://content.time.com/time/magazine/article/0,9171,1983970,00.html.

6. The so-called Stonewall Riots of 1969 were perhaps an inevitable collision between law enforcement and the LGBTQ community in New York City. In the 1960s, Mayor John Lindsay spearheaded a crackdown on the city's increasing numbers of gay men, lesbians, and non-gender-conforming people. Arrests for "vice" were common, as were raids on bars that catered to what we would now call a queer clientele. The raid on the Stonewall Inn—a popular spot for drag queens, among others—was the last straw for many of its fed-up patrons. They fought back, and their defiance is now popularly thought of a turning point in the gay rights movement. A standout among the many excellent accounts of the event is History.com, "Stonewall Riots," May 31, 2017, updated May 31, 2022, https://www.history.com/topics/gay-rights/the-stonewall-riots. See also David Carter, *Stonewall: The Riots That Sparked the Gay Revolution* (St. Martin's Griffin, 2004).

7. E. B. Saunders, "Reformer's Choice: Marriage License or Just License?," *One*, Aug. 1953, at 10, http://queermusicheritage.com/jun2008one.html.

8. One, Inc. v. Olesen, 355 U.S. 371 (1958).

9. Garance Franke-Ruta, "The Prehistory of Gay Marriage: Watch a 1971 Protest at NYC's Marriage License Bureau, *The Atlantic*, Mar. 26, 2013, https://www.theatlantic.com/politics/archive/2013/03/the-prehistory-of-gay-marriage-watch-a-1971-protest-at-nycs-marriage-license-bureau/274357/.

10. Not all expressive conduct is protected by the First Amendment, but overtly political acts such as the protest discussed in the text would clearly qualify based on Supreme Court precedent. See Hurley v. Irish-American Gay, Lesbian and Bisexual Group of Boston, 515 U.S. 557 (1995) (a parade is expressive "enough" to be protected by the First Amendment, even if the message conveyed is neither clear nor coherent). I criticize the expansive, sometimes inconsistent jurisprudence of expressive conduct as "speech" in John G. Culhane, "The Right to Say, but Not to Do: Balancing First Amendment Freedom of Expression with the Anti-discrimination Imperative," 24 *Widener L. Rev.* 235 (2018).

11. Jones v. Hallahan, 501 S.W.2d 588 (Ky. 1973); Baker v. Nelson, 191 N.W.2d 185 (Minn. 1971); Singer v. Hara, 522 P.2d 1187 (Wash. Ct. App. 1974). In 1972, an appeal from the decision in *Baker* went to the Supreme Court, which dismissed it "for want of a substantial federal question." Baker v. Nelson, 409 U.S. 810 (1972). Other gay and lesbian couples brought a number of less direct challenges to marriage laws that excluded them. For example, in DeSanto v. Barnsley, 476 A.2d 952 (Pa. Super. Ct. 1984), a Pennsylvania appellate court rejected a man's claim that he and another man had entered into a common-law marriage. The claimant sought a divorce and alimony payments. The court noted that, although no Pennsylvania law at the time explicitly forbade same-sex marriages, the entire architecture of the marriage laws presumed a "husband" and a "wife." Id. at 954. Since ceremonial marriages were therefore restricted to different-sex couples, the court declined to extend common-law marriages beyond that traditional dyad. In 2017, the same Pennsylvania court recognized that the decision had been abrogated by the 2015 decision in *Obergefell v. Hodges* and other "subsequent decisional law." In re Estate of Carter, 159 A.3d 970, 975 n.4 (Pa. Super. Ct. 2017). Early cases that indirectly involved the issue include Anonymous v. Anonymous, 325 N.Y.S.2d 982 (N.Y. Sup. Ct. 1971) (court agreed with a man's claim that his marriage was a nullity because his spouse was male; man asserted he had been tricked into believing that the spouse was female at the time of the ceremony); M.T. v. J.T., 355 A.2d 204 (N.J. Super. Ct. 1976) (man claimed that his wife was a man and that their marriage was therefore void; court found that, as the wife had undergone sexual reassignment surgery before the couple married, she was legally a woman); Adams v. Howertown, 486 F. Supp. 1119 (C.D. Calif. 1980), aff'd, 673 F.2d 1036 (9th Cir. 1982) (same-sex couple not married for immigration purposes).

12. *Advocate*, "'Non-believers' Seek License to Wed," Nov. 10, 1971.

13. 522 P.2d at 1192.

14. 501 S.W.2d at 589.

15. Michael Klarman, *From the Closet to the Altar: Courts, Backlash, and the Struggle for Same-Sex Marriage*, 19 (Oxford University Press, 2013). See generally David K. Johnson, *The Lavender Scare: The Cold War Persecution of Gays and Lesbians in the Federal Government* (University of Chicago Press, 2004).

16. Marvin v. Marvin, 557 P.2d 106 (Calif. 1976).

17. Id. at 122.

18. Id. at 110.

19. Id.

20. Id. at 109.

21. Jones v. Daly, 122 Calif. App. 3d 500, 505 (Cal. Ct. App. 1981).

22. Whorton v. Dillingham, 202 Calif. App. 3d 447 (Calif. Ct. App. 1988).

23. Id. at 450.

24. Wallace Turner, "Partnership Law Vetoed on Coast," *N.Y. Times*, Dec. 10, 1982, https://www.nytimes.com/1982/12/10/us/partnership-law-vetoed-on -coast.html.

25. Tom Brougham, interview by Ron Schlitter, *Out and Elected in the USA, 1974–2004*, last visited July 13, 2022, https://outhistory.org/exhibits/show/out -and-elected/late-1980s/tom-brougham. This article provides some of the information contained in the account in the text and supplements what I learned from our interviews.

26. Centers for Disease Control and Prevention, *"Pneumocystis* Pneumonia— Los Angeles," 30 *MMWR* 250 (June 5, 1981). The report profiled five young men, "all active homosexuals," who had died between October 1980 and May 1981 of a rare type of pneumonia. It further noted that the disease in the United States was "almost exclusively limited to severely immunosuppressed patients." The underlying cause would eventually be identified as human immunodeficiency virus (HIV).

27. There are many excellent accounts of the early social and medical history of HIV/AIDS and its effect on the gay male community, but the best of these remains Randy Shilts, *And the Band Played On: Politics, People and the AIDS Epidemic* (St. Martins, 1987). A film of the same name was release in 1993, and the images depicted in it and in the much more recent *How to Survive a Plague* (2012) bear powerful visual witness to the toll of the disease.

28. Centers for Disease Control and Prevention, "HIV Stigma and Discrimination," reviewed June 1, 2021, https://www.cdc.gov/hiv/basics/hiv-stigma /index.html.

29. Phila. Code § 19-405 (28) (1997), now at Phila. Fair Practices Ord. §§ 9-1102 (q) & (r) (definitions), 9-1123 (verification), 9-1124 (termination), last visited July 13, 2022, https://berneylaw.com/wp-content/uploads/Berney-Law- The-Philadelphia-Fair-Practices-Ordinance.pdf.

30. Carly Karlberg, "Philadelphia's Life Partnership Ordinance: Broadening the Same-Sex Marriage Debate and Implications for Federalism," 11 *Rutgers J.L. & Religion* 508, 508–9 (2010). Of course, many unmarried couples, groups of friends, and family members make similar commitments.

31. Judith Scherr, "Berkeley, Activists Set Milestone for Domestic Partnerships in 1984," *East Bay Times*, June 28, 2013, https://www.eastbaytimes .com/2013/06/28/ berkeley-activists-set-milestone-for-domestic-partnerships-in-1984/.

32. West Hollywood, Calif., Ord. 22 (Feb. 21, 1985).

33. S.F., Calif., Ord. 176-89, § 4002 (a) (June 5, 1989) (repealed Nov. 7, 1989). See also NeJaime, "Before Marriage," 135–44, for an in-depth chronicle of the advocacy for and against domestic partnerships and of the measure's final approval.

34. See S.F., Calif., Mun. Code § 62.1 (1991).

35. See David L. Chambers, "Tales of Two Cities: AIDS and the Legal Recognition of Domestic Partnerships in San Francisco and New York," 2 *Law & Sexuality* 181, 191 (1992).

36. Calif. Fam. Code § 297 (Deering, 2021). See generally NeJaime, "Before Marriage," 87 (examining the development and history of domestic partnerships in California).

37. NeJaime, "Before Marriage," 136; Cynthia Gorney, "Making It Official: The Law Live-Ins," *Washington Post*, July 5, 1989, https://www.washingtonpost.com/archive/lifestyle/1989/07/05/making-it-official-the-law-live-ins/a11543fc-4a0d-4761-b4cb-032e5716cbab/ (discussing the Catholic Church's opposition since 1982).

38. 2004 Va. Acts 983 (2004): "A civil union, partnership contract or other arrangement between persons of the same sex purporting to bestow the privileges or obligations of marriage is prohibited. Any such civil union, partnership contract or other arrangement entered into by persons of the same sex in another state or jurisdiction shall be void in all respects in Virginia and any contractual rights created thereby shall be void and unenforceable."

39. Arizona Together v. Brewer, 149 P.3d 742 (Ariz. 2007) (holding that a proposition defining marriage and prohibiting the state and its political subdivisions from creating or recognizing a legal status for unmarried persons similar to that of marriage did not violate the Arizona constitution, which requires that a ballot initiative address only one concern).

40. In 1992, Levi Strauss offered health benefits to unmarried couples, becoming the first Fortune 500 company to do so. Amy Joyce, "Majority of Large Firms Offer Employees Domestic Partner Benefits," *Washington Post*, June 30, 2006, https://www.washingtonpost.com/wp-dyn/content/article/2006/06/29/AR2006062902049.html. By 1993, there were only 10 Fortune 500 companies offering domestic partner health benefits. In 2000 that number reached 124, and by 2006 it was 249. Samir Luther, "Domestic Partner Benefits Employer Trends and Benefits Equivalency for the GLBT Family" (Washington, DC: Human Rights Campaign Foundation, 2006). Since the achievement of marriage equality, though, that number has fluctuated and been difficult to determine, as corporations reexamine their commitment to domestic partner benefits.

41. In an earlier work, I discussed the recent history of legislative and judicial progress and pushback in the drive toward the legal recognition of same-sex couples in the areas of tort and contract, as well as marriage. John G. Culhane, "Marriage, Tort, and Private Ordering: Rhetoric and Reality in LGBT Rights," 84 *Chi.-Kent L. Rev.* 437 (2009).

42. Andrew Strickler, "BigLaw Belt Tightening Squeezes Domestic Partner Benefits," Law360, Dec. 8, 2016, https://www.law360.com/articles/869585/biglaw-belt-tightening-squeezes-domestic-partner-benefits.

43. Tara Siegel Bernard, "Fate of Domestic Partner Benefits in Question after Marriage Ruling," *N.Y. Times*, June 28, 2015, https://www.nytimes.com /2015/06/29/your-money/fate-of-domestic-partner-benefits-in-question-after -marriage-ruling.html.

44. Michael Dresser & Carrie Wells, "With Same-Sex Marriage Now Available, State to End Benefits for Domestic Partners," *Baltimore Sun*, May 3, 2013, http://articles.baltimoresun.com/2013–05–03/features/bs-md-domestic-benefits -20130502_1_domestic-partners-health-benefits-state-employees. The administration of Gov. Martin O'Malley explained that fairness required gay and lesbian employees who wanted to retain their benefits to marry, since domestic partnerships were not available to different-sex couples.

45. Laura Lorenzetti, "Looking to Stay on Your Partner's Insurance? It May Be Time to Get Married," *Fortune*, June 26, 2015, https://fortune.com/2015/06 /26/same-sex-benefits-marriage/.

46. Any number of historical accounts of the establishment and subsequent strengthening of statewide domestic partnerships in California are available, but that given by the California Supreme Court in In re Marriage Cases, 183 P.3d 384, 413–16 (Calif. 2008), is a good, compact place to start. The court clearly details how the domestic partnership law, first put into effect in 1999, began with "limited substantive benefits" and then gradually expanded until it conferred all the rights that were available to married couples under California state law. Id. at 413. As the court recognized, DOMA meant that there were no federal benefits available to same-sex couples, no matter what the state's domestic partnership law purported to do. Id. at 418. Proposition 8 vacated the court's decision in this case in 2008, but the historical account remains cogent.

47. The Arizona amendment was the second attempt to fence out same-sex marriages. An amendment introduced in 2006 would have prohibited other forms of same-sex relationship recognition as well. The statute provided, "The State of Arizona and its cities, towns, counties or districts shall not create or recognize a legal status for unmarried persons that is similar to marriage." It failed, garnering only 48 percent of the total vote. This was the first defeat anywhere in the United States for a statewide measure prohibiting same-sex unions. Kevin Vance, "Why Arizona Flipped on Gay Marriage," CBS News, Dec. 2, 2008, https://www.cbsnews.com/news/why-arizona-flipped-on-gay-marriage/.

48. City of Scottsdale, "Domestic Partner Coverage," last visited Mar. 9, 2022, https://www.scottsdaleaz.gov/hr/benefits/domestic-partner.

49. Sedona, Ariz., Ord. No. 2013-05 (2013). The Arizona situation is unusual for another reason: several of the localities use the term *civil union* rather than *domestic partnership* to describe the relationship. This is an odd lexical choice because *civil union* is otherwise universally used for the very specific purpose of describing a statewide legal status that conveys all of the rights and responsibilities of marriage but by a different name. (Civil unions are the subject of the next chapter.)

50. Greg Lucas, "Domestic Partners Bill Sent to Davis / Lawmakers Also OK Needle Exchange Law," SFGATE, Sept. 10, 1999, https://www.sfgate.com/politics /article/Domestic-Partners-Bill-Sent-to-Davis-Lawmakers-2909885.php.

51. Calif. Fam. Code § 297 (b)(4) (amended 2020). This difference in consequences between remarriage and domestic partnership was true at the time. When the California law later expanded to make domestic partnership more closely mirror marriage, though, this work-around to retain social security benefits became imperiled. See discussion in chapter 5.

52. In 2019, Governor Gavin Newsom signed into law the expansion of eligibility for domestic partnership status, which went into effect on January 1, 2020. CBS Sacramento, "Domestic Partnerships Are Not Just for Same-Sex Couples in California Anymore," July 30, 2019, https://sacramento.cbslocal.com/2019 /07/30/domestic-partnerships-are-not-just-for-same-sex-couple-in-california -anymore/.

53. Bernard, "Fate of Domestic Partner Benefits."

54. Id.

55. Nora Daly, "Single? So Are the Majority of U.S. Adults," PBS NewsHour, Sept. 11, 2014, https://www.pbs.org/newshour/nation/single-youre-not-alone. In early 2018, it was reported that about 45 percent of all adults were single in 2016. Francesca Friday, "More Americans Are Single Than Ever Before—and They're Healthier, Too," *Observer*, Jan. 16, 2018, https://observer.com/2018/01 /more-americans-are-single-than-ever-before-and-theyre-healthier-too/, citing US Census Bureau, "America's Families and Living Arrangements: 2016," revised Oct. 8, 2021, https://www.census.gov/data/tables/2016/demo/families /cps-2016.html.

56. It is unclear whether this "trick" will continue to work now that the Social Security Administration (SSA) has stated that it recognizes certain kinds of domestic partnerships, including California's, as marriages for purposes of benefits. As will be discussed in chapter 5, the SSA has been less clear about the effect of these relationships on different-sex couples than on same-sex couples. See Heidi L. Brady & Robin Fretwell Wilson, "The Precarious Status of Domestic Partnerships for the Elderly in a Post-*Obergefell* World," 24 *Elder L. J.* 49 (2016).

57. Clarkdale, Ariz., Town Code, Ch. 8, Business Regs., Article 8-6, Civil Unions (2013); Sedona, Ariz., Ord. No. 2013-05 (2013).

58. It's true that couples can already enter into agreements like these, so in a way these laws don't add much. But they can be expected to help in the arena where they're most likely to be contested: when disputes between partners end up in court. The track record of judicial enforcement is mixed, so collecting a set of otherwise diffuse agreements under one legal roof seems like a good idea to persuade an otherwise skeptical judge that contracts of this sort are to be taken seriously and enforced.

59. *Huffington Post,* "Florida Abandons Statewide Domestic Partnership Registry and LGBT Civil Protections," May 8, 2013, huffpost.com/entry /florida-domestic-registry-lgbt-rights_n_3237475.

CHAPTER 2. CIVIL UNIONS

Epigraphs. Stacy Jolles, quoted in David Goodman, "A More Civil Union," *Mother Jones,* July–Aug. 2000, https://www.motherjones.com/politics/2000/07 /more-civil-union/; Leah Whitesel, Skype interview, Oct. 10, 2011.

1. Bowers v. Hardwick, 478 U.S. 186 (1986). For an indispensable guide to the long history of antisodomy laws in both England and the United States, see William N. Eskridge Jr., *Dishonorable Passions: Sodomy Laws in America, 1861–2003* (Penguin, 2008).

2. 478 U.S. at 194.

3. Id. at 197 (Burger, C.J., concurring). See Steve Sanders, "Dignity and Social Meaning: *Obergefell, Windsor,* and *Lawrence* as Constitutional Dialogue," 87 *Fordham L. Rev.* 2069, 2096, n.219 (2019). For another possible explanation of Blackstone's phrase, see Kendall Thomas, "The Eclipse of Reason: A Rhetorical Reading of *Bowers v. Hardwick,*" 79 *Va. L. Rev.* 1805, 1822 (1993): "Unlike rape, sex between men represents an assault on the normative order of male heterosexuality—indeed, an abdication of masculine identity *as such*" (emphasis in original).

4. One notorious example of the pernicious effect of the court's holding came from Georgia, the very state whose law the court had upheld. Robin Shahar was a bright and talented young attorney who had an offer to work in the office of the state attorney general—ironically, as it would turn out, the same Michael Bowers who had defended the sodomy law. But Bowers withdrew the offer after Shahar expressed her intention to have a lesbian commitment ceremony with her partner. For him, this was enough to show her propensity to engage in illegal actions (certainly inappropriate for an enforcer of the law!). Shahar challenged this view, but a federal appeals court validated Bowers's crazy decision, citing *Bowers v. Hardwick.* Shahar v. Bowers, 114 F.3d 1097 (11th Cir. 1997) (en banc). See Linda Greenhouse, "Gay Rights Case Fails in Bid for Supreme Court Hearing," *N.Y. Times,* Jan. 13, 1998, https://www.nytimes.com/1998/01/13/us/gay-rights-case-fails-in-bid-for-supreme-court-hearing.html.

5. Andrew Sullivan, "Here Comes the Groom: A (Conservative) Case for Gay Marriage," *New Republic,* Aug. 28, 1989, https://newrepublic.com/article/79054 /here-comes-the-groom; Sullivan, *Virtually Normal: An Argument about Homosexuality* (Vintage, 1995).

6. The landmark attack on Sullivan came from Michael Warner. In *The Trouble with Normal: Sex, Politics, and the Ethics of Queer Life* (Free Press, 1999),

Warner inveighed against what he thought to be Sullivan's misplaced reverence for normalcy, which, for Warner, betrayed the deeper promises and potential of a progressive LGBTQ rights movement that should present a challenge to the dominant, patriarchal structure that underlies marriage.

7. See Sasha Issenberg, *The Engagement: America's Quarter-Century Struggle over Same-Sex Marriage* (Pantheon, 2021) for a comprehensive legal and political history of the marriage equality movement.

8. Evan Wolfson, probably the central figure in the decades-long judicial struggle toward marriage equality, stepped in as Foley's co-counsel on the appeal. His account of *Baehr v. Lewin*, the case that led to the developments described in the text, is given in lapidary detail in Wolfson, *Why Marriage Matters*, 28–32 (Simon and Schuster, 2004).

9. Baehr v. Lewin, 852 P.2d 44, 67 (Haw. 1993) (the law fencing gay and lesbian couples out of marriage "is presumed to be unconstitutional . . . unless . . . the State of Hawaii can show that [a] the statute's sex-based classification is justified by compelling state interests and [b] the statute is narrowly drawn to avoid unnecessary abridgements of the applicant couples' constitutional rights").

10. Id. at 68. The case, later renamed Baehr v. Miike, 1999 Haw. LEXIS 391 (Dec. 9, 1999), was ultimately and summarily remanded for entry of judgment in favor of Miike (the state official who had succeeded Lewin) and against the plaintiffs. There was no arguing with the state's newly amended constitution. The developments in Hawaii garnered the most attention, but another case from the same period served as a reminder that the marriage equality movement continued to simmer. Although its plaintiffs also lost, one judge on the federal appellate court that ruled against them signaled an emerging willingness to take marriage claims seriously. Dean v. District of Columbia, 653 A.2d 307, 309 (D.C. 1995) (Ferren, J., concurring in part and dissenting in part: "A trial is required to determine whether same-sex couples comprise a 'suspect' or a 'quasi-suspect' class entitled either to 'strict' or to 'intermediate' scrutiny of governmental discrimination against them").

11. 110 Stat. 2419 (1996) (section 3 of which has since been declared unconstitutional). See also Richard Socarides, "Why Bill Clinton Signed the Defense of Marriage Act," *New Yorker*, Mar. 8, 2013, https://www.newyorker.com/news/news-desk/why-bill-clinton-signed-the-defense-of-marriage-act; Michelle Ye Hee Lee, "Fact Checker: Hillary Clinton's Claim That DOMA Had to Be Enacted to Stop an Anti-Gay Marriage Amendment to the U.S. Constitution," *Washington Post*, Oct. 28, 2015, https://www.washingtonpost.com/news/fact-checker/wp/2015/10/28/hillary-clintons-claim-that-doma-had-to-be-enacted-to-stop-an-anti-gay-marriage-amendment-to-the-u-s-constitution/.

12. The provision in 28 U.S.C. § 1738 (c) (1996) was added by DOMA, § 2.

13. DOMA, § 3 amended the Dictionary Act, 1 U.S.C. §7 (2021), to provide the following definitions of *marriage* and *spouse*: "In determining the meaning

of any Act of Congress, or of any ruling, regulation, or interpretation of the various administrative bureaus and agencies of the United States, the word 'marriage' means only a legal union between one man and one woman as husband and wife, and the word 'spouse' refers only to a person of the opposite sex who is a husband or a wife."

14. Mike Maciag, "State Same Sex Marriage State Laws Map," Governing, Mar. 25, 2013, http://www.governing.com/archive/same-sex-marriage-civil -unions-doma-laws-by-state.html.

15. Andrew Koppelman, "Interstate Recognition of Same-Sex Marriages and Civil Unions: A Handbook for Judges," 153 *U. Pa. L. Rev.* 2143, 2165 (2005) (the appendix has a collection of the laws); Barbara J. Cox, "Same-Sex Marriage and the Public Policy Exception in Choice-of-Law: Does It Really Exist?," 16 *Quinnipiac L. Rev.* 61 (1996) (discussing the public policy exception).

16. The best example of the nonrecognition of interracial marriages comes from a lower court decision in the *Loving* case itself. In Loving v. Virginia, 388 U.S. 1, 3 (1967), the Supreme Court quoted the trial judge's statement that "Almighty God created the races white, black, yellow, malay and red, and he placed them on separate continents. And but for the interference with his arrangement there would be no cause for such marriages. The fact that he separated the races shows that he did not intend for the races to mix." The trial judge had refused to recognize the interracial couple's marriage, which had been celebrated in the District of Columbia, and had upheld the Virginia statute criminalizing such actions by its residents.

17. See, e.g., Ghassemi v. Ghassemi, 998 So.2d 731, 749–50 (La. Ct. App. 2008) ("Although Louisiana law expressly prohibits the marriages of first cousins, such marriages are not so 'odious' as to violate a strong public policy of this state. Accordingly, a marriage between first cousins, if valid in the state or country where it was contracted, will be recognized as valid"); In re Estate of Loughmiller, 629 P.2d 156, 161 (Kans. 1981) ("Although our statutes prohibit first cousin marriages and impose criminal penalties where such marriages are contracted in Kansas, we cannot find that a first cousin marriage validly contracted elsewhere is odious to the public policy of this state").

18. Haw. Const. Art. I, § 23 ("The legislature shall have the power to reserve marriage to opposite-sex couples").

19. CNN, "Hawaii Gives Legislature Power to Ban Same-Sex Marriage," Nov. 3, 1998, http://edition.cnn.com/ALLPOLITICS/stories/1998/11/04/same.sex .ballot/.

20. Alaska Const. Art. I, § 25 ("To be valid or recognized in this State, a marriage may exist only between one man and one woman"); Brause v. Bureau of Vital Statistics, 1998 WL 88743, at 6* (Alaska Super. Ct. 1998).

21. Noah, who was born with a heart defect, died in 1997 at age two—just one month after the lawsuit was filed. This tragedy only stiffened the spines of Beck and Jolles, who felt that he was with them throughout the whole legal ordeal.

22. 15A Vt. Stat. Ann. § 1-102 (2022) (current statute).

23. Baker v. State, 744 A.2d 864 (Vt. 1999). The other couples were Stan Baker and Peter Harrigan, and Holly Puterbaugh and Lois Farnham.

24. Indeed, throughout its *Baker* decision, the Vermont Supreme Court cited many of the laws and rulings that had favored same-sex couples and their children and had extended civil rights protections to the LGBTQ community.

25. MacCallum v. Seymour, 686 A.2d 935 (Vt. 1996).

26. For a good summary of activism in Vermont leading up to the lawsuit, see Greg Johnson, "Vermont Civil Unions: The New Language of Marriage," 25 *Vt. L. Rev.* 15, 24–33 (2000).

27. 744 A.2d at 867 (quoting unpublished trial court opinion).

28. Oral argument in *Baker v. State* (audiotape, Nov. 18, 1998), quoted in Michael Mello, *Legalizing Gay Marriage*, 34 (Temple University Press, 2004).

29. Carey Goldberg, "Vermont High Court Backs Rights of Same-Sex Couples," *N.Y. Times*, Dec. 20, 1999, A1.

30. Vt. Const. Art. VII, ch. 1.

31. 744 A.2d at 886.

32. Id. at 888. He was responding to this statement: "The majority elects to send plaintiffs to an uncertain fate in the political cauldron." Id. at 898 (Johnson, J., dissenting).

33. Perhaps the court was also affected by the very term the Vermont Constitution uses to guarantee equality: "common benefits." The majority of the court appears to have taken the phrase literally, requiring the legislature to equalize the benefits, under whatever name it chose.

34. See Mello, *Legalizing Gay Marriage*; David Moats, *Civil Wars: A Battle for Gay Marriage* (Harcourt, 2004). These two excellent, comprehensive books cover the same general territory from two slightly different perspectives. Mello is a law professor, and he delves deeply into the complex legal issues but anchors them in the real-life stories of the many couples affected by the Vermont civil union battle. Moats is a Pulitzer Prize–winning journalist who covered the legislative and public debate for the *Rutland Herald*. For a comprehensive scholarly treatment of the subject, there is no better place to start than the symposium "Vermont Civil Unions," which ran as the *Vermont Law Review*'s first issue of 2000. That issue also contains the *Baker* ruling and the text of the civil union statute enacted in response.

35. The statement appeared in the *Rutland Herald*, of which Moats was the editorial page editor, and is reported in his *Civil Wars*, 161.

36. Beck, quoted in Moats, *Civil Wars*, 227.

37. Id., 162.

38. Donna Lescoe, quoted in id., 174.

39. This account draws on William N. Eskridge Jr., *Equality Practice: Civil Unions and the Future of Gay Rights*, 62 (Routledge, 2002).

40. Washington's and Nevada's domestic partnership laws, for instance, were really civil union laws by another name, conferring all the rights, benefits, and obligations of marriage. Wash. Stat. 26.60.015 (2022) ("Any privilege, immunity, right or benefit granted by statute, administrative or court rule, policy, common law or any other law to an individual because the individual is or was married, or because the individual is or was an in-law in a specified way to another individual, is granted on equivalent terms, substantive and procedural, to an individual because the individual is or was in a domestic partnership or because the individual is or was, based on a domestic partnership, related in a specified way to another individual"); Nev. Rev. Stat. § 122A.200 (2021). Oregon's statute, by contrast, provides a more limited set of benefits. Or. Rev. Stat. § 106.340 (1) (2022) (listing benefits). This is still a good law, as are the laws in Nevada and Washington.

41. See, e.g., 2005 Conn. Pub. Acts No. 05-10; 13 Del. C. § 212 (2012); N.J. Stat. Ann. § 37:1-31 (West 2021). All but New Jersey's civil union law have since been repealed.

42. The Massachusetts Supreme Judicial Court seems to have had the *civil* modifier in mind when it became the first state high court to take the final step of declaring that same-sex couples were entitled to marriage licenses. In Goodridge v. Department of Public Health, 798 N.E.2d 941 (Mass. 2003), the court referred consistently to "civil marriage" as the institution to which the plaintiffs sought entry. *Goodridge* was an important step on the trail leading to nationwide marriage equality. The decision benefited from the Supreme Court's decision in Lawrence v. Texas, 539 U.S. 558 (2003), a few months earlier, overruling *Bowers v. Hardwick* and committing the Supreme Court to "respect" for the lives of gay and lesbian people. The Massachusetts Supreme Court adverted to *Bowers* on this point: "The State's action [in denying marriage equality to same-sex couples] confers an official stamp of approval on the destructive stereotype that same-sex relationships are inherently unstable and inferior to opposite-sex relationships and are not worthy of respect." 798 N.E.2d at 962.

43. See, e.g., United States v. Windsor, 570 U.S. 744, 766 (2013) ("State laws defining and regulating marriage, of course, must respect the constitutional rights of persons . . . but, subject to those guarantees, 'regulation of domestic relations' is 'an area that has long been regarded as a virtually exclusive province of the States,'" quoting Sosna v. Iowa, 419 U.S. 393, 404 [1975]).

44. Vermont had moved to full marriage equality by then, establishing that right legislatively in 2009.

45. Garden State Equality v. Dow, 79 A.2d 1036, 1043 (N.J. 2013) ("The state's statutory scheme effectively denies committed same-sex partners in New Jersey the ability to receive federal benefits now afforded to married couples"); Salvador Rizzo, "Christie Withdraws Appeal of Gay Marriage Ruling," NJ.com, Oct. 21, 2013, https://www.nj.com/politics/2013/10/christie_withdraws_appeal_of_gay_marriage_ruling.html.

46. 15 Vt. Stat. Ann. § 1204 (enacted 2000).

47. 15 Vt. Stat. Ann. § 1201 (enacted 2000).

48. 744 A.2d at 901: "Absent 'compelling' reasons that dictate otherwise, it is not only the prerogative but the duty of courts to provide prompt relief for violations of individual civil rights" (Johnson, J., dissenting).

49. The Massachusetts Supreme Judicial Court stressed this disparity in 2004, responding with a big, fat no to the state attorney general's question of whether a civil union law could meet the equality mandate in *Goodridge*. Opinion of the Justices to the Senate, 802 N.E.2d 565 (Mass. 2004). Judges on both sides tried to enlist Shakespeare to their ranks, but only the majority seemed to recall that *Romeo and Juliet* was a tragedy. The dissenters thought that a civil union would do, because, after all, "what's in a name? That which we call a rose / by any other name would smell as sweet." But as those familiar with the play well know, the last names Montague and Capulet did mean something: the enmity between the two families led to the tragic deaths of both protagonists. As the majority stated, "The bill's absolute prohibition of the use of the word 'marriage' by 'spouses' who are the same sex is more than semantic. The dissimilitude between the terms 'civil marriage' and 'civil union' is not innocuous; it is a considered choice of language that reflects a demonstrable assigning of same-sex, largely homosexual, couples to second-class status. . . . The bill would have the effect of maintaining and fostering a stigma of exclusion that the Constitution prohibits." Id. at 1207–8.

50. The law had such wide legislative support that it was enacted over the veto of the state's governor, Jim Douglas. David Abel, "Vermont Legalizes Same-Sex Marriage," *Boston Globe*, Apr. 8, 2009, http://archive.boston.com/news/local /massachusetts/articles/2009/04/08/vermont_legalizes_same_sex_marriage/.

51. Vermont Office of Legislative Council, Vermont Commission on Family Recognition and Protection, "Report of the Vermont Commission on Family Recognition and Protection," Apr. 21, 2008, http://www.leg.state.vt.us /WorkGroups/FamilyCommission/VCFRP_Report.pdf, 10.

52. Id., 29.

53. Langan v. St. Vincent's Hospital, 802 N.Y.S.2d 476 (App. Div. 2005).

54. William N. Eskridge Jr., *Gaylaw: Challenging the Apartheid of the Closet*, 320 (Harvard University Press, 1999).

55. 539 U.S. 558 (2003). *Lawrence v. Texas* was a milestone decision not only because of its holding that states could not criminalize private consensual sexual relations between adults but also because of the language Justice Anthony Kennedy employed throughout the opinion. For example: "Adults may choose to enter upon this relationship in the confines of their homes and their own private lives and still retain their dignity as free persons. When sexuality finds overt expression in intimate conduct with another person, the conduct can be but one element in a personal bond that is more enduring. The liberty protected

by the Constitution allows homosexual persons the right to make this choice." Id. at 567.

56. 798 N.E.2d at 948.

57. 2005 Conn. Pub. Acts No. 05-10; N.J. Stat. Ann. § 37:1-31 (West 2007); N.H. Rev. Stat. Ann. § 457:1-A (2007); 13 Del. C. § 212 (2012); R.I. Gen. Stat. Ann. § 15-3.1-12 (2011). New Jersey is the one state where the legislature acted in response to a decision by the state's supreme court. In Lewis v. Harris, 908 A.2d 196 (N.J. 2006), the New Jersey Supreme Court unanimously held that same-sex couples were entitled to the benefits of marriage, but a bare majority of the justices followed the lead of the Vermont Supreme Court and decided that the remedy was up to the legislature. Not surprisingly, the New Jersey lawmakers took the same path as their kin to the north and enacted a civil union law.

58. 13 Del. C. § 129 (2021); Doug Denison, "Delaware Becomes 11th State with Gay Marriage," *USA Today,* May 7, 2013, https://www.usatoday.com/story /news/nation/2013/05/07/delaware-gay-marriage/2142703/.

59. Nev. Const. Art. 1, § 21; Nev. Rev. Stat. § 122A.200 (2021).

60. John Kennedy's views and statements are drawn from an event I moderated in Chicago on Apr. 10, 2012, on civil unions in Illinois, hosted by the American Constitution Center for Law and Society. He was a panelist.

61. Tom Gibson (pseud.), telephone conversation, Feb. 3, 2013.

62. Office of Cook County Clerk David Orr, "Opposite-Sex Civil Unions: Motives for Not Marrying" (on file with the author), Nov. 28, 2011, 1, n.2.

63. Id., 1.

64. Id., 3.

65. Id., 6 (35 yes, 11 no).

66. Id.

67. Id., 1.

68. Id., 2, n.6.

69. Id., 2, table 1.

70. Quotations and narrative from Leah Whitesel and Justin Gates are drawn from a Skype interview on Oct. 10, 2011.

71. Quotes and discussion from Jennifer Tweeton and Alex Rifman are drawn from a Skype interview on Oct. 18, 2011.

72. Quotations and narrative from Emil Roe and Margaret Koe are drawn from a Skype interview on Oct. 25, 2011.

73. Vermont Judiciary, "Civil Union and Dissolution," last visited July 22, 2022, https://vermontjudiciary.org/family/divorce/civil-union-and-dissolution.

74. See, e.g., Conn. Gen. Stat. Ann. § 46b-38rr (2021); 13 Del. C. § 218 (2021).

75. Varnum v. Brien, 763 N.W.2d 862 (Iowa 2009).

76. In two appendices (A & B) to its decision, the Supreme Court in Obergefell v. Hodges, 576 U.S. 644, 681–686 (2015), provided a compendium of state laws and judicial rulings on marriage equality current to that date.

77. Martine Powers, "Maine Votes to Legalize Same-Sex Marriage," Boston .com, Nov. 6, 2012, https://www.boston.com/uncategorized/noprimarytagmatch /2012/11/06/maine-votes-to-legalize-same-sex-marriage; 576 U.S. at 693 (Roberts, C.J., dissenting: "In 2012, voters in Maine . . . revers[ed] the result of a referendum just three years earlier in which they had upheld the traditional definition of marriage").

78. See introduction, including Ginsburg's quote in n. 14.

79. Rev. Rul. 2013-17, 2013-2 C.B. 201.

80. Garden State Equality v. Dow, 82 A.3d 336 (N.J. Super. Ct. Law Div. 2013).

81. Id. at 359, 367.

82. Office of Cook County Clerk David Orr, "Report," appendix, p. 2. The weird duality the civil union creates is somewhat like the problems with common-law marriage, a status so hard to determine that a Pennsylvania court once memorably referred to it as a "legal raincoat" that couples could put on or take off as the (legal) weather changed. PNC Bank Corp. v. Workers' Compensation Appeal Board (Stamos), 831 A.2d 1269, 1281 (Pa. Commonwealth Ct. 2003). That's because common-law marriages are not publicly documented, and their existence is demonstrated by meeting requirements that are hard to pin down. (Generally, the couple has to have the "intent" to marry and must "hold themselves out" to the community as spouses, to name the two slipperiest requirements.) See Sarah Primrose, "The Decline of Common Law Marriage & the Unrecognized Cultural Effect," 34 *Whittier L. Rev.* 187, 202–5 (2013).

83. Social Security Administration, "GN 00210.004: Same-Sex Relationships—Non-marital Legal Relationships," Feb. 10, 2016, https://secure.ssa.gov /poms.nsf/lnx/0200210004. See also chapter 5.

84. Lisa Goodman, telephone conversation, Mar. 4, 2014.

85. For a description of this batty process, see Carrie Stone & John G. Culhane, *Same-Sex Legal Kit for Dummies*, 134–35 (John Wiley & Sons, 2013).

86. JustLanded, "Marriage & Divorce in France: Procedures, Statistics and Tips," last visited July 5, 2022, https://www.justlanded.com/english/France /Articles/Visas-Permits/Marriage-Divorce-in-France.

87. Sheila Blackburn, email, June 7, 2016.

88. E.g., Commonwealth of Virginia, "Application for Marriage License," last visited July 25, 2022, https://media.alexandriava.gov/docs-archives/clerkofcourt /webappfillable.pdf; Vermont Department of Health, "Application for Vermont License of Civil Marriage," last visited July 25, 2022, https://www.healthvermont .gov/sites/default/files/documents/pdf/HS_VR_App_CivilMarriage.pdf.

89. Ryan Wilson, "Kentucky Legislative Session Comes to a Close; Fails to Pass Anti-LGBT Legislation," Human Rights Campaign, Apr. 19, 2016.

90. I wrote about this carnival of events at the time: John G. Culhane, "Kim Davis Is No Rosa Parks," *Politico*, Sept. 8, 2015, https://www.politico.com

/magazine/story/2015/09/kim-davis-is-no-rosa-parks-213127/. The issue was resolved by the expedient of removing the clerk's name from all wedding licenses. Tal Kopan, "Kentucky Governor Removes Clerk Names from Marriage Licenses," CNN, Dec. 23, 2015, https://edition.cnn.com/2015/12/23/politics/kentucky-marriage-licenses-matt-bevin-kim-davis/index.html.

91. See, e.g., 798 N.E.2d at 948: "The question before us is whether, consistent with the Massachusetts Constitution, the Commonwealth may deny the protections, benefits, and obligations conferred by civil marriage to two individuals of the same sex who wish to marry"; "[The Commonwealth] has failed to identify any constitutionally adequate reason for denying civil marriage to same-sex couples."

92. State of New Jersey Department of Health, "Civil Union Licenses," reviewed Sept. 18, 2017, https://www.nj.gov/health/vital/registration-vital/civil-union-licenses/.

93. Sheila Blackburn, telephone conversation, June 8, 2016.

94. Kaiponanea T. Matsumura, "A Right Not to Marry," 84 *Fordham L. Rev.* 1509 (2016).

95. Id., 1531.

96. Herman Melville, "Bartleby," in *The Piazza Tales*, 31 (Dix & Edwards, 1856).

97. Lisa Goodman, telephone conversation, Mar. 4, 2014.

CHAPTER 3. THE DESIGNATED BENEFICIARY AGREEMENT ACT

1. All statements from Colorado State Senator Pat Steadman are drawn from a telephone conversation on July 25, 2014.

2. Colo. Rev. Stat. § 15-22-105 (3)(c) (West 2022) (beneficiary of retirement systems, pensions, and health and life insurance), (3)(e) (hospital visitation), (3)(f) (medical decisions), (3)(h) (anatomical gifts), (3)(l) (direct the disposition of the other's remains), (3)(a)(hold property jointly), (3)(i) (inherit property through intestate succession), (3)(k) (sue for wrongful death on behalf of other beneficiary), (3)(c)(IV) (workers' compensation); § 15-22-107 (the document is filed with the county clerk's office).

3. Colo. Rev. Stat. § 15-22-104 (1)(a)(I).

4. At the time of the law's enactment, civil unions were not available in Colorado. But now that they are, the disqualification extends to both civil unions and marriages. Colo. Rev. Stat. § 15-22-104 (1)(a)(III), (1)(a)(III.5).

5. Colo. Rev. Stat. § 15-22-104. The law was in fact created largely as a way of affording some rights and responsibilities to Colorado residents in same-sex relationships.

6. Colo. Rev. Stat., Const. Art. 2, § 3b. The amendment was declared unconstitutional in Romer v. Evans, 517 U.S. 620 (1996).

7. The amendment read as follows: "No Protected Status Based on Homosexual, Lesbian or Bisexual Orientation. Neither the State of Colorado, through any of its branches or departments, nor any of its agencies, political subdivisions, municipalities or school districts, shall enact, adopt or enforce any statute, regulation, ordinance or policy whereby homosexual, lesbian or bisexual orientation, conduct, practices or relationships shall constitute or otherwise be the basis of or entitle any person or class of persons to have or claim any minority status, quota preferences, protected status or claim of discrimination. This Section of the Constitution shall be in all respects self-executing." Colo. Rev. Stat., Const. Art. 2, § 3b.

8. See 517 U.S. at 623–624.

9. Id. at 620. The *Romer* court found that Amendment 2 violated the constitutional guarantee of equal protection under the law. Although declining to hold that legal distinctions based on sexual orientation should be regarded with the same suspicion as laws discriminating on the basis of such characteristics as race or gender, it developed the point that laws based on animus toward a particular group violate the very notion of equality. So once the court decided that the law was mostly an antigay measure, it was doomed. *Romer* was the first case to apply the "animus principle" to LGBTQ rights, but the court had used that approach earlier, most notably in Department of Agriculture v. Moreno, 413 U.S. 538 (1973), where it wrote that "a bare congressional desire to harm a politically unpopular group" offends principles of equality. Id. at 534. (In that case, the group targeted was "hippies." Really.) This approach turned out to be of great importance in *United States v. Windsor*, because Justice Kennedy (again writing for the court, as he did in all of the major gay rights cases) found that DOMA was the product of antigay animus. That determination was fatal to the law. I have traced the lineage of the gay rights cases and their fusion of equal protection and liberty (or "due process") doctrine in John G. Culhane, "Ball of Con(stitutional) Fusion: The Supreme Court's Evolving Gay Rights Jurisprudence," in *Controversies in Equal Protection Cases in America: Race, Gender and Sexual Orientation* 183(Anne Richardson Oakes ed., Ashgate, 2015).

10. *Loving v. Virginia*, 388 U.S. 1 (1967). I discussed the progressively more restrictive antimiscegenation laws in John G. Culhane, "Uprooting the Arguments against Same-Sex Marriage," 20 *Cardozo L. Rev.* 1119, 1165–69 (1999).

11. Kevin Simpson, "Colorado Amendment 43: Gay Marriage Banned; Domestic Partnerships Also Defeated," *Denver Post*, Nov. 8, 2006, https://www.denverpost.com/2006/11/08/colorado-amendment-43-gay-marriage-banned-domestic-partnerships-also-defeated/.

12. "Upon the issuance of a certificate of reciprocal beneficiary relationship, the parties named in the certificate shall be entitled to those rights and obligations provided by the law to reciprocal beneficiaries. Unless otherwise expressly

provided by law, reciprocal beneficiaries shall not have the same rights and obligations under the law that are conferred through marriage under chapter 572." Haw. Rev. Stat. Ann. § 572C-6 (2012). For a summary of the rights conferred, see National Center for Lesbian Rights, "Marriage, Domestic Partnerships, and Civil Unions: Same-Sex Couples within the United States" (2020), https://www.nclrights.org/wp-content/uploads/2015/07/Relationship-Recognition.pdf.

13. Haw. Rev. Stat. Ann. § 572C-4 (3) (2022).

14. 15 Vt. Stat. Ann. §§ 1301–1306 (West 2017) (repealed).

15. 2013 Vt. Legis. Serv. 164 (LexisNexis) ("Since enactment in 2000, no reciprocal beneficiary relationship has been established in Vermont").

16. Claire Trageser, "Designated Beneficiary Rules Grant Unmarried Pairs Decision-Making Power," *Denver Post*, June 30, 2009, https://www.denverpost.com/2009/06/30/designated-beneficiary-rules-grant-unmarried-pairs-decision-making-power/.

17. Colo. Rev. Stat. § 15-22-102 (d).

18. In chapter 5, I discuss prenuptial agreements in greater depth.

19. All statements from Patricia Yarrow and Liz Gettings are drawn from a Skype interview on July 14, 2014.

20. The federal Family and Medical Leave Act, which allows employees to take time off from work to care for sick relatives, does not regard unmarried couples as relatives. 29 U.S.C. § 2611 (West 2018). This remains a disqualification even today (including for couples in "virtual marriage" relationships such as civil unions), but marriage equality has at least eliminated the problem for those same-sex couples who do choose to wed. The U.S. Department of Labor confirms these conclusions: "Frequently Asked Questions: FMLA Final Rule," question 15, last visited July 26, 2022, https://www.dol.gov/agencies/whd/fmla/spouse/faq#15.

21. Colo. Rev. Stat. § 15-22-105.

22. Colo. Rev. Stat. § 14-15-107 (5)(i) (West 2022). Generally, the civil union confers all the benefits of marriage, while the DBA is more limited—and especially stingy when it comes to benefits that the state has to pay for.

23. Griego v. Oliver, 316 P.3d 865, 872 (N.M. 2013) ("We hold that the State of New Mexico is constitutionally required to allow same-gender couples to marry and must extend to them the rights, protections, and responsibilities that derive from civil marriage under New Mexico law").

24. Jessica R. Feinberg, "Gradual Marriage," 20 *Lewis & Clark L. Rev.* 1 (2016).

25. All statements from Marilyn McCord are drawn from a telephone conversation on July 24, 2014.

26. The Social Security Administration's 2016 guidance, had it been in effect at the time when the couple entered into their DBA, might have caused them to hesitate before granting each other rights of intestate succession. It states that

those in DBAs will be treated as married unless they opt out of the intestate succession provision. Social Security Administration, "GN 00210.004: Same-Sex Relationships—Non-marital Legal Relationships," Feb. 10, 2016, https://secure .ssa.gov/poms.nsf/lnx/0200210004. As discussed in chapter 5, though, it is unclear whether this applies to different-sex couples.

27. Any legal document, whenever executed, that conflicts with a DBA is considered "superseding" and nullifies the DBA to the extent of the conflict: "'Superseding legal document' means a legal document, regardless of the date of execution, that is valid and enforceable and conflicts with all or a portion of a designated beneficiary agreement and, therefore, causes the designated beneficiary agreement in whole or in part to be replaced or set aside. To the extent there is a conflict between a superseding legal document and a designated beneficiary agreement, the superseding legal document controls." Colo. Rev. Stat. § 15-22-103 (3).

28. All of the data on civil unions and DBAs were gleaned from Denver's Office of the Clerk and Recorder, Denver Clerk & Recorder Online Services, last visited July 27, 2022, https://countyfusion3.kofiletech.us/countyweb /loginDisplay.action?countyname=Denver. Because these records are maintained at the county level, it was not possible to obtain statewide statistics. Denver was chosen for illustrative purposes, inasmuch as it is the most populous county. In another large county, Boulder, I counted 122 total DBAs from 2009 to 2017: 97 were (probably) entered into by same-sex couples and 21 by opposite-sex couples; 4 were impossible to determine. For civil unions, the Boulder numbers from 2013–17 were 213 for same-sex couples, with the vast majority (179) taking place in 2013, when the status became available, and 32 for opposite-sex couples, with steady but low numbers (between 4 and 9) every year. Boulder County Office of the Clerk & Recorder, Boulder County Recording Division Online Services, last visited July 27, 2022, https://recorder.bouldercounty.org /countyweb/loginDisplay.action?countyname=Boulder.

CHAPTER 4. WHAT IS MARRIAGE, ANYWAY?

1. May Doe and April Doe (pseuds.), live interview, April 3, 2014. The sisters' account is substantially excerpted and analyzed throughout this chapter.

2. For a brisk summary of how these two types of taxes differ, see Mark R. Siegel, "Who Should Bear the Bite of Estate Taxes on Non-probate Property?," 43 *Creighton L. Rev.* 747 (2010).

3. 26 U.S.C. § 2056 (2022) governs the federal estate tax, while 72 Pa. Cons. Stat. § 9116 (2021) sets forth the inheritance tax rates for all categories of legally recognized relationships in Pennsylvania.

4. That amount, adjusted for inflation, will remain in effect until Jan. 1, 2026. 26 U.S.C. § 2010 (c)(3)(C) (2022).

5. Judge Richard Posner cited this Indiana law in Baskin v. Bogan, 766 F.3d 648, 662 (7th Cir. 2014) to emphasize the inconsistency of the state's argument against allowing same-sex couples to marry: "How to explain Indiana's decision to carve an exception to its prohibition against marriage of close relatives for first cousins 65 or older—a population guaranteed to be infertile because women can't conceive at that age? Ind. Code § 31-11-1-2. If the state's only interest in allowing marriage is to protect children, why has it gone out of its way to permit marriage of first cousins *only after* they are provably infertile? The state must think marriage valuable for something other than just procreation—that even non-procreative couples benefit from marriage."

6. Courtney Megan Cahill, "Same-Sex Marriage, Slippery Slope Rhetoric, and the Politics of Disgust: A Critical Perspective on Contemporary Family Discourse and the Incest Taboo," 99 *Nw. L. Rev.* 1543, 1570 (2005).

7. Smith v. State, 6 S.W.3d 512, 518 (Tenn. Ct. Crim. App. 1999).

8. The statements in this section are the result of separate interviews of Terry McKeon (Skype, July 31, 2014) and Anne Quinn (telephone, June 10, 2016).

9. DNA Diagnostics Center, "Introduction to DNA Testing History," last visited July 29, 2022, https://dnacenter.com/history-dna-testing/.

10. For an analytical, historical account of this presumption, see Jane C. Murphy, "Legal Images of Fatherhood: Welfare Reform, Child Support Enforcement, and Fatherless Children," 81 *Notre Dame L. Rev.* 325 (2005). The power of this presumption has waned somewhat in recent years, as some courts have moved toward a more expansive analysis of who should count as parents. See, e.g., K.E.M. v. P.C.S., 38 A.3d 798, 806–807 (Pa. 2012) ("As to the presumption of paternity, we note only that recent Pennsylvania decisions have relegated it to a substantially more limited role, by narrowing its application to situations in which the underlying policy of supporting the best interest of the child will be advanced").

11. The law regarding stepparents is in a state of flux as courts and legislatures struggle to update policy to conform to the increasing complexity of family structures. For a good summary of the law as it had evolved up to the mid-aughts, see Margaret M. Mahoney, "Stepparents as Third Parties in Relation to their Stepchildren," 40 *Fam. L. Q.* 81 (2006). Since then, the law has looked to the functionality and strength of adult-child relationships to determine whether a person qualifies as a "parent." A dramatic example is Brooke S.B. v. Elizabeth A.C.C., 61 N.E.3d 488 (N.Y. 2016), where the New York Court of Appeals allowed adults who had been involved in same-sex relationships standing to petition for custody and visitation of the children they had agreed to raise together, even though the parties seeking these orders were neither the biological nor the adoptive parents. In so doing, the court overruled Alison D. v. Virginia M., 572 N.E.2d 27 (N.Y. 1991), which had rejected a similar request.

12. Calif. Fam. Code § 7601 (2021), which went into effect on Jan. 1, 2014. California's law also provides guidance about how custody and visitation are to

be decided: "In cases where a child has more than two parents, the court shall allocate custody and visitation among the parents based on the best interest of the child, including, but not limited to, addressing the child's need for continuity and stability by preserving established patterns of care and emotional bonds. The court may order that not all parents share legal or physical custody of the child if the court finds that it would not be in the best interest of the child." Calif. Fam. Code § 3040 (2021).

13. See Jacob v. Shultz-Jacob, 923 A.2d 473 (Pa. Super. Ct. 2007). In this case, the court held that two women who had been in a romantic relationship and contributed to raising children together and the man who had been the sperm donor for one of the children all had a stake in that child's well-being. It thus remanded the case to the lower court to determine how best to allocate support and visitation obligations and rights among all three. Id. at 482.

14. A couple of years before the California law was passed (see n. 12), I argued (with a coauthor) against such a measure, in part because of concerns about how decision-making would be allocated among multiple parents. Elizabeth Marquardt & John Culhane, "California Should Not Pass 'Multiple Parents' Bill," *Huffington Post*, Aug. 17, 2012, https://www.huffingtonpost.com/entry/multiple -parents-bill_b_1791709.html. Since then, I have come to the position that it's better to manage those issues than to deprive a child of an adult whose legal status as a parent is protected, where that relationship is best for the child's well-being. But it remains true that the three- (or more) parent model can give rise to additional problems in custody, support, and decision-making.

15. All statements from John Hunter and Hal Kooden are drawn from a Skype interview on Aug. 3, 2011.

16. This was Edie Windsor and Thea Spyer's situation: their marriage was recognized in New York but had taken place in a different jurisdiction (in their case Canada). United States v. Windsor, 570 U.S. 744, 753 (2013).

17. The history of members of the LGBTQ community in the military is complex. President Bill Clinton's effort in the 1990s to lift the ban on gay service members backfired, leading to the disastrous "Don't Ask, Don't Tell" policy, which permitted them to continue in the military as long as they were willing to shut up about their sexuality. For a good discussion of the history and this policy to the start of the Obama administration, see Nathaniel Frank, *Unfriendly Fire: How the Gay Ban Undermines the Military and Weakens America* (Thomas Dunne Books, 2009). The Don't Ask, Don't Tell Repeal Act of 2010, Pub. L. No. 111-321, set out a process for reviewing the ban with an eye toward ending it, which happened the following year. After that, gays could serve openly in the military. Elizabeth Bumiller, "Obama Ends 'Don't Ask, Don't Tell' Policy," *N.Y. Times*, July 22, 2011, https://www.nytimes.com/2011/07/23/us/23military.html. Since then, attention has shifted to whether transgender men and women should be allowed to join the military. The Trump administration put a ban on their service, but the

Biden administration repealed it shortly after taking office. As of April 30, 2021, members of the trans community can serve openly. Ellie Kaufman & Barbara Starr, "Pentagon Announces New Policies to Abolish Trump Administration's Transgender Military Ban," CNN, March 31, 2021, https://edition.cnn .com/2021/03/31/politics/transgender-military-ban-policies/index.html.

18. Calif. Const. Art. 1, § 7.5. In Strauss v. Horton, 207 P.3d 48 (Calif. 2009), the California Supreme Court, in upholding Proposition 8 against a challenge to its constitutionality, drew attention to the fact that full domestic partnership benefits were still available to same-sex couples under existing California law.

19. Most of these cases have been resolved in favor of the same-sex couple seeking wedding services. In 2018, the US Supreme Court dodged the question of whether the owner of a bakery can refuse to create a custom cake for a gay couple based on the baker's "freedom of expression" or religious beliefs. Masterpiece Cakeshop, Ltd. v. Colorado Civil Rights Commission, 138 S. Ct. 1719 (2018). The case was expected to have important implications for the issue of so-called conscience exemptions from the antidiscrimination imperative, but the justices sided with the baker, 7–2, on the grounds that the Colorado Civil Rights Commission, which had considered the case, had been biased against him. In concurring opinions, Justices Elena Kagan and Neil Gorsuch battled over whether religious claims should prevail over civil rights in future instances. John G. Culhane, "The Supreme Court Punts on Cakes for Same-Sex Couples," *Politico*, June 4, 2018, https://www.politico.com/magazine/story/2018/06/04/the-supreme-court-punts-on-cakes-for-same-sex-couples-218591.

20. A law enacted in Mississippi is the worst of the lot. H.B. 1523 (2016) states that any of the following three anti-LGBTQ (usually religious) beliefs constitutes a permissible reason to refuse a wide range of services to that community: "(a) Marriage is or should be recognized as the union of one man and one woman; (b) Sexual relations are properly reserved to such a marriage; and (c) Male (man) or female (woman) refer to an individual's immutable biological sex as objectively determined by anatomy and genetics at time of birth." The federal court of appeals refused to consider the merits of a challenge to this law, on the grounds that the plaintiffs had not shown a concrete injury. Barber v. Bryant, 860 F.3d 345 (5th Cir. 2017), petition for rehearing en banc denied, 872 F.3d 671 (2017). The Supreme Court also declined to hear the appeal, 138 S. Ct. 652 (2018), so the law is still in effect.

21. The best known of these cases involved the Kentuckian Kim Davis, who claimed that issuing marriage licenses to same-sex couples would violate her religious beliefs. This created a national firestorm, with Davis's supporters calling her a civil rights hero and her opponents claiming that she was unwilling to do her job. John G. Culhane, "Kim Davis Is No Rosa Parks," *Politico*, Sept. 8, 2015, https://www.politico.com/magazine/story/2015/09/kim-davis-is-no-rosa-parks-213127. The case was ultimately resolved by a new policy, put into

force through an executive order from the governor, that removed the county clerk's name from the wedding certificate. Associated Press, "Kentucky Bows to Clerk Kim Davis and Changes Marriage License Rules," *L.A. Times*, Dec. 23, 2015, http://www.latimes.com/nation/nationnow/la-na-nn-kentucky-kim-davis-20151223-story.html. But Kentucky is hardly the only state to grapple with this issue. In Alabama, a number of counties got out of the marriage business entirely because clerks there responded to marriage equality by simply refusing to grant licenses to anyone. This course of conduct persisted for years. Phil Ammann, "Two Years Later, 7 Alabama Counties Still Not Issuing Marriage Licenses to Same-Sex, Other Couples," Alabama Today, June 29, 2017, http://altoday.com/archives/17555-two-years-later-7-alabama-counties-still-not-issuing-marriage-licences-sex-couples. The clerks had this authority because of an old law that was passed in response to the Supreme Court's decision in Loving v. Virginia, 388 U.S. 1 (1967), which required states to recognize interracial marriages. By giving clerks the option to stop issuing marriage licenses, the state maneuvered around this antidiscrimination imperative. In May 2019, Alabama came up with a final workaround: do away with the license altogether and simply have couples sign an affidavit that they met the requirements for marriage. Rhuaridh Marr, "Alabama Republicans Want to Abolish Marriage Licenses so Homophobes Don't Have to Issue Them to Gays," *Metro Weekly*, May 28, 2019, https://www.metroweekly.com/2019/05/alabama-republicans-want-to-abolish-marriage-licenses-so-homophobes-dont-have-to-issue-them-to-gays/.

22. In 2017, the Supreme Court ruled that the decision in Obergefell v. Hodges, 576 U.S. 644 (2015), which declared that same-sex couples have a constitutional right to marry, means that a state can't refuse to list a child's nonbiological parent on the birth certificate when the parents are legally married: "As we explained [in *Obergefell*], a State may not 'exclude same-sex couples from civil marriage on the same terms and conditions as opposite-sex couples.' Indeed, in listing those terms and conditions—the 'rights, benefits, and responsibilities' to which same-sex couples, no less than opposite-sex couples, must have access— we expressly identified 'birth and death certificates.'" Pavan v. Smith, 137 S. Ct. 2075 (2017), quoting *Obergefell* (internal citations omitted).

23. Fulton v. City of Philadelphia, 141 S. Ct. 1868 (2021).

24. E. J. Graff, *What Is Marriage For?*, xix (Beacon, 2004).

25. These grounds still exist in many states, although they now stand alongside the much more commonly used no-fault divorce. For cases, commentary, and representative statutes about fault-based divorce, see D. Kelly Weisberg & Susan Frelich Appleton, *Modern Family Law*, 484–97 (6th ed., 2016).

26. Alimony is a fascinating subject. It was once a way for a still legally married husband to support a wife from whom he had a separation but not a divorce; this was the only option for wives who could not divorce in England under ecclesiastical law that applied until 1857. Since then, the rationale for alimony

splintered into fragments, among which is its purported deterrent effect on divorce and wrongful conduct. Danielle Morone, "A Short History of Alimony in England and the United States," 20 *J. Contemporary Legal Issues* 3 (2011–12).

27. These unions are somewhat easier to get out of than they would have been during the fault-based era, though. Covenant marriage laws are in place in only three states: Arkansas, A.C.A § 9-11-803 (2021); Arizona, A.R.S. § 25-901 (2021); and Louisiana, LSA-R.S. § 9:272 (2021). For a discussion of their impact on women, see Cynthia M. VanSickle, "A Return to the Anti-feminist Past of Divorce Law: The Implications of the Covenant or Marriage Laws as Applied to Women," 6 *J. L. Society* 154 (2005).

28. Very few couples in any of the three states that offer covenant marriage have opted for it. Divorce Knowledgebase, "What Is a Covenant Marriage?," Sept. 11, 2014, https://www.divorceknowledgebase.com/blog/covenant-marriage/.

29. The rationales for requiring one ex-spouse to support the other are shifting and not always clear. One justification is that a decision is made in some relationships for only one spouse to participate in paid market work while the other remains at home (often to care for children). Alimony payments may be permanent (barring some event such as the recipient's remarriage), but the overwhelming legislative and judicial preference today is for "rehabilitative alimony" (or "rehabilitative support"), which is temporary and intended to provide the recipient with the resources to get (back) into the labor force. For a succinct discussion of this issue, see Daniel Jones, "Rehabilitative Alimony—the Goal of Self Support," 20 *J. Contemporary Legal Issues* 25 (2011–12).

30. Mary Ann Case, "'The Very Stereotype the Law Condemns': Constitutional Sex Discrimination as a Quest for Perfect Proxies," 85 *Cornell L. Rev.* 1447, 1489 (2000).

31. Courts call such misrepresentation one that goes to the "essence" of marriage: willingness to engage in sexual relations. See, e.g., Janda v. Janda, 984 So.2d 434 (Ala. Civ. App. 2007).

32. 576 U.S. at 669. . Indeed, even the conservative Justice Antonin Scalia, in his dissenting opinion in Lawrence v. Texas, 539 U.S. 558 (2003), was dismissive of the idea that procreation could be used as a way to separate different-sex and same-sex couples. If morality wasn't a sufficient reason to deny gay and lesbian couples the right to wed, he wondered what remained: "Surely not the encouragement of procreation, since the sterile and the elderly are allowed to marry." Id. at 604 (Scalia, J., dissenting).

33. George's argument is developed at length in "What Is Marriage?," 34 *Harv. J. L. & Public Pol'y* 245 (2010), coauthored with Sherif Girgis & Ryan T. Anderson.

34. "The critical public or 'civil' task of marriage is to regulate sexual relationships between men and women in order to reduce the likelihood that children . . . will face the burdens of fatherlessness." Maggie Gallagher, "The Case against

Same-Sex Marriage," in John Corvino & Maggie Gallagher, *Debating Same-Sex Marriage*, 96 (Oxford University Press, 2012).

35. A video in which Santorum makes this argument is summarized in an article by Igor Volsky, "Rick Santorum Pledges to Defund Contraception: 'It's Not Okay, It's a License to Do Things,'" Think Progress, Oct. 19, 2011, https://thinkprogress.org/rick-santorum-pledges-to-defund-contraception-its-not-okay-it-s-a-license-to-do-things-a9a9b04f0761/. For an excellent, historically grounded account of laws against nonprocreative sex, see William N. Eskridge Jr., *Dishonorable Passions: Sodomy Laws in America, 1861–2003* (Penguin, 2008).

36. The idea that human beings engage in sexual relations only for procreative purposes is inaccurate, both as a matter of fact and for reasons of sociobiological evolution. Christopher Ryan, "What Rick Santorum Doesn't Know about Sex," *Psychology Today*, Jan. 6, 2012, https://www.psychologytoday.com/us/blog/sex-dawn/201201/what-rick-santorum-doesn-t-know-about-sex.

37. "By giving recognition and legal structure to their parents' relationship, marriage allows children to understand the integrity and closeness of their own family and its concord with other families in their community and in their daily lives." 576 U.S. at 668, quoting 570 U.S. at 772. "Marriage also affords the permanency and stability important to children's best interests." 576 U.S. at 668.

38. See, e.g., Social Trends Institute, "World Family Map 2017: Mapping Family Change and Child Well-Being Outcomes" (2017) (summarizing statistics from the United States and European nations), http://worldfamilymap.ifstudies.org/2017/files/WFM-2017-FullReport.pdf.

39. US birthrates have been falling for decades and continue to decline. National Center for Health Statistics, "Births: Final Data for 2020," National Vital Statistics Reports 70, no. 17, Feb. 7, 2022, https://www.cdc.gov/nchs/data/nvsr/nvsr70/nvsr70-17.pdf.

40. Research has shown, however, that first marriages are more likely to last than second, third, or fourth marriages. Ben Steverman, "Boomers Are Making Sure the Divorces Keep Coming," *Bloomberg*, June 17, 2016, https://www.bloomberg.com/news/articles/2016-06-17/boomers-are-making-sure-the-divorces-keep-coming.

41. See, e.g., Patrick Lee & Robert P. George, "What Male-Female Complementarity Makes Possible: Marriage as a Two-in-One-Flesh Union," 69 *Theological Studies* 641 (2008).

42. Professor Maura I. Strassberg has written persuasively about the arguments for and against polygamy—in both the criminal and the marriage context. In a 2016 article, she offered a deep dive into the illegality of consensual polygamous relationships, ultimately concluding that more evidence was needed to determine whether such criminalization was the least restrictive means to discourage these arrangements, which she believed there were legitimate reasons

for doing. Strassberg, "Can We Still Criminalize Polygamy: Strict Scrutiny of Polygamy Laws under State Religious Freedom Restoration Acts after *Hobby Lobby*," 2016 *U. Ill. L. Rev.* 1605 (2016). The judicial affirmation of the antipolygamy principle originated in Reynolds v. United States, 98 U.S. 145 (1879), a decision that has been much criticized but never reexamined by the Supreme Court. In Brown v. Buhman, 947 F. Supp. 2d 1170 (D. Utah 2013), a federal trial court judge determined that the criminal prosecution of people living in polygamous relationships could not be defended under modern constitutional principles, but the appellate court vacated the judgment as moot, because of the Utah County attorney's commitment to refrain from prosecuting such cases in the future. Brown v. Buhman, 822 F.3d 1151 (10th Cir. 2016).

43. World Bank, "Fertility Rate, Total (Births per Woman)—United States," last visited June 28, 2018, https://data.worldbank.org/indicator/SP.DYN.TFRT.IN?end=2016&locations=US&start=1960&view=chart. For a dramatic visual depiction of the declining birth rate in the United States over the past 220 years, see Aaron O'Neill, "Crude Birth Rate in the United States from 1800 to 2020," Statista, June 21, 2022, https://www.statista.com/statistics/1037156/crude-birth-rate-us-1800-2020/.

44. After the FDA approved it in 1960, the birth control pill became widely available over the following decade. Tracee Cornforth, "A Brief History of the Birth Control Pill," Verywell Health, updated May 6, 2020, https://www.verywellhealth.com/a-brief-history-on-the-birth-control-pill-3522634.

45. While only a minority of states gave women broad power to terminate their pregnancies before 1973, the Supreme Court's decision in Roe v. Wade, 410 U.S. 113 (1973), made abortion a matter of constitutional right. In 1992, however, the court's decision in Planned Parenthood v. Casey, 505 U.S. 833 (1992), allotted states greater authority to regulate that right. Since then, and especially during the past decade or so, some aggressively pushed the boundaries of what is permissible. For a reliably up-to-date map of state laws on the issue, see Guttmacher Institute, "An Overview of Abortion Laws," updated Aug. 1, 2022, https://www.guttmacher.org/state-policy/explore/overview-abortion-laws. This website also provides demographic data on the people who have abortions, reflecting these laws' disproportionate effect on access for the poor. Following Brett Kavanaugh's seating on the Supreme Court in 2018, thereby cementing its conservative majority, states became even more emboldened to enact laws that clearly violate the strictures imposed by *Casey*. They were hopeful that the court would overrule that case and permit them to ban abortion completely. K. K. Rebecca Lai, "Abortion Bans: 9 States Have Passed Bills to Limit the Procedure This Year," *N.Y. Times*, updated May 29, 2019, https://www.nytimes.com/interactive/2019/us/abortion-laws-states.html. Their optimism grew in late 2020, when the Senate confirmed Amy Coney Barrett, known to have conservative views on abortion, to fill the seat on the Supreme Court created when Justice

Ruth Bader Ginsburg died in September of that year. Then, in 2021, the Supreme Court agreed to decide a case that many feared would severely limit or even overturn a woman's constitutional right to terminate her pregnancy. Adam Liptak, "Supreme Court to Hear Abortion Case Challenging *Roe v. Wade*," *N.Y. Times*, May 27, 2021, https://www.nytimes.com/2021/05/17/us/politics/supreme-court-to-hear-abortion-case-challenging-roe-v-wade.html. These fears were fully justified. In late June 2022, the Supreme Court overruled both *Roe* and *Casey*, holding that women do not have a constitutionally protected right to terminate their pregnancies. Dobbs v. Jackson Women's Health Organization, 142 S. Ct. 2228 (2022).

46. Bridget Brennan, "Why Has Women's Economic Power Surged? Five Stats You Need to Know," *Forbes*, Jan. 31, 2017, https://www.forbes.com/sites/bridgetbrennan/2017/01/31/why-has-womens-economic-power-surged-five-stats-you-need-to-know/.

47. Ariana Eunjung Cha, "The U.S. Fertility Rate Just Hit a Historic Low. Why Some Demographers Are Freaking Out," *Washington Post*, June 30, 2017), https://www.washingtonpost.com/news/to-your-health/wp/2017/06/30/the-u-s-fertility-rate-just-hit-a-historic-low-why-some-demographers-are-freaking-out/.

48. National Center for Health Statistics, "Unmarried Childbearing," reviewed May 16, 2022, https://www.cdc.gov/nchs/fastats/unmarried-childbearing.htm.

49. Pew Research Center, "Immigration's Impact on Past and Future U.S. Population Change," Sept. 28, 2015, https://www.pewresearch.org/hispanic/2015/09/28/chapter-2-immigrations-impact-on-past-and-future-u-s-population-change/, chapter 2 of *Modern Immigration Wave Brings 59 Million to U.S., Driving Population Growth and Change through 2065*.

50. The American Law Institute's approach to recharacterizing separate property as marital property in marriages of long duration reflects this insight. American Law Institute, *Principles of the Law of Family Dissolution: Analysis and Recommendations*, § 4.12, comment a (American Law Institute Publishers, 2002).

51. G. W. F. Hegel, *The Philosophy of History*, trans. J. Sibree, 42 (Dover, 1956). For an excellent and accessible account of Hegel's view of marriage and how it supports monogamy, see Maura I. Strassberg, "Distinctions of Form or Substance: Monogamy, Polygamy and Same-Sex Marriage," 75 *N.C.L. Rev.* 1501 (1997).

52. Turner v. Safley, 482 U.S. 78, 95 (1987). The court found that the state had a potential interest in denying marriage in the prison context but had shown no reasonable relationship between penology and this restriction. The child support debtor case is Zablocki v. Redhail, 434 U.S. 374 (1978). There, the Supreme Court found that the state of Wisconsin could not, consistent with constitutional requirements, place a direct and substantial obstacle in the path of marriage by

withholding licenses from those who were in arrears on child support—even though the state was understandably frustrated by the difficulty of holding certain parents accountable for supporting children from their previous marriages.

53. Litigation to obtain limited benefits is another strategy. See, e.g., Braschi v. Stahl Associates, 543 N.E.2d 49 (N.Y. 1989) (allowing a man to gain the benefits of New York City's rent control law as a successor to his deceased male partner, even though the couple could not marry). For a good discussion of the promise and limitations of using litigation in this way, see Melissa Murray, "*Obergefell v. Hodges* and Nonmarriage Inequality," 104 *Calif. L. Rev.* 1207, 1240 (2016).

54. On intestacy, see Lawrence M. Friedman, *Dead Hands: A Social History of Wills, Trusts, and Inheritance Law* (Stanford University Press, 2009).

55. Before no-fault divorce, the at-fault party was often barred from receiving property, or the division was skewed in the innocent party's direction. McKinley Irvin Family Law, "Understanding 'Fair and Equitable' Division of Property in a No-Fault Divorce," Sept. 25, 2013, https://www.mckinleyirvin.com/family-law -blog/2013/september/understanding-fair-and-equitable-division-of-pro/. Under current law in most states, property division is not generally affected by who is at fault. Since property is thus more equitably divided, there is less need in some cases for courts to award support payments. In fact, some states now have a presumption against permanent alimony. See, e.g., Fla. Stat. Ann. § 61.08 (8) (West 2021). Support payments are more typically tied to specific goals, such as reimbursing a spouse for uncompensated value during marriage, as in Ohio Rev. Code Ann. § 3105.18 (j) (West 2021), or rehabilitating a spouse who has left the workforce—often to care for children—as in Ohio Rev. Code Ann. § 3105.18 (k) (West 2021).

56. I discussed the "pro-marriage" research in John G. Culhane, "Beyond Rights and Morality: The Overlooked Public Health Argument for Same-Sex Marriage," 17 *Law & Sexuality* 7 (2008). Much of the argument for the superiority of marriage over "nonmarriage" summarizes the pro-marriage position in Linda J. Waite & Maggie Gallagher, *The Case for Marriage* (Broadway, 2001). These authors discuss scores of social science studies relating to the various categories of advantages that have been associated with marriage. A few caveats are in order. First, benefits to the couple are not necessarily evenly distributed between men and women (in the different-sex marriages the authors examined; marriage equality had not yet been achieved, so there were no same-sex married couples). Second, the authors compare marriage to cohabitation and "nonmarriage" more generally in a society that has the marriage option. Would the benefits be revealed as illusory (to at least some extent) if marriage were no longer recognized? The question is impossible to answer unless marriage were in fact abolished, but this prospect is highly unlikely, at least in the near future. For an able discussion of this intractable limitation on studies of this kind, see Anita Bernstein, "For and against Marriage: A Revision," 102 *Mich. L. Rev.* 129, 159–67 (2003). I return to this point in chapter 5.

57. Macroeconomic forces also play a significant role in determining who ends up getting married. In June Carbone & Naomi Cahn, *Marriage Markets: How Inequality Is Remaking the American Family* (Oxford University Press, 2014), the authors marshal an impressive body of evidence in support of their conclusion that the availability of suitable (different-sex) marriage partners has a dramatic effect on who chooses to take this legal step. In sum, marriage is much likelier and more stable where men have higher income and greater education than where the opposite is true. The authors persuasively demonstrate that overall inequality plays a substantial role in this imbalance; for this reason, creating legal protections for the unmarried takes on an important dimension of fairness that runs counter to the concern that such protections will detract from the central position marriage occupies—for many, that position is simply not reality.

58. An Act Relating to Civil Unions, 2000 Vt. Laws P.A. 91 (H. 847).

59. Kerry Abrams, "Marriage Fraud," 100 *Calif. L. Rev.* 1 (2012).

60. Id., 6.

CHAPTER 5. MATCHING RELATIONSHIP LAW TO REALITY

Epigraph. J. Bryan Lowder, "What Was Gay?," *Slate*, May 12, 2015, https://slate .com/news-and-politics/2015/05/can-you-be-homosexual-without-being-gay-the-future-of-cruising-drag-and-camp-in-a-post-closet-world.html.

1. The marriage alternative movement has recently come back to life, at least in a limited way. California expanded the domestic partnership option to all legal couples in 2020, as mentioned in chapter 1. As another example, the Uniform Law Commission drafted model legislation to deal with the economic rights of unmarried cohabitants, which was approved by the full commission in July 2021. (I have been involved with this project as an approved observer.) Uniform Law Commission, Uniform Cohabitants' Economic Remedies Act, July 13, 2021, https://www .uniformlaws.org/HigherLogic/System/DownloadDocumentFile.ashx?Document FileKey=eed76273-b2b7-eea1-953f-a657b9535820.

2. Thinking about a world without formal legal marriage is nonetheless a helpful exercise, as doing so can bring into sharp relief some of the institution's problems and issues. For such a thought experiment, see Elizabeth S. Scott, "A World without Marriage," 41 *Fam. L. Q.* 537 (Fall 2007). Among those who favor the registration of different kinds of relationships and understandings over an obsessive focus on marriage, Nancy Polikoff has been the most influential. Her groundbreaking book *Beyond (Straight and Gay) Marriage: Valuing All Families under the Law* (Beacon, 2008) is required reading for anyone interested in a serious discussion of how exalting marriage above other adult relationships creates and supports an unfair caste system of sorts. In *Against Marriage: An*

Egalitarian Defense of the Marriage-Free State (Oxford University Press, 2017), Clare Chambers recently argued for the elimination of marriage in favor of regulating individual practices—akin to my call for an expanded designated beneficiary agreement law.

3. Mary Lyndon Shanley & Linda McClain, "Should States Abolish Marriage?," *Legal Affairs*, May 16, 2005, http://www.legalaffairs.org/webexclusive /debateclub_m0505.msp.

4. John G. Culhane, "Public Health and Marriage (Equality)," in *Reconsidering Law and Policy Debates: A Public Health Perspective*, 89, 104–5 (Culhane ed., Cambridge University Press, 2011): "There is cost to [those] who might wish to marry but have not done so because they are unable to find a suitable partner. . . . Those unable to find a suitable partner for marriage may feel themselves somehow 'apart,' as well, in a society that even today so values marriage."

5. For a persuasive discussion of how some of the benefits that accrue to marriage might be peeled off, see Kerry Abrams, "Marriage Fraud," 100 *Calif. L. Rev.* 1, 54–66 (2012).

6. On benefits as an incentive, see, e.g., William N. Eskridge Jr., "Family Law Pluralism: The Guided-Choice Regime of Menus, Default Rules, and Override Rules," 100 *Geo. L. Rev.* 1881 (2012). As we'll see, there is a clear distinction between marriage's add-on benefits and the protections for both spouses that have long come with marriage and are more intrinsically tied to it. The law recognizes the commitment that the couple makes to each other, and protects their expectations with an extensive set of default rules, including assumptions of inheritance at death, status as proxy decision-maker, and equitable division of assets if the marriage dissolves.

7. W. Bradford Wilcox, Angela Rachidi, & Joseph Price, "Marriage, Penalized: Does Social-Welfare Policy Affect Family Formation?," American Enterprise Institute & Institute for Family Studies, July 26, 2016, https://www.aei.org /research-products/report/marriage-penalized-does-social-welfare-policy-affect-family-formation/. About one in three respondents reported knowing someone who had decided not to marry for fear of losing benefits.

8. Abrams, "Marriage Fraud," 42–43.

9. Same-sex friends (and sexual intimates) could live together, but no benefits were accrued thereby. In "Family Law Pluralism," Professor William Eskridge offers a thorough account of the recent history of relationship definition and recognition and situates the decreasing enforcement and final abolition of these laws before changes such as no-fault divorce and the elimination of the mixed-race marriage bans.

10. This history is expertly chronicled by Abrams, "Marriage Fraud," 40–47.

11. Some point to economic drivers for the decrease in marriage, while others press the argument that a breakdown of social norms, except among the upper economic class, is principally responsible. For two opposing views, compare Amy

L. Wax, "Engines of Inequality: Class, Race, and Family Structure," 41 *Fam. L. Q.* 567, 582–99 (Fall 2007), emphasizing family disintegration and other social factors, with Andrew J. Cherlin, *Labor's Love Lost: The Rise and Fall of the Working-Class Family in America* (Russell Sage Foundation, 2014), blaming the decline in part on the loss of well-paying manufacturing jobs. Most agree, though, that the falling marriage rate is caused by multiple economic and social factors. For a clear discussion, see Rachel Sheffield, "What's Driving the Marriage Divide?," *Public Discourse* (Witherspoon Institute), Aug. 31, 2015, https:// www.thepublicdiscourse.com/2015/08/14792/.

12. For a succinct description of the enactment of the Social Security Act, see Kathryn L. Moore, "Privatization of Social Security: Misguided Reform," 71 *Temple L. Rev.* 131, 133–35 (1998).

13. Social Security Act, Pub. L. No. 74-271, 49 Stat. 620 (1935).

14. Moore, "Privatization of Social Security," 134. As the author notes, these amendments also moved the date at which benefits would be available from 1942 to 1940.

15. Anne L. Alstott, "Updating the Welfare State: Marriage, the Income Tax, and Social Security in the Age of Individualism," 66 *Tax L. Rev.* 695, 701 (2013).

16. The age of full retirement is being increased from sixty-five to sixty-seven, in a process that will be complete once those who "attain . . . early retirement age after December 31, 2021," have been accounted for. 42 U.S.C. § 216 (l) (1) (2021).

17. Survivor benefits can also go to the children of the deceased and, in cases of dependence, to the parents of the deceased if they are over the age of sixty-two. Social Security Administration, "If You Are the Survivor," last visited Aug. 5, 2022, https://www.ssa.gov/benefits/survivors/ifyou.html#h3.

18. AARP, "How Do Survivor Benefits Work?," updated July 1, 2022, https:// www.aarp.org/retirement/social-security/questions-answers/how-do-survivor-benefits-work.html.

19. Social Security Administration, "Benefits for Your Family," last visited Aug. 5, 2022, https://www.ssa.gov/benefits/retirement/planner/applying7.html.

20. Jim Borland, "Will Remarrying Affect My Social Security Benefits?," Social Security Matters, Sept. 5, 2017, updated Oct. 14, 2021, https://blog.ssa .gov/will-remarriage-affect-my-social-security-benefits/.

21. Social Security Administration, *Understanding the Benefits*, Publication No. 05-10024, 13 (Jan. 2022), https://ssa.gov/pubs/EN-05-10024.pdf.

22. Douglas E. Abrams et al., *Contemporary Family Law*, 698–99 (4th ed., West Academic Publishing, 2015).

23. For a concise and comprehensive look at the dismaying figures for senior citizens, see Heidi L. Brady & Robin Fretwell Wilson, "The Precarious Status of Domestic Partnerships for the Elderly in a Post-*Obergefell* World," 24 *Elder L. J.* 49, 62–65 (2016). For social security income, see Wendy Connett, "What Is the Maximum Social Security Retirement Benefit?," Investopedia, updated June 28,

2022, https://www.investopedia.com/ask/answers/102814/what-maximum-i-can-receive-my-social-security-retirement-benefit.asp.

24. See Brady & Wilson, "Precarious Status," 53–61 (discussing the creation and expansion of these laws and their current status).

25. As long as domestic partnerships conferred only a subset of the benefits of marriage, there was no prospect that entering into them would cause otherwise eligible divorced spouses to forfeit their share of their exes' retirement benefits. But when the law expanded them to marriage-like status, the situation changed—even though the shift has gone largely unnoticed. The Social Security Act has an odd provision along these lines:

> (1)(A)(i) An applicant is the wife, husband, widow, or widower of a fully or currently insured individual . . . if the courts of the State in which such insured individual is domiciled . . . would find that such applicant and such insured individual were validly married at the time such applicant files such application or, if such insured individual is dead, at the time he died.
>
> (ii) If such courts would not find that such applicant and such insured individual were validly married at such time, such applicant shall, nevertheless, be deemed to be the wife, husband, widow, or widower . . . of such insured individual if such applicant would, under the laws applied by such courts in determining the devolution of intestate personal property, have the same status with respect to the taking of such property as a wife, husband, widow, or widower of such insured individual.

This provision, found at 42 U.S.C. § 416 (h) (2021), is puzzling, given that in 1939, when it was put into force, no other status was seen as equivalent to that of legally married spouses—but it may have to do with equitable doctrines, such as spouse by estoppel (prevents a person from arguing against being married to a current "spouse" when they know of a previously existing marriage but continue to act as though legally married to that spouse; see Lowenschuss v. Lowenschuss, 579 A.2d 377 [Pa. Super. Ct. 1990]). For an early case interpreting this provision (but deciding that the ceremonially married widow's rights should defeat the claim of an earlier "spouse" whose common-law marriage was not recognized in the state), see Sanders v. Altmeyer, 58 F. Supp. 67 (W.D. Tenn. 1944). Thus, where the law equates a nonmarital status to marriage in respect to the rights available, relationships such as civil unions, which are intended to be state law equivalents to marriage—and trigger full inheritance benefits—should in principle also create entitlement to social security benefit eligibility, as the SSA's 2016 guidance provides. But that same relationship status threatens disqualification from that eligibility: once people marry or do something equivalent, they should lose SSA benefits under this provision—even though the guidance does not explicitly so state.

26. For an article that expertly discusses and analyzes the research on cohabitating couples and finds that many merge their economic lives in ways that look a great deal like the typical married couple (while others do not), see Alicia Brokars Kelly, "Navigating Gender in Modern Intimate Partnership Law," 14 *J. L. & Fam. Stud.* 1, 20–26 (2012). A searching question is what should happen

to the property of couples in nonmarital relationships when they dissolve. See Albertina Antognini, "The Law of Nonmarriage," 58 *B.C.L. Rev.* 1 (2017) (arguing for a fact-based inquiry on this issue, which is currently constrained by gendered judicial views of the roles of men and women).

27. While this firm line may have been justified when the great majority of surviving partners were married to the decedents, today these statutes can result in grave inequity. See John G. Culhane, "Even More Wrongful Death: Statutes Divorced from Reality," 32 *Fordham Urb. L. J.* 171 (2005). Michigan has provided a partial workaround that allows other parties to bring a claim: anyone named as a beneficiary in the decedent's will also has standing to sue under the law. Id., 176, analyzing Mich. Comp. Laws Ann. 600.2922 §3 (c) (2022).

28. I discussed and criticized these wrongful death laws in some detail in John G. Culhane, "A 'Clanging Silence': Same-Sex Couples and Tort Law," 89 *Ky. L. J.* 911 (2000–2001).

29. The social security program is not theoretically coherent. While it is true that it was enacted in the depths of the Depression as a way of ensuring financial security for senior citizens, payments go to all who qualify as survivors or retirees, no matter how high their income. Since the program is funded by payroll deductions (up to a determined limit), those who receive higher payments are generally also those who pay more into the system, which can give them a perhaps understandable sense of entitlement.

30. John G. Culhane, "Tort, Compensation, and Two Kinds of Justice," 55 *Rutgers L. Rev.* 1027, 1095 (2003): "The residual risk that vaccinations themselves create is, from a broad societal perspective, a small price for such a large gain."

31. Social Security Administration, "Frequently Asked Questions," "What Are the Marriage Requirements to Receive Social Security Spouse's Benefits?," modified July 26, 2022, https://faq.ssa.gov/en-us/Topic/article/KA-01999.

32. This is a controversial suggestion, of course, since some believe that a means-tested approach to social security would be a breach of faith with workers who have been contributing to the program for decades with the expectation that their payouts will reflect this. Others focus on the insurance aspect and point to the savings that would be realized through the implementation of such a test. For a concise version of the debate, see David John & Virginia Reno, "Reforming Social Security: Option: Begin Means-Testing Social Security Benefits," Perspectives 22, AARP Public Policy Institute report (June 2012), https://aarp.org/content/dam/aarp/research/public_policy_institute/econ_sec/2012/option-means-test-social-security-benefits-AARP-ppi-econ-sec.pdf.

33. The ideas in this paragraph are inspired by Anne L. Alstott, "Updating the Welfare State: Marriage, the Income Tax, and Social Security in the Age of Individualism," 66 *Tax L. Rev.* 695, 756–57 (2013).

34. Mich. Comp. Laws Ann. 600.2922 (2021). See also Culhane, "Even More Wrongful Death," 176–78, discussing Michigan's law as a partial solution to the problem of statutory exclusion of dependent parties.

35. IRS, "Employee Benefits," updated Aug. 5, 2022, https://www.irs.gov /businesses/small-businesses-self-employed/employee-benefits.

36. This is hardly the place for a debate on the Affordable Care Act and its seemingly perpetually uncertain fate. After the Republican Congress narrowly failed to repeal the law in 2017 but effectively removed the individual mandate to purchase insurance, the act was challenged yet again in federal court. The plaintiffs succeeded at the trial court level but ultimately failed at the Supreme Court, which ruled that the plaintiffs lacked standing to contest the law. California v. Texas, 141 S. Ct. 2104 (2021). This was but the latest legal skirmish in a long and dispiriting battle to undo the will of Congress regarding the ACA. The first significant challenge ended in 2012, when a 5–4 majority in National Federation of Independent Business v. Sebelius, 567 U.S. 519 (2012), held that the law was a valid exercise of Congress's power to tax. Perhaps it is sufficient to point out that the ACA, for all the challenges, detractors, and political meddling it has faced, has drastically reduced the number and percentage of Americans who lack health insurance. It's a substantial yet incomplete move in the right direction. For a comprehensive look at the statistics, complete with instructive charts and graphs, see Jennifer Tolbert, Kendal Orgera, & Anthony Damico, "Key Facts about the Uninsured Population," Kaiser Family Foundation, Nov. 6, 2020, https://www.kff.org/uninsured/issue-brief/key-facts-about-the-uninsured-population/.

37. At one time, only the nine so-called community property states—Arizona, California, Idaho, Louisiana, Nevada, New Mexico, Texas, Washington, and Wisconsin—treated the income earned by either spouse as belonging to the couple (the marital "community"). In recent years, though, the so-called title states—which, as the name implies, considered each spouse to own only the property to which they had "title" (including income earned in their own name)—have moved to the equitable distribution system, whereby most of the property acquired during the marriage is considered fair game for distribution, no matter whose name it's in. Common exceptions (in both community property and the former title states) include gifts made to either party, inheritances, and sometimes the increase in value of property acquired before marriage. For a good summary of the law, see Abrams et al., *Contemporary Family Law*, 575–78.

38. Id., 474.

39. States typically have a statutory list of factors that courts are supposed to consider in making the property division. In the broadest sense, these are meant to achieve fairness and equity between the parties. For instance, the law in Pennsylvania mentions, among other things, the marriage's length, prior marriages of either spouse, each spouse's age and ability to gain employment after divorce,

contributions the spouses made to each other's education or training, the parties' standard of living, and, perhaps most significant, "the economic circumstances of each party." 23 Pa. Cons. Stat. § 3502 (2021).

40. Alicia Brokars Kelly, "Rehabilitating Marriage as a Theory of Wealth Distribution at Divorce: In Recognition of a Shared Life," 19 *Wis. Women's L.J.* 141, 168 (2004): "Almost unfettered judicial discretion has opened the door for courts to betray partnership's core values of joint contribution and equality, which the law ... purports to embrace. Judges, empowered to measure contribution, have ... systematically devalued the contributions of women, particularly home labor."

41. This number is drawn from an analysis of the Current Population Survey: Renee Stepler, "Number of U.S. Adults Cohabiting with a Partner Continues to Rise, Especially among Those 50 and Older," Pew Research Center, Apr. 6, 2017,https://www.pewresearch.org/fact-tank/2017/04/06/number-of-u-s-adults-cohabiting-with-a-partner-continues-to-rise-especially-among-those-50-and-older/.

42. June Carbone & Naomi Cahn, *Marriage Markets: How Inequality Is Remaking the American Family* (Oxford University Press, 2014).

43. Kelly, "Navigating Gender," 20–26. Demographics play an important role here. For couples who have attained a high level of education and income, cohabitation often leads to marriage. For others, marriage is less likely to ensue. Cohabitation in such cases may be a matter of convenience or economic necessity. For a comprehensive treatment of the variety of cohabiting couples, see Sharon Sassler & Amanda Jayne Miller, *Cohabitation Nation: Gender, Class, and the Remaking of Relationships* (University of California Press, 2017). See generally Cynthia Grant Bowman, *Unmarried Couples, Law, and Public Policy* (Oxford University Press, 2010).

44. Kelly, "Navigating Gender."

45. Uniform Law Commission, Uniform Premarital and Marital Agreements Act, Jan. 2, 2013, https://www.uniformlaws.org/HigherLogic/System/DownloadDocumentFile.ashx?DocumentFileKey=f5d36125-9433-c7d8-28ec-6244f4a316e6, §§ 2–3 (listing the permissible subjects of a prenuptial agreement).

46. American Law Institute, *Principles of the Law of Family Dissolution: Analysis and Recommendations* (American Law Institute Publishers, 2002). The recommendations are discussed more fully later in this chapter.

47. Australian Family Law Act of 1975, as amended, § 4AA (2016).

48. See, e.g., Crowley & Pappas, [2013] FamCA 783, Family Court of Australia, http://www.austlii.edu.au/cgi-bin/viewdoc/au/cases/cth/FamCA/2013/783.html.

49. American Law Institute, *Principles*, § 603, comments a & b.

50. Id., comment b.

51. Id.

52. Id., § 603.

53. Id., § 603 (7).

54. Id., § 603 (7)(j).

55. Id., § 603 (3).

56. Id., § 603 (6).

57. Although it has not expressly adopted the ALI approach, Washington has come the closest to recognizing that the relationships between longtime cohabitants are subject to the same rights and expectations as marriage. There, couples in a relationship that resembles marriage are entitled to claim the property acquired by either or both during the relationship as "marital property," subject to the same kind of division. See Olver v. Fowler, 168 P.3d 348 (Wash. 2007) (en banc). For a thorough discussion of this point and a trenchant analysis of the emerging rules on nonmarital relationships, see June Carbone & Naomi Cahn, "Nonmarriage," 76 *Md. L. Rev.* 55 (2016).

58. Australian Family Law Act, § 4AA (2) (listing circumstances relevant to determining whether "persons have a relationship as a couple"). This law applies throughout the country, with the partial exception of the state of Western Australia.

59. [2013] FamCA 783.

60. Id. at 3 (footnote references omitted). The pinpoint citations used throughout the discussion of this case refer to the page numbers in the Westlaw report.

61. Id. at 4.

62. Id. at 7. The court went into unnecessarily lurid detail about the couple's sexual relationship.

63. Id. at 13.

64. Id. at 12.

65. Id.

66. The ALI *Principles* occasioned any number of symposia in which legal academics and others debated what they perceived as its virtues and vices. A hefty representation of the literature can be found in Mary Kay Kisthardt, "The AAML Model for a Parenting Plan," 19 *J. Am. Acad. Matrimonial Lawyers* 223, 223 n.2 (2005) (listing several symposia and their individual contributions). One of the symposium articles, Lynn D. Wardle, "Deconstructing Family: A Critique of the American Law Institute's 'Domestic Partners' Proposal," 2001 *B.Y.U. L. Rev.* 1189, 1221, contains a dire warning: "Legalizing domestic partnership as proposed by [the ALI] could significantly weaken marriage. The overwhelming majority of young people today yearn to get married, yet they are also frightened of marriage because they have personally experienced or witnessed repeatedly in the lives of their loved ones and friends the personal trauma of marital failure and divorce. These vulnerable young people may be drawn to the dangerous alternative of non-marital domestic partnership if it is legalized."

67. American Law Institute, *Principles*, § 602, comment b.

68. William Eskridge is concerned that, under an approach like the ALI's, some couples will find themselves involuntarily declared to have been in a relationship with legal consequences, and maintains that "lack of notice to the citizenry is intolerable for a pluralistic family law." "Family Law Pluralism," 1979. I agree that conscripting couples into a legal relationship they did not choose is a serious concern. Kaiponanea T. Matsumura expresses the same concern and suggests that a more fact-specific approach to consent is needed in "Consent to Intimate Regulation," 96 *N.C. L. Rev.* 1013 (2018). This approach could be useful for determining the obligations of both the couple to each other and the government to the couple, in extending state-conferred benefits otherwise available only to married people. At a minimum, there is a pressing need for better public education about marriage alternatives, including cohabiting relationships that might amount to domestic partnerships. One hard question is whether the couple should have to opt in to the status or opt out. It's also important to recognize that there is another side to this "conscription" story: whatever their knowledge of their legal status, people in committed relationships do at least sometimes establish mutual reliance, and a law that takes no steps to protect the economically vulnerable party is "tolerable" only to the other partner.

69. Family and Medical Leave Act, 29 U.S.C. § 2601 (2018). Section 2611 defines the terms "parent," "son or daughter," and "spouse" and leaves no room for other relations in the subsequent sections that provide protection for those who miss work because of a family member's health.

70. Attiwill & Secretary, Department of Education, Employment and Workplace Relations, 2013 WL 1152047 (Administrative Appeals Tribunal, Adelaide).

71. Id. at ¶ 30.

72. American Law Institute, *Principles*, § 6.03 (6) (a person seeking recognition as the domestic partner of someone related by blood or adoption "bears the burden of proof that for a significant period of time the parties shared a primary residence and a life together as a couple").

73. Daniel Borrillo, "The '*Pacte Civil de Solidarité*' in France: Midway between Marriage and Cohabitation," in *Legal Recognition of Same-Sex Partnerships*, 475, 481 (Robert Wintemute & Mads Andenæs eds., Hart, 2001).

74. Quantitative studies are necessary but can take us only so far. For a compelling, narrative-rich account of why some women choose not to marry (even when they have children with men with whom they are in relationships), see Kathryn Edin & Maria Kefalas, *Promises I Can Keep: Why Poor Women Put Motherhood before Marriage* (University of California Press, 2005). The authors interviewed 162 poor women in Philadelphia and nearby Camden, New Jersey, and gained rare insight into their lives—both individually and as members of unmarried couples. Although the book is now nearly twenty years old, these stories provide a window onto the continued value that is placed on marriage—

which many of these women viewed as a sort of luxury they might never achieve. Motherhood, in contrast, was seen as a necessity for many.

75. 42 U.S.C. §667 (a)–(b) (2021); Adoption and Safe Families Act, Pub. L. No. 105-89, 111 Stat. 2115 (effective 1997; codified in sections of 42 U.S.C.). For a critical look at ASFA, including the mandate, see Cynthia Godsoe, "Parsing Parenthood," 17 *Lewis & Clark L. Rev.* 113 (2013).

76. See, e.g., 23 Pa. Cons. Stat. § 3301 (d) (1) (2021) (requiring that the parties live "separate and apart" for one year, which can be satisfied even if they remain in the same home, as long as they lead separate lives).

77. Courts have not always been sympathetic to the claim that one party was taken advantage of. The Pennsylvania case Simeone v. Simeone, 581 A.2d 162 (Pa. 1990), evinces a particularly tone-deaf approach, validating a prenuptial agreement that was signed the night before the wedding. Id. at 167. As part of a recent project to rewrite family law opinions from a feminist perspective, my colleague Alicia Kelly and I suggested an analysis that trains a much more searching light on prenuptial contracts, policing them to make sure they are fair both procedurally and in their terms. Kelly & Culhane, "Rewritten Opinion, *Simeone v. Simeone*," in *Feminist Judgments: Family Law Opinions Rewritten*, 243 (Rachel Rebouché ed., Cambridge University Press, 2020).

78. Because such agreements are not legally registered, reliable statistics are hard to find. Anecdotal reports from attorneys suggest that the number is small but rising. See Heather Mahar, "Why Are There So Few Prenuptial Agreements?," John M. Olin Center for Law, Economics, and Business, Discussion Paper No. 436 (Sept. 2003), http://www.law.harvard.edu/programs/olin_center/papers /pdf/436.pdf.

79. Some states, such as Pennsylvania, require only that the agreement has been executed fairly—with full disclosure of assets—and voluntarily. 581 A.2d 162. Others, like Iowa, require that the agreement also be fair, on the merits, to the economically weaker party who is seeking to resist enforcement. In re Marriage of Shanks, 758 N.W.2d 506 (Iowa 2008).

80. Law Commission of Canada, *Beyond Conjugality: Recognizing and Supporting Close Personal Adult Relationships* (2001), https://papers.ssrn.com /sol3/papers.cfm?abstract_id=1720747 (abstract, with link to full report). For its time, this report is a remarkable document. The question of whether to recognize same-sex marriages was one of the motivating forces behind the call for it, but its recommendations went far beyond a brief for formal marriage equality. The drafters recognized that the percentage of people in marriage was declining and that many couples—and not just "conjugal" couples—were in relationships that required and merited the law's protection. One change for which they advocated was the creation of a registration system that would permit consenting adults to structure their rights and responsibilities inter se in ways that would recognize and protect their expectations, even without marriage: "Registration should pro-

vide options to registrants: for example, models of predetermined rights and responsibilities reflecting a conjugal relationship or a variety of caregiving relationships." Id., xvii (Executive Summary). Perhaps because the drafters were equivocal about whether marriage should survive as "a legal institution" (id., xviii), the document was attacked as radical. See, e.g., Stanley Kurtz, "The Conspiracy to Abolish Marriage: Martha Bailey and the Law Reform Commission," Free Library, Sept. 1, 2006, https://www.thefreelibrary.com/The+conspiracy+to+abolish+marriage%3a+Martha+Bailey+and+the+Law+Reform...-a0151394664.

81. Jessica R. Feinberg, "The Survival of Non-marital Relationship Statuses in the Same-Sex Marriage Era: A Proposal," 87 *Temp. L. Rev.* 47 (2014).

82. Eskridge, "Family Law Pluralism," 1965–67. Eskridge draws support for maintaining the civil union from Robin West, who argues that this specific marriage alternative is a useful way to throw patriarchy off the bus. West, *Marriage, Sexuality, and Gender* (Routledge, 2007). In chapter 2, I explained why, even though the civil union has some value as a tool for subverting patriarchy and the religious associations of marriage, it is probably not worth saving.

83. American Law Institute, *Principles*, § 4.12, comment a. The ALI's proposal is justified as follows:

> After many years of marriage, spouses typically do not think of their separate-property assets as separate, even if they would be so classified under the technical property rules. Both spouses are likely to believe, for example, that such assets will be available to provide for their joint retirement, for a medical crisis of either spouse, or for other personal emergencies. The longer the marriage the more likely it is that the spouses will have made decisions about their employment or the use of their marital assets that are premised in part on such expectations about the separate property of both spouses.

84. The proposal here borrows from Jessica R. Feinberg, "Gradual Marriage," 20 *Lewis & Clark L. Rev.* 1 (2016). In the "gradual marriage" process suggested there, the couple's ownership of property would automatically become more integrated at specified intervals, before which the parties would be notified of the impending change so they could choose to opt out.

85. Sally F. Goldfarb, "Legal Recognition of Plural Unions: Is a Nonmarital Relationship Status the Answer to the Dilemma?," 58 *Fam. Ct. Rev.* 33 (2020). Goldfarb argues for allowing adults to enter into multiparty relationships through marriage alternatives—including those discussed in this book—as a way of creating their legal statuses without marriage, which in her view provides for the systemic oppression of women and children.

86. See, e.g., Laura A. Rosenbury, "Friends with Benefits?," 106 *Mich. L. Rev.* 189 (2007). The author describes how focusing on family caregiving relationships further ensconces gender roles, and proposes that recognizing caregiving relationships between friends is both intrinsically good and a way of deconstructing those assumptions about gender and caring. She floats the idea of allowing people to designate a legal "best friend" in addition to a spouse and then

asks whether such a designation would create a hierarchy of its own. Id., 230–32. The expanded designated beneficiary agreement proposed here is one way of applying Rosenbury's insights: friends can recognize and protect each other through this vehicle, and do so with multiple friends at the same time.

87. IRS, "IRS Provides Tax Inflation Adjustments for Tax Year 2020," updated Nov.2,2021,https://www.irs.gov/newsroom/irs-provides-tax-inflation-adjustments-for-tax-year-2020.

88. Megan Garber, "The Old-Fashioned, Modern Marriage of Ina and Jeffrey," *The Atlantic*, Oct. 25, 2016, https://www.theatlantic.com/entertainment/archive/2016/10/the-old-fashioned-modern-marriage-of-ina-and-jeffrey/505277/.

References

INTERVIEWS AND STATEMENTS

Sheila Blackburn, email, June 7, 2016; telephone conversation, June 8, 2016.

Tom Brougham, interview by Ron Schlitter, *Out and Elected in the USA, 1974–2004*, last visited July 13, 2022, https://outhistory.org/exhibits/show /out-and-elected/late-1980s/tom-brougham.

Tom Brougham and Barry Warren, Skype interviews, September 2011.

May Doe and April Doe (pseuds.), live interview, April 3, 2014.

Tom Gibson (pseud.), telephone conversation, February 3, 2013.

Lisa Goodman, telephone conversation, March 4, 2014.

John Hunter and Hal Kooden, Skype interview, August 3, 2011.

John Kennedy, statement as panelist on civil unions, Chicago, April 10, 2012.

Marilyn McCord, telephone conversation, July 24, 2014.

Terry McKeon, Skype interview, July 31, 2014.

Anne Quinn, telephone conversation, June 10, 2016.

Emil Roe and Margaret Koe (pseuds.), Skype interview, October 25, 2011.

Colorado State Senator Pat Steadman, telephone conversation, July 25, 2014.

Jennifer Tweeton and Alex Rifman, Skype interview, October 18, 2011.

Leah Whitesel, email, February 6, 2014.

Leah Whitesel and Justin Gates, Skype interview, October 10, 2011.

Patricia Yarrow and Liz Gettings, Skype interview, July 14, 2014.

BOOKS AND CHAPTERS

Abrams, Douglas E., et al., *Contemporary Family Law* (4th ed., West Academic Publishing, 2015).

American Law Institute, *Principles of the Law of Family Dissolution: Analysis and Recommendations* (American Law Institute Publishers, 2002).

Borrillo, Daniel, "The *'Pacte Civil de Solidarité'* in France: Midway between Marriage and Cohabitation," in *Legal Recognition of Same-Sex Partnerships*, 475 (Robert Wintemute & Mads Andenæs eds., Hart, 2001).

Bowman, Cynthia Grant, *Unmarried Couples, Law, and Public Policy* (Oxford University Press, 2010).

Brake, Elizabeth (ed.), *After Marriage: Rethinking Marital Relationships* (Oxford University Press, 2016).

Brandon, Mark E., *States of Union* (University Press of Kansas, 2013).

Carbone, June, & Naomi Cahn, *Marriage Markets: How Inequality Is Remaking the American Family* (Oxford University Press, 2014).

Carter, David, *Stonewall: The Riots That Sparked the Gay Revolution* (St. Martin's Griffin, 2004).

Chambers, Claire, *Against Marriage: An Egalitarian Defense of the Marriage-Free State* (Oxford University Press, 2017).

Cherlin, Andrew J., *Labor's Love Lost: The Rise and Fall of the Working-Class Family in America* (Russell Sage Foundation, 2014).

Culhane, John G., "Public Health and Marriage (Equality)," in *Reconsidering Law and Policy Debates: A Public Health Perspective*, 89 (Culhane ed., Cambridge University Press, 2011).

Den Otter, Ronald C., *In Defense of Plural Marriage* (Cambridge University Press, 2015).

Edin, Kathryn, & Maria Kefalas, *Promises I Can Keep: Why Poor Women Put Motherhood before Marriage* (University of California Press, 2005)

Eskridge, William N., Jr., *Dishonorable Passions: Sodomy Laws in America, 1861–2003* (Penguin, 2008).

———, *Equality Practice: Civil Unions and the Future of Gay Rights* (Routledge, 2002).

———, *Gaylaw: Challenging the Apartheid of the Closet*, 320 (Harvard University Press, 1999).

Eskridge, William N., Jr., & Christopher R. Riano, *Marriage Equality: From Outlaws to In-Laws* (Yale University Press, 2020).

Francoz Terminal, Laurence, "Registered Partnerships in France," in *The Future of Registered Partnerships: Family Recognition beyond Marriage*, 153 (Jens M. Scherpe & Andy Hayward eds., Intersentia, 2017).

Frank, Nathaniel, *Unfriendly Fire: How the Gay Ban Undermines the Military and Weakens America* (Thomas Dunne Books, 2009).

Franke, Katherine, *Wedlocked: The Perils of Marriage Equality* (NYU Press, 2015).

Friedan, Betty, *The Feminine Mystique* (W. W. Norton, 1963).

Friedman, Lawrence M., *Dead Hands: A Social History of Wills, Trusts, and Inheritance Law* (Stanford University Press, 2009).

Gallagher, Maggie, "The Case against Same-Sex Marriage," in John Corvino & Gallagher, *Debating Same-Sex Marriage*, 91 (Oxford University Press, 2012).

Graff, E. J., *What Is Marriage For?* (Beacon, 2004).

Hegel, G. W. F., *The Philosophy of History*, translated by J. Sibree (Dover, 1956).

Issenberg, Sasha, *The Engagement: America's Quarter-Century Struggle over Same-Sex Marriage* (Pantheon, 2021).

Johnson, David K., *The Lavender Scare: The Cold War Persecution of Gays and Lesbians in the Federal Government* (University of Chicago Press, 2004).

Kelly, Alicia, & John G. Culhane, "Rewritten Opinion, *Simeone v. Simeone*," in *Feminist Judgments: Family Law Opinions Rewritten*, 243 (Rachel Rebouché ed., Cambridge University Press, 2020).

Klarman, Michael, *From the Closet to the Altar: Courts, Backlash, and the Struggle for Same-Sex Marriage* (Oxford University Press, 2013).

Mello, Michael, *Legalizing Gay Marriage* (Temple University Press, 2004).

Melville, Herman, "Bartleby," in *The Piazza Tales*, 31 (Dix & Edwards, 1856).

Metz, Tamara, *Untying the Knot* (Princeton University Press, 2010).

Moats, David, *Civil Wars: A Battle for Gay Marriage* (Orlando, FL: Harcourt, 2004).

Oakes, Anne Richardson (ed.), *Controversies in Equal Protection Cases in America: Race, Gender and Sexual Orientation* (Ashgate, 2015).

Polikoff, Nancy, *Beyond (Straight and Gay) Marriage: Valuing All Families under the Law* (Beacon, 2008).

Sassler, Sharon, & Amanda Jayne Miller, *Cohabitation Nation: Gender, Class, and the Remaking of Relationships* (University of California Press, 2017).

Scherpe, Jens M., & Andy Hayward (eds.), *The Future of Registered Partnerships: Family Recognition beyond Marriage* (Intersentia, 2017).

Shakespeare, William, Sonnet 116, in *The Complete Works of William Shakespeare*, vol. 6 (Bantam, 1980).

———, *Romeo and Juliet* (Folger, 1992).

Shilts, Randy, *And the Band Played On: Politics, People and the AIDS Epidemic* (St. Martins, 1987).

Stone, Carrie, & John G. Culhane, *Same-Sex Legal Kit for Dummies* (John Wiley & Sons, 2013).

Sullivan, Andrew, *Virtually Normal: An Argument about Homosexuality* (Vintage, 1995).

Waite, Linda M., & Maggie Gallagher, *The Case for Marriage* (Broadway, 2001).

Warner, Michael, *The Trouble with Normal: Sex, Politics, and the Ethics of Queer Life* (Free Press, 1999).

Weisberg, D. Kelly, & Susan Frelich Appleton, *Modern Family Law* (6th ed., 2016).

West, Robin, *Marriage, Sexuality, and Gender* (Routledge, 2007).

Wintermute, Robert, & Mads Andenaes, *Legal Recognition of Same-Sex Partnerships* (Bloomsbury Academic, 2001).

Wolfson, Evan, *Why Marriage Matters* (Simon and Schuster, 2004).

ACADEMIC ARTICLES AND REPORTS

Abrams, Kerry, "Marriage Fraud," *California Law Review* 100 (2012): 1.

Aloni, Erez, "The Puzzle of Family Law Pluralism," *Harvard Journal of Law and Gender* 39 (2016): 317.

Alstott, Anne L., "Updating the Welfare State: Marriage, the Income Tax, and Social Security in the Age of Individualism," *Tax Law Review* 66 (2013): 695.

Antognini, Albertina, "The Law of Nonmarriage," *Boston College Law Review* 58 (2017): 1.

——, "Nonmarital Contracts," *Stanford Law Review* 73 (2021): 67.

Barnhart, Gwendolyn, "The Stigma of HIV/AIDS," *American Psychological Association*, December 2014.

Bernstein, Anita, "For and against Marriage: A Revision," *Michigan Law Review* 102 (2003): 129.

Brady, Heidi L., & Robin Fretwell Wilson, "The Precarious Status of Domestic Partnerships for the Elderly in a Post-*Obergefell* World," *Elder Law Journal* 24 (2016): 49.

Cahill, Courtney Megan, "Same-Sex Marriage, Slippery Slope Rhetoric, and the Politics of Disgust: A Critical Perspective on Contemporary Family Discourse and the Incest Taboo," *Northwestern Law Review* 99 (2005): 1543.

Cahn, Naomi, & June Carbone, "Blackstonian Marriage, Gender, and Cohabitation," *Arizona State Law Journal* 51 (2019): 1247.

Carbone, June, & Naomi Cahn, "Nonmarriage," *Maryland Law Review* 76 (2016): 55.

Carroll, Mary Charlotte Y., "When Marriage Is Too Much: Reviving the Registered Partnership in a Diverse Society," *Yale Law Journal* 130 (2020): 748.

Case, Mary Ann, "'The Very Stereotype the Law Condemns': Constitutional Sex Discrimination as a Quest for Perfect Proxies," *Cornell Law Review* 85 (2000): 1447.

Centers for Disease Control and Prevention, "*Pneumocystis* Pneumonia—Los Angeles," *Morbidity and Mortality Weekly Report* 30 (June 5, 1981): 250.

Chambers, David L., "Tales of Two Cities: AIDS and the Legal Recognition of Domestic Partnerships in San Francisco and New York," *Law & Sexuality* 2 (1992): 181.

Coolidge, David Orgon, & William C. Duncan, "Reaffirming Marriage: A Presidential Priority," *Harvard Journal of Law and Public Policy* 24 (2001): 623.

Cox, Barbara J., "Same-Sex Marriage and the Public Policy Exception in Choice-of-Law: Does It Really Exist?," *Quinnipiac Law Review* 16 (1996): 61.

Culhane, John G., "Ball of Con(stitutional) Fusion: The Supreme Court's Evolving Gay Rights Jurisprudence," in *Controversies in Equal Protection Cases in America: Race, Gender and Sexual Orientation* 183 (Anne Richardson Oakes ed., Ashgate, 2015).

———, "Beyond Rights and Morality: The Overlooked Public Health Argument for Same-Sex Marriage," *Law & Sexuality* 17 (2008): 7.

———, "A 'Clanging Silence': Same-Sex Couples and Tort Law," *Kentucky Law Journal* 89 (2000–2001): 911.

———, "Cohabitation, Registration, and Reliance: Creating a Comprehensive and Just Scheme for Protecting the Interests of Couples' Real Relationships," *Family Court Review* 58 (2020): 145.

———, "Even More Wrongful Death: Statutes Divorced from Reality," *Fordham Urban Law Journal* 32 (2005): 171.

———, "Marriage, Tort, and Private Ordering: Rhetoric and Reality in LGBT Rights," *Chicago-Kent Law Review* 84 (2009): 437.

———, "The Right to Say, but Not to Do: Balancing First Amendment Freedom of Expression with the Anti-discrimination Imperative," *Widener Law Review* 24 (2018): 235.

———, "Tort, Compensation, and Two Kinds of Justice," *Rutgers Law Review* 55 (2003): 1027.

———, "Uprooting the Arguments against Same-Sex Marriage," *Cardozo Law Review* 20 (1999): 1119.

Eskridge, William N., "Family Law Pluralism: The Guided-Choice Regime of Menus, Default Rules, and Override Rules," *Georgetown Law Review* 100 (2012): 1881.

Feinberg, Jessica R., "Gradual Marriage," *Lewis & Clark Law Review* 20 (2016): 1.

———, "The Survival of Non-marital Relationship Statuses in the Same-Sex Marriage Era: A Proposal," *Temple Law Review* 87 (2014): 47.

Gallagher, Maggie, "What Is Marriage For? The Public Purposes of Marriage Law," *Louisiana Law Review* 62 (2002): 773.

Girgis, Sherif, Robert George, & Ryan T. Anderson, "What Is Marriage?," *Harvard Journal of Law and Public Policy* 34 (2010): 245.

Godsoe, Cynthia, "Parsing Parenthood," *Lewis & Clark Law Review* 17 (2013): 113.

Goldfarb, Sally F., "Legal Recognition of Plural Unions: Is a Nonmarital Relationship Status the Answer to the Dilemma?," *Family Court Review* 58 (2020): 33.

Higdon, Michael J., "(In)formal Marriage Equality," *Fordham Law Review* 89 (2021): 1351.

John, David, & Virginia Reno, "Reforming Social Security: Option: Begin Means-Testing Social Security Benefits," Perspectives 22, AARP Public Policy Institute report (June 2012), https://aarp.org/content/dam/aarp/research/public_policy_institute/econ_sec/2012/option-means-test-social-security-benefits-AARP-ppi-econ-sec.pdf.

Johnson, Greg, "Vermont Civil Unions: The New Language of Marriage," *Vermont Law Review* 25 (2000): 15.

Jones, Daniel, "Rehabilitative Alimony—the Goal of Self Support," *Journal of Contemporary Legal Issues* 20 (2011–12): 25.

Joslin, Courtney G., "Autonomy in the Family," *UCLA Law Review* 66 (2019): 912.

———, "Family Choices," *Arizona State Law Review* 51 (2016): 1286.

Karlberg, Carly, "Philadelphia's Life Partnership Ordinance: Broadening the Same-Sex Marriage Debate and Implications for Federalism," *Rutgers Journal of Law and Religion* 11 (2010): 508.

Kelly, Alicia Brokars, "Navigating Gender in Modern Intimate Partnership Law," *Journal of Law and Family Studies* 14 (2012): 1.

———, "Rehabilitating Marriage as a Theory of Wealth Distribution at Divorce: In Recognition of a Shared Life," *Wisconsin Women's Law Journal* 19 (2004): 141.

Kim, Ji Hyun, Scott A. Oliver, & Margaret Ryznar, "The Rise of PACS: A New Type of Commitment from the City of Love," *Washburn Law Review* 56 (2017): 69.

Kisthardt, Mary Kay, "The AAML Model for a Parenting Plan," *Journal of the American Academy of Matrimonial Lawyers* 19 (2005): 223.

Koppelman, Andrew, "Interstate Recognition of Same-Sex Marriages and Civil Unions: A Handbook for Judges," *University of Pennsylvania Law Review* 153 (2005): 2143.

Lee, Patrick, & Robert P. George, "What Male-Female Complementarity Makes Possible: Marriage as a Two-in-One-Flesh Union," *Theological Studies* 69 (2008): 641.

Mahar, Heather, "Why Are There So Few Prenuptial Agreements?," John M. Olin Center for Law, Economics, and Business, Discussion Paper No. 436 (September 2003), http://www.law.harvard.edu/programs/olin_center/papers/pdf/436.pdf.

Mahoney, Margaret M., "Stepparents as Third Parties in Relation to their Stepchildren," *Family Law Quarterly* 40 (2006): 81.

Matsumura, Kaiponanea T., "Beyond Property: The Other Legal Consequences of Informal Relationships," *Arizona State Law Journal* 51 (2019): 1325.

———, "Breaking Down Status," *Washington Law Review* 98 (2021): 671.

———, "Consent to Intimate Regulation," *North Carolina Law Review* 96 (2018): 1013.

———, "The Integrity of Marriage," *William and Mary Law Review* 61 (2019): 453.

———, "A Right Not to Marry," *Fordham Law Review* 84 (2016): 1509.

McClain, Linda, "The Other Marriage Equality Problem," *Boston University Law Review* 93 (2013): 921.

Moore, Kathryn L., "Privatization of Social Security: Misguided Reform," *Temple Law Review* 71 (1998): 131.

Morone, Danielle, "A Short History of Alimony in England and the United States," *Journal of Contemporary Legal Issues* 20 (2011–12): 3.

Murphy, Jane C., "Legal Images of Fatherhood: Welfare Reform, Child Support Enforcement, and Fatherless Children," *Notre Dame Law Review* 81 (2005): 325.

Murray, Melissa, "*Obergefell v. Hodges* and Nonmarriage Inequality," *California Law Review* 104 (2016): 1207.

NeJaime, Douglas, "Before Marriage: The Unexplored History of Nonmarital Recognition and Its Relationship to Marriage," *California Law Review* 102 (2014): 87.

———, "Marriage Equality and the New Parenthood," *Harvard Law Review* 129 (2016): 1185.

Primrose, Sarah, "The Decline of Common Law Marriage & the Unrecognized Cultural Effect," *Whittier Law Review* 34 (2013): 187.

Rosenbury, Laura A., "Friends with Benefits?," *Michigan Law Review* 106 (2007): 189.

Sanders, Steve, "Dignity and Social Meaning: *Obergefell*, *Windsor*, and *Lawrence* as Constitutional Dialogue," *Fordham Law Review* 87 (2019): 2069.

Scott, Elizabeth S., "A World without Marriage," *Family Law Quarterly* 41 (Fall 2007): 537.

Shanley, Mary Lyndon, & Linda McClain, "Should States Abolish Marriage?," *Legal Affairs*, May 16, 2005, http://www.legalaffairs.org/webexclusive /debateclub_m0505.msp.

Sheffield, Rachel, "What's Driving the Marriage Divide?," *Public Discourse* (Witherspoon Institute), August 31, 2015, https://www.thepublicdiscourse .com/2015/08/14792/.

Siegel, Mark R., "Who Should Bear the Bite of Estate Taxes on Non-probate Property?," *Creighton Law Review* 43 (2010): 747.

Strassberg, Maura I., "Can We Still Criminalize Polygamy: Strict Scrutiny of Polygamy Laws under State Religious Freedom Restoration Acts after *Hobby Lobby*," *University of Illinois Law Review* (2016): 1605.

———, "Distinctions of Form or Substance: Monogamy, Polygamy and Same-Sex Marriage," *North Carolina Law Review* 75 (1997): 1501.

Thomas, Kendall, "The Eclipse of Reason: A Rhetorical Reading of *Bowers v. Hardwick*," *Virginia Law Review* 79 (1993): 1805.

VanSickle, Cynthia M., "A Return to the Anti-feminist Past of Divorce Law: The Implications of the Covenant or Marriage Laws as Applied to Women," *Journal of Law in Society* 6 (2005): 154.

Wardle, Lynn D., "Deconstructing Family: A Critique of the American Law Institute's 'Domestic Partners' Proposal," 2001 *Brigham Young University Law Review*: 1189.

Wax, Amy L., "Engines of Inequality: Class, Race, and Family Structure," *Family Law Quarterly* 41 (Fall 2007): 567.

Wilcox, W. Bradford, Angela Rachidi, & Joseph Price, "Marriage, Penalized: Does Social-Welfare Policy Affect Family Formation?," American Enterprise Institute & Institute for Family Studies, July 26, 2016, https://www.aei.org/research-products/report/marriage-penalized-does-social-welfare-policy-affect-family-formation/.

PERIODICALS AND NEWS REPORTS

Abel, David, "Vermont Legalizes Same-Sex Marriage," *Boston Globe*, April 8, 2009, http://archive.boston.com/news/local/massachusetts/articles/2009/04/08/vermont_legalizes_same_sex_marriage/.

Advocate, "'Non-believers' Seek License to Wed," November 10, 1971.

Ammann, Phil, "Two Years Later, 7 Alabama Counties Still Not Issuing Marriage Licenses to Same-Sex, Other Couples," *Alabama Today*, June 29, 2017.

Associated Press, "Kentucky Bows to Clerk Kim Davis and Changes Marriage License Rules," *Los Angeles Times*, December 23, 2015, http://www.latimes.com/nation/nationnow/la-na-nn-kentucky-kim-davis-20151223-story.html.

Bernard, Tara Siegel, "Fate of Domestic Partner Benefits in Question after Marriage Ruling," *New York Times*, June 28, 2015, https://www.nytimes.com/2015/06/29/your-money/fate-of-domestic-partner-benefits-in-question-after-marriage-ruling.html.

Brennan, Bridget, "Why Has Women's Economic Power Surged? Five Stats You Need to Know," *Forbes*, January 31, 2017, https://www.forbes.com/sites/bridgetbrennan/2017/01/31/why-has-womens-economic-power-surged-five-stats-you-need-to-know/.

Bumiller, Elizabeth, "Obama Ends 'Don't Ask, Don't Tell' Policy," *New York Times*, July 22, 2011, https://www.nytimes.com/2011/07/23/us/23military.html.

CBS Sacramento, "Domestic Partnerships Are Not Just for Same-Sex Couples in California Anymore," July 30, 2019, https://sacramento.cbslocal.com/2019 /07/30/domestic-partnerships-are-not-just-for-same-sex-couple-in-california-anymore/.

Cha, Ariana Eunjung, "The U.S. Fertility Rate Just Hit a Historic Low. Why Some Demographers Are Freaking Out," *Washington Post*, June 30, 2017, https://www.washingtonpost.com/news/to-your-health/wp/2017/06/30 /the-u-s-fertility-rate-just-hit-a-historic-low-why-some-demographers-are-freaking-out/.

Chereb, Sandra, "Amended Gay Marriage Bill Approved in Nevada Senate," *Las Vegas Review-Journal*, May 1, 2017.

CNN, "Hawaii Gives Legislature Power to Ban Same-Sex Marriage," November 3, 1998, http://edition.cnn.com/ALLPOLITICS/stories/1998/11/04/same .sex.ballot/.

Culhane, John G., "The Cake Controversy That Just Won't Go Away," *Politico*, August 16, 2018, https://www.politico.com/magazine/story/2018/08/16 /masterpiece-cakeshop-controversy-219365/.

———, "Kim Davis Is No Rosa Parks," *Politico*, September 8, 2015, https://www .politico.com/magazine/story/2015/09/kim-davis-is-no-rosa-parks-213127/.

———, "The Most Important Cake in America," *Politico*, December 4, 2017, https://www.politico.com/magazine/story/2017/12/04/cake-supreme-court-case-gay-marriage-216006.

———, "The Supreme Court Punts on Cakes for Same-Sex Couples," *Politico*, June 4, 2018, https://www.politico.com/magazine/story/2018/06/04/the-supreme-court-punts-on-cakes-for-same-sex-couples-218591/.

Daly, Nora, "Single? So Are the Majority of U.S. Adults," PBS NewsHour, September 11, 2014, https://www.pbs.org/newshour/nation/single-youre-not-alone.

Denison, Doug, "Delaware Becomes 11th State with Gay Marriage," *USA Today*, May 7, 2013, https://www.usatoday.com/story/news/nation/2013/05/07 /delaware-gay-marriage/2142703/.

Dresser, Michael, & Carrie Wells, "With Same-Sex Marriage Now Available, State to End Benefits for Domestic Partners," *Baltimore Sun*, May 3, 2013, http://articles.baltimoresun.com/2013–05–03/features/bs-md-domestic-benefits-20130502_1_domestic-partners-health-benefits-state-employees.

Florida, Richard, "Singles Now Make Up More Than Half the U.S. Adult Population. Here's Where They Live," Bloomberg, CityLab, September 15, 2014, https://www.citylab.com/equity/2014/09/singles-now-make-up-more-than-half-the-us-adult-population-heres-where-they-all-live /380137/.

Franke-Ruta, Garance, "The Prehistory of Gay Marriage: Watch a 1971 Protest at NYC's Marriage License Bureau," *The Atlantic*, March 26, 2013, https://

www.theatlantic.com/politics/archive/2013/03/the-prehistory-of-gay-marriage-watch-a-1971-protest-at-nycs-marriage-license-bureau/274357/.

Friday, Francesca, "More Americans Are Single Than Ever Before—and They're Healthier, Too," *Observer*, January 16, 2018, https://observer.com/2018/01/more-americans-are-single-than-ever-before-and-theyre-healthier-too/.

Garber, Megan, "The Old-Fashioned, Modern Marriage of Ina and Jeffrey," *The Atlantic*, October 25, 2016, https://www.theatlantic.com/entertainment/archive/2016/10/the-old-fashioned-modern-marriage-of-ina-and-jeffrey/505277/.

Goldberg, Carey, "Vermont High Court Backs Rights of Same-Sex Couples," *New York Times*, December 20, 1999, A1.

Goodman, David, "A More Civil Union," *Mother Jones*, July–August 2000, https://www.motherjones.com/politics/2000/07/more-civil-union/.

Gorney, Cynthia, "Making It Official: The Law Live-Ins," *Washington Post*, July 5, 1989, https://www.washingtonpost.com/archive/lifestyle/1989/07/05/making-it-official-the-law-live-ins/a11543fc-4a0d-4761-b4cb-032e5716cbab/.

Greenhouse, Linda, "Gay Rights Case Fails in Bid for Supreme Court Hearing," *New York Times*, January 13, 1998, https://www.nytimes.com/1998/01/13/us/gay-rights-case-fails-in-bid-for-supreme-court-hearing.html.

Huffington Post, "Florida Abandons Statewide Domestic Partnership Registry and LGBT Civil Protections," May 8, 2013, https://www.huffpost.com/entry/florida-domestic-registry-lgbt-rights_n_3237475.

Joyce, Amy, "Majority of Large Firms Offer Employees Domestic Partner Benefits," *Washington Post*, June 30, 2006, https://www.washingtonpost.com/wp-dyn/content/article/2006/06/29/AR2006062902049.html.

Kaufman, Ellie, & Barbara Starr, "Pentagon Announces New Policies to Abolish Trump Administration's Transgender Military Ban," CNN, March 31, 2021, https://edition.cnn.com/2021/03/31/politics/transgender-military-ban-policies/index.html.

Kelly, Amita, "Texas Supreme Court Rules against Benefits for Same-Sex Couples," NPR, June 30, 2017, https://www.npr.org/2017/06/30/535021154/texas-supreme-court-rules-against-benefits-for-same-sex-couples.

Kitsap Sun, "Alaska: Judge Rules against Same-Sex Marriage Ban," February 28, 1998.

Kopan, Tal, "Kentucky Governor Removes Clerk Names from Marriage Licenses," CNN, December 23, 2015, https://edition.cnn.com/2015/12/23/politics/kentucky-marriage-licenses-matt-bevin-kim-davis/index.html.

Kurtz, Stanley, "The Conspiracy to Abolish Marriage: Martha Bailey and the Law Reform Commission," Free Library, September 1, 2006, https://www.thefreelibrary.com/The+conspiracy+to+abolish+marriage%3A+Martha+Bailey+and+the+Law+Reform...-a0151394664.

Lai, K. K. Rebecca, "Abortion Bans: 9 States Have Passed Bills to Limit the Procedure This Year," *New York Times*, updated May 29, 2019, https://www .nytimes.com/interactive/2019/us/abortion-laws-states.html.

Lee, Michelle Ye Hee, "Fact Checker: Hillary Clinton's Claim That DOMA Had to Be Enacted to Stop an Anti-Gay Marriage Amendment to the U.S. Constitution," *Washington Post*, October 28, 2015, https://www.washingtonpost.com /news/fact-checker/wp/2015/10/28/hillary-clintons-claim-that-doma-had-to-be-enacted-to-stop-an-anti-gay-marriage-amendment-to-the-u-s-constitution/.

Levy, Ariel, "The Perfect Wife," *New Yorker*, September 30, 2013, http://www .newyorker.com/magazine/2013/09/30/the-perfect-wife.

Lorenzetti, Laura, "Looking to Stay on Your Partner's Insurance? It May Be Time to Get Married," *Fortune*, June 26, 2015, https://fortune.com/2015 /06/26/same-sex-benefits-marriage/.

Lowder, J. Bryan, "What Was Gay?," *Slate*, May 12, 2015, https://slate.com /news-and-politics/2015/05/can-you-be-homosexual-without-being-gay-the-future-of-cruising-drag-and-camp-in-a-post-closet-world.html.

Lucas, Greg, "Domestic Partners Bill Sent to Davis / Lawmakers Also OK Needle Exchange Law," SFGATE, September 10, 1999, https://www.sfgate .com/politics/article/Domestic-Partners-Bill-Sent-to-Davis-Lawmakers-2909885.php.

Maciag, Mike, "State Same Sex Marriage State Laws Map," Governing, March 25, 2013, http://www.governing.com/archive/same-sex-marriage-civil-unions-doma-laws-by-state.html.

Marquardt, Elizabeth, & John Culhane, "California Should Not Pass 'Multiple Parents' Bill," *Huffington Post*, August 17, 2012, https://www.huffpost.com /entry/multiple-parents-bill_b_1791709.

Marr, Rhuaridh, "Alabama Republicans Want to Abolish Marriage Licenses So Homophobes Don't Have to Issue Them to Gays," *Metro Weekly*, May 28, 2019, https://www.metroweekly.com/2019/05/alabama-republicans-want-to-abolish-marriage-licenses-so-homophobes-dont-have-to-issue-them-to-gays/.

McFadden, Robert D., "Edie Windsor, Whose Same-Sex Marriage Fight Led to Landmark Ruling, Dies at 88," *New York Times*, September 12, 2017, https:// www.nytimes.com/2017/09/12/us/edith-windsor-dead-same-sex-marriage-doma.html.

National Center for Health Statistics, "Births: Final Data for 2020," National Vital Statistics Reports 70, no. 17. February 7, 2022, https://www.cdc.gov /nchs/data/nvsr/nvsr70/nvsr70-17.pdf.

Ose, Erik, "Jesse Helms' Shameful Legacy Can't Be Whitewashed," *Huffington Post*, July 21, 2008, https://www.huffpost.com/entry/jesse-helms-shameful -lega_b_111791.

Pew Research Center, "Immigration's Impact on Past and Future U.S. Population Change," September 28, 2015, https://www.pewresearch.org/hispanic /2015/09/28/chapter-2-immigrations-impact-on-past-and-future-u-s-population-change/. Chapter 2 of *Modern Immigration Wave Brings 59 Million to U.S., Driving Population Growth and Change through 2065.*

Powers, Martine, "Maine Votes to Legalize Same-Sex Marriage," Boston.com, November 6, 2012, https://www.boston.com/uncategorized/noprimary tagmatch/2012/11/06/maine-votes-to-legalize-same-sex-marriage/.

Rizzo, Salvador, "Christie Withdraws Appeal of Gay Marriage Ruling," NJ.com, October 21, 2013, https://www.nj.com/politics/2013/10/christie_withdraws _appeal_of_gay_marriage_ruling.html.

Ryan, Christopher, "What Rick Santorum Doesn't Know about Sex," *Psychology Today*, January 6, 2012, https://www.psychologytoday.com/us/blog/sex-dawn/201201/what-rick-santorum-doesn-t-know-about-sex.

Saunders, E. B., "Reformer's Choice: Marriage License or Just License?," *One*, August 1953, http://queermusicheritage.com/jun2008one.html.

Scherr, Judith, "Berkeley, Activists Set Milestone for Domestic Partnerships in 1984," *East Bay Times*, June 28, 2013, https://www.eastbaytimes.com/2013 /06/28/berkeley-activists-set-milestone-for-domestic-partnerships-in-1984/.

Simpson, Kevin, "Colorado Amendment 43: Gay Marriage Banned; Domestic Partnerships Also Defeated," *Denver Post*, November 8, 2006, https://www .denverpost.com/2006/11/08/colorado-amendment-43-gay-marriage-banned-domestic-partnerships-also-defeated/.

Socarides, Richard, "Why Bill Clinton Signed the Defense of Marriage Act," *New Yorker*, March 8, 2013, https://www.newyorker.com/news/news-desk /why-bill-clinton-signed-the-defense-of-marriage-act.

Steverman, Ben, "Boomers Making Sure the Divorces Keep Coming," *Bloomberg*, June 17, 2016, https://www.bloomberg.com/news/articles/2016-06-17 /boomers-are-making-sure-the-divorces-keep-coming.

Strickler, Andrew, "BigLaw Belt Tightening Squeezes Domestic Partner Benefits," Law360, December 8, 2016, https://www.law360.com/articles /869585/biglaw-belt-tightening-squeezes-domestic-partner-benefits.

Sullivan, Andrew, "Here Comes the Groom: A (Conservative) Case for Gay Marriage," *New Republic*, August 28, 1989.

Swanson, Ana, "144 Years of Marriage and Divorce in the United States, in One Chart," *Washington Post*, June 23, 2015, https://www.washingtonpost.com /news/wonk/wp/2015/06/23/144-years-of-marriage-and-divorce-in-the-united-states-in-one-chart/.

Time, "A Brief History of Birth Control: From Early Contraception to the Birth of the Pill," May 3, 2010, http://content.time.com/time/magazine/article /0,9171,1983970,00.html.

Trageser, Claire, "Designated Beneficiary Rules Grant Unmarried Pairs Decision-Making Power," *Denver Post*, June 30, 2009, https://www.denverpost.com /2009/06/30/designated-beneficiary-rules-grant-unmarried-pairs-decision-making-power/.

Turner, Wallace, "Partnership Law Vetoed on Coast," *New York Times*, December 10, 1982, https://www.nytimes.com/1982/12/10/us/partnership-law-vetoed-on-coast.html.

Vance, Kevin, "Why Arizona Flipped on Gay Marriage," CBS News, December 2, 2008, https://www.cbsnews.com/news/why-arizona-flipped-on-gay-marriage/.

Vermont Commission on Family Recognition and Protection, "Report of the Vermont Commission on Family Recognition and Protection," April 21, 2008, http://www.leg.state.vt.us/WorkGroups/FamilyCommission/VCFRP_Report.pdf.

Volsky, Igor, "Rick Santorum Pledges to Defund Contraception: 'It's Not Okay, It's a License to Do Things,'" Think Progress, October 19, 2011, https:// thinkprogress.org/rick-santorum-pledges-to-defund-contraception-its-not-okay-it-s-a-license-to-do-things-a9a9b04f0761/.

Wilson, Ryan, "Kentucky Legislative Session Comes to a Close; Fails to Pass Anti-LGBT Legislation," Human Rights Campaign, April 19, 2016.

CASES

U.S. Federal

Adams v. Howertown, 486 F. Supp. 1119 (C.D. Calif. 1980), aff'd, 673 F.2d 1036 (9th Cir. 1982).

Baker v. Nelson, 409 U.S. 810 (1972) (dismissing appeal from Minnesota case).

Barber v. Bryant, 860 F.3d 345 (5th Cir. 2017), petition for rehearing enc ban denied, 872 F.3d 671 (2017), cert. denied, 138 S. Ct. 652 (2018).

Bowers v. Hardwick, 478 U.S. 186 (1986) (overruled by *Lawrence v. Texas*).

Brown v. Buhman, 822 F.3d 1151 (10th Cir. 2016).

Brown v. Buhman, 947 F. Supp. 2d. 1170 (D. Utah 2013).

California v. Texas, 141 S. Ct. 2104 (2021).

Davis v. Ermold, 141 S. Ct. 3 (2020).

Department of Agriculture v. Moreno, 413 U.S. 538 (1973).

Dobbs v. Jackson Women's Health Organization, 142 S. Ct. 2228 (2022).

Fulton v. City of Philadelphia, 141 S. Ct. 1868 (2021).

Hurley v. Irish-American Gay, Lesbian and Bisexual Group of Boston, 515 U.S. 557 (1995).

Lawrence v. Texas, 539 U.S. 558 (2003).

Loving v. Virginia, 388 U.S. 1 (1967).

Masterpiece Cakeshop, Ltd. v. Colorado Civil Rights Commission, 138 S. Ct. 1719 (2018).

National Federation of Independent Business v. Sebelius, 567 U.S. 519 (2012).

Obergefell v. Hodges, 576 U.S. 644 (2015).

One, Inc. v. Oleson, 355 U.S. 371 (1958).

Pavan v. Smith, 137 S. Ct. 2075 (2017).

Planned Parenthood v. Casey, 505 U.S. 833 (1992).

Reynolds v. United States, 98 U.S. 145 (1879).

Roe v. Wade, 410 U.S. 113 (1973).

Romer v. Evans, 517 U.S. 620 (1996).

Sanders v. Altmeyer, 58 F. Supp. 67 (W.D. Tenn. 1944).

Shahar v. Bowers, 114 F.3d 1097 (11th Cir. 1997).

Sosna v. Iowa, 419 U.S. 393 (1975).

Turner v. Safley, 482 U.S. 78 (1987).

United States v. Windsor, 570 U.S. 744 (2013).

Whole Women's Health v. Hellerstedt, 136 S. Ct. 2292 (2016).

Zablocki v. Redhail, 434 U.S. 374 (1978).

U.S. State

Alison D. v. Virginia M., 572 N.E.2d 27 (N.Y. 1991).

Anonymous v. Anonymous, 325 N.Y.S.2d 982 (N.Y. Sup. Ct. 1971).

Arizona Together v. Brewer, 149 P.3d 742 (Ariz. 2007).

Baehr v. Lewin, 852 P.2d 44 (Haw. 1993).

Baehr v. Miike, 1999 Haw. LEXIS 391.

Baker v. Nelson, 191 N.W.2d 185 (Minn. 1971).

Baker v. State, 744 A.2d 864 (Vt. 1999).

Baskin v. Bogan, 766 F.3d 648 (7th Cir. 2014).

Braschi v. Stahl Associates, 543 N.E.2d 49 (N.Y. 1989).

Brause v. Bureau of Vital Statistics, 1998 WL 88743 (Alaska Super. Ct. 1998).

Brooke S.B. v. Elizabeth A.C.C., 61 N.E. 3d 488 (N.Y. 2016).

Dean v. District of Columbia, 653 A.2d 307 (D.C. 1995).

DeSanto v. Barnsley, 476 A.2d 952 (Pa. Super. Ct. 1984).

Garden State Equality v. Dow, 79 A.2d 1036 (N.J. 2013).

Garden State Equality v. Dow, 82 A.3d 336 (N.J. Super. Ct. Law Div. 2013).

Ghassemi v. Ghassemi, 998 So.2d 731 (La. Ct. App. 2008).

Goodridge v. Department of Public Health, 798 N.E.2d 941 (Mass. 2003).

Griego v. Oliver, 316 P.3d 865 (N.M. 2013).

In re Estate of Carter, 159 A.3d 970 (Pa. Super. Ct. 2017).

In re Estate of Loughmiller, 629 P.2d 156 (Kans. 1981).

In re Marriage Cases, 183 P.3d 384 (Calif. 2008).

In re Marriage of Shanks, 758 N.W.2d 506 (Iowa 2008).

Jacob v. Shultz-Jacob, 923 A.2d 473 (Pa. Super. Ct. 2007).

Janda v. Janda, 984 So.2d 434 (Ala. Civ. App. 2007).

Jones v. Daly, 122 Calif. App. 3d 500 (Calif. Ct. App. 1981).

Jones v. Hallahan, 501 S.W.2d 588 (Ky. 1973).

K.E.M. v. P.C.S., 38 A.3d 798 (Pa. 2012).

Langan v. St. Vincent's Hospital, 802 N.Y.S.2d 476 (App. Div. 2005).

Lewis v. Harris, 908 A.2d 196 (N.J. 2006).

Lowenschuss v. Lowenschuss, 579 A.2d 377 (Pa. Super. Ct. 1990).

MacCallum v. Seymour, 686 A.2d 935 (Vt. 1996).

Marvin v. Marvin, 557 P.2d 106 (Calif. 1976).

M.T. v. J.T., 355 A.2d 204 (N.J. Super. Ct. 1976).

Olver v. Fowler, 168 P.3d 348 (Wash. 2007).

Opinion of the Justices to the Senate, 802 N.E.2d 565 (Mass. 2004).

Pidgeon v. Turner, 538 S.W.3d 73 (Tex. 2017).

PNC Bank Corp. v. Workers' Compensation Appeal Board (Stamos), 831 A.2d 1269 (Pa. Commonwealth Ct. 2003).

Simeone v. Simeone, 581 A.2d 162 (Pa. 1990).

Singer v. Hara, 522 P.2d 1187 (Wash. Ct. App. 1974).

Smith v. State, 6 S.W.3d 512 (Tenn. Ct. Crim. App. 1999).

Strauss v. Horton, 207 P.3d 48 (Calif. 2009).

Varnum v. Brien, 763 N.W.2d 862 (Iowa 2009).

Whorton v. Dillingham, 202 Calif. App. 3d 447 (Calif. Ct. App. 1988).

Australian

Attiwill & Secretary, Department of Education, Employment and Workplace Relations, 2013 WL 1152047 (Administrative Appeals Tribunal, Adelaide).

Crowley & Pappas, [2013] FamCA 783, Family Court of Australia, http://www .austlii.edu.au/cgi-bin/viewdoc/au/cases/cth/FamCA/2013/783.html.

French

Cass. Civ. 3, Dec. 17, 1997, no. 95-20779.

Cass. Soc., July 11, 1989, no. 86-10665.

Conseil constitutionnel, Décision no. 99-419 DC, 1999.

UNITED STATES LAWS

Federal

1 U.S.C. §7.

8 U.S.C. § 1153.

26 U.S.C. § 1.
26 U.S.C. § 2010
26 U.S.C. § 2056.
28 U.S.C. § 1738.
29 U.S.C. §§ 2601 et seq.
42 U.S.C. § 216 (l) (1).
42 U.S.C. § 402.
42 U.S.C. § 416 (h).
42 U.S.C. § 667.
110 Stat. 2419, Defense of Marriage Act.
Pub. L. No. 74-271, 49 Stat. 620, Social Security Act.
Pub. L. No. 105-89, 111 Stat. 2115, Adoption and Safe Families Act.
Pub. L. No. 111-321, Don't Ask, Don't Tell Repeal Act of 2010.
Rev. Rul. 2013-17, 2013-2 C.B. 201.

State

Constitutional Provisions
Alaska Const. Art. I, § 25.
Calif. Const. Art. 1, § 7.5 (Proposition 8).
Colo. Rev. Stat., Const. Art. 2, § 3b.
Haw. Const. Art. I, § 23.
Nev. Const. Art. 1, § 21.
Vt. Const. Art. VII, ch. 1.

Statutes
A.C.A. § 9-11-803.
A.R.S. § 25-901.
Calif. Fam. Code § 297.
Calif. Fam. Code § 3040.
Calif. Fam. Code § 7601.
Colo. Rev. Stat. §§ 14-15-104 et seq., Civil Union Act.
Colo. Rev. Stat. §§ 15-22-101 et seq.
Conn. Gen. Stat. Ann. § 46-b.
2005 Conn. Pub. Acts No. 05-10.
13 Del. C. § 129.
13 Del. C. § 212.
13 Del. C. § 218.
Fla. Stat. Ann. § 61.08.
Haw. Rev. Stat. Ann. § 572.
750 Ill. Comp. Stat. Ann. § 75/10.
Iowa Code Ann. § 598.21.

LSA-R.S. § 9:272.
Me. Rev. Stat. Ann. 19A, § 951-A.
Mich. Comp. Laws Ann. 600.2922.
Miss. Code Ann. § 11-62-3.
N.D. Cent. Code Ann. § 14-05.24.1.
Nev. Rev. Stat. § 122A.200.
N.H. Rev. Stat. Ann. § 457:1-A.
N.J. Stat. Ann. § 37:1-31.
Ohio Rev. Code Ann. § 3105.18.
Or. Rev. Stat. § 106.340.
23 Pa. Cons. Stat. § 3301.
23 Pa. Cons. Stat. § 3502.
72 Pa. Cons. Stat. § 9116.
R.I. Gen. Stat. Ann. § 15-3.1-12.
2004 Va. Acts 983.
1999 Vt. Acts & Resolves 91.
2000 Vt. Laws P.A. 91 (H. 847), An Act Relating to Civil Unions.
2013 Vt. Legis. Serv. 164 (LexisNexis).
15 Vt. Stat. Ann. §§ 1201 et seq.
15 Vt. Stat. Ann. §§ 1301 et seq.
15A Vt. Stat. Ann. § 1-102.
Wash. Rev. Code § 26.60.
Wash. Stat. 26.60.015.
Wis. Stat. Ann. § 767.511.

Local Ordinances

Berkeley, Calif., Mun. Code, chapter 13.28.
Clarkdale, Ariz., Town Code, Ch. 8, Business Regs., Article 8-6.
Phila. Fair Practices Ord. §§ 9-101 et seq.
Sedona, Ariz., Ord. No. 2013-05.
S.F., Calif., Mun. Code § 62.1.
S.F., Calif., Ord. 176-89, § 4002(a).
West Hollywood, Calif., Ord. 22.

FOREIGN STATUTORY AUTHORITIES

Australian Family Law Act of 1975 (amended, 2016).
Du pacte civil de solidarité et du concubinage, Loi n° 99/944 du 15 novembre 1999 (since amended), https://www.legifrance.gouv.fr/jorf/id/JORFTEXT 000000761717.

French Civil Code, Art. 515 (Titre XIII: Du pacte civil de solidarité et du concubinage), https://www.legifrance.gouv.fr/codes/section_lc/LEGI-TEXT000006070721/LEGISCTA000006118360/2020-08-30/; translation in David Gruning, Alain R. Levasseur, John Randy Trahan, and Estelle Roy, *Traduction du Code civil français en anglais version bilingue* (2015), halshs-01385107, https://halshs.archives-ouvertes.fr/halshs-01385107/document.

OTHER SOURCES

AARP, "How Do Survivor Benefits Work?," updated July 1, 2022, https://www.aarp.org/retirement/social-security/questions-answers/how-do-survivor-benefits-work.html.
Borland, Jim, "Will Remarrying Affect My Social Security Benefits?," Social Security Matters, September 5, 2017, updated October 14, 2021, https://blog.ssa.gov/will-remarriage-affect-my-social-security-benefits/.
Centers for Disease Control and Prevention, "HIV Stigma and Discrimination," reviewed June 1, 2021, https://www.cdc.gov/hiv/basics/hiv-stigma/index.html.
Commonwealth of Virginia, "Application for Marriage License," last visited July 25, 2022, https://media.alexandriava.gov/docs-archives/clerkofcourt/webappfillable.pdf.
Connett, Wendy, "What Is the Maximum Social Security Retirement Benefit?," Investopedia, updated June 28, 2022, https://www.investopedia.com/ask/answers/102814/what-maximum-i-can-receive-my-social-security-retirement-benefit.asp.
Cornforth, Tracee, "A Brief History of the Birth Control Pill," Verywell Health, updated May 6, 2020, https://www.verywellhealth.com/a-brief-history-on-the-birth-control-pill-3522634.
Divorce Knowledgebase, "What Is a Covenant Marriage?," September 11, 2014, https://www.divorceknowledgebase.com/blog/covenant-marriage/.
DNA Diagnostics Center, "Introduction to DNA Testing History," last visited July 29, 2022, https://dnacenter.com/history-dna-testing/.
France in the United States, Embassy of France in Washington, D.C., "Marriage in France," Ministère de l'Europe et des affaires étrangères, November 13, 2007, https://franceintheus.org/spip.php?article387.
Guttmacher Institute, "An Overview of Abortion Laws," updated August 1, 2022, https://www.guttmacher.org/state-policy/explore/overview-abortion-laws.
Hamilton, Brady E., et al., "Births: Provisional Data for 2017," Division of Vital Statistics, National Center for Health Statistics (May 2018), https://stacks.cdc.gov/view/cdc/55172.

History.com, "Stonewall Riots," May 31, 2017, updated May 31, 2022, https://www.history.com/topics/gay-rights/the-stonewall-riots.

IRS, "IRS Provides Tax Inflation Adjustments for Tax Year 2020," updated November 2, 2021, https://www.irs.gov/newsroom/irs-provides-tax-inflation-adjustments-for-tax-year-2020.

JustLanded.com, "Marriage & Divorce in France: Procedures, Statistics and Tips," last visited July 5, 2022, https://www.justlanded.com/english/France/Articles/Visas-Permits/Marriage-Divorce-in-France.

Law Commission of Canada, *Beyond Conjugality: Recognizing and Supporting Close Personal Adult Relationships* (2001), https://papers.ssrn.com/sol3/papers.cfm?abstract_id=1720747.

Luther, Samir, "Domestic Partner Benefits: Employer Trends and Benefits—Equivalency for the GLBT Family," Washington, DC: Human Rights Campaign Foundation, 2006.

McKinley Irvin Family Law, "Understanding 'Fair and Equitable' Division of Property in a No-Fault Divorce," September 25, 2013, https://www.mckinleyirvin.com/family-law-blog/2013/september/understanding-fair-and-equitable-division-of-pro/.

Movement Advancement Project, "Local Nondiscrimination Ordinances," last visited March 9, 2022, http://www.lgbtmap.org/equality-maps/non_discrimination_ordinances/policies.

National Center for Health Statistics, "Unmarried Childbearing," reviewed May 16, 2022, https://www.cdc.gov/nchs/fastats/unmarried-childbearing.htm.

National Center for Lesbian Rights, "Marriage, Domestic Partnerships, and Civil Unions: Same-Sex Couples within the United States" (2020). https://www.nclrights.org/wp-content/uploads/2015/07/Relationship-Recognition.pdf.

New Jersey Civil Union Review Commission, *First Interim Report of the New Jersey Civil Union Review Commission*, February 19, 2008.

Office of Cook County Clerk David Orr, "Opposite-Sex Civil Unions: Motives for Not Marrying," November 28, 2011.

O'Neill, Aaron, "Crude Birth Rate in the United States from 1800 to 2020," Statista, June 21, 2022, https://www.statista.com/statistics/1037156/crude-birth-rate-us-1800-2020/.

Pew Research Center, "The Decline of Marriage and Rise of New Families," November 18, 2010, https://www.pewresearch.org/social-trends/2010/11/18/the-decline-of-marriage-and-rise-of-new-families/.

Sawe, Benjamin Elisha, "Religious Demographics of France," WorldAtlas, March 13, 2018, https://www.worldatlas.com/articles/religious-demographics-of-france.html.

Social Security Administration, "Benefits For Your Family," last visited August 5, 2022, https://www.ssa.gov/benefits/retirement/planner/applying7.html.

———, "Frequently Asked Questions," "What Are the Marriage Requirements to Receive Social Security Spouse's Benefits?," modified July 26, 2022, https://faq.ssa.gov/en-us/Topic/article/KA-01999.

———, "GN 00210.004: Same-Sex Relationships—Non-marital Legal Relationships," February 10, 2016, https://secure.ssa.gov/poms.nsf/lnx/0200210004.

———, "If You Are the Survivor," last visited August 5, 2022, https://www.ssa.gov/benefits/survivors/ifyou.html#h3.

———, *Understanding the Benefits*. Publication No. 05-10024 (January 2022), https://ssa.gov/pubs/EN-05-10024.pdf.

Social Trends Institute, "World Family Map 2017: Mapping Family Change and Child Well-Being Outcomes" (2017), http://worldfamilymap.ifstudies.org/2017/files/WFM-2017-FullReport.pdf.

State of New Jersey Department of Health, "Civil Union Licenses," reviewed September 18, 2017, https://www.nj.gov/health/vital/registration-vital/civil-union-licenses/.

Stepler, Renee, "Number of U.S. Adults Cohabiting with a Partner Continues to Rise, Especially among Those 50 and Older," Pew Research Center, April 6, 2017, https://www.pewresearch.org/fact-tank/2017/04/06/number-of-u-s-adults-cohabiting-with-a-partner-continues-to-rise-especially-among-those-50-and-older/.

Tolbert, Jennifer, Kendal Orgera, & Anthony Damico, "Key Facts about the Uninsured Population," Kaiser Family Foundation, November 6, 2020, https://www.kff.org/uninsured/issue-brief/key-facts-about-the-uninsured-population/.

Uniform Law Commission, Uniform Cohabitants' Economic Remedies Act, July 13, 2021, https://www.uniformlaws.org/HigherLogic/System/Download-DocumentFile.ashx?DocumentFileKey=eed76273-b2b7-eea1-953f-a657b9535820.

———, Uniform Premarital and Marital Agreements Act, January 2, 2013, https://www.uniformlaws.org/HigherLogic/System/DownloadDocument-File.ashx?DocumentFileKey=f5d36125-9433-c7d8-28ec-6244f4a316e6.

US Census Bureau, "America's Families and Living Arrangements: 2016," revised October 8, 2021, https://www.census.gov/data/tables/2016/demo/families/cps-2016.html.

U.S. Department of Labor, "Frequently Asked Questions: FMLA Final Rule," question 15, last visited July 26, 2022, https://www.dol.gov/agencies/whd/fmla/spouse/faq#15.

U.S. Government Accountability Office, "Defense of Marriage Act," GAO-04-353R, January 23, 2004.

Vermont Department of Health, "Application for Vermont License of Civil Marriage," last visited July 25, 2022, https://www.healthvermont.gov/sites/default/files/documents/pdf/HS_VR_App_CivilMarriage.pdf.

Vermont Judiciary, "Civil Union and Dissolution," last visited July 22, 2022, https://vermontjudiciary.org/family/divorce/civil-union-and-dissolution.

World Bank, "Fertility Rate, Total (Births per Woman)—United States," last visited June 28, 2018, https://data.worldbank.org/indicator/SP.DYN.TFRT .IN?end=2016&locations=US&start=1960&view=chart.

Index

Page references followed by the letter *t* indicate a table.

Founded in 1893,
UNIVERSITY OF CALIFORNIA PRESS
publishes bold, progressive books and journals
on topics in the arts, humanities, social sciences,
and natural sciences—with a focus on social
justice issues—that inspire thought and action
among readers worldwide.

The UC PRESS FOUNDATION
raises funds to uphold the press's vital role
as an independent, nonprofit publisher, and
receives philanthropic support from a wide
range of individuals and institutions—and from
committed readers like you. To learn more, visit
ucpress.edu/supportus.